2 TIMOTHY
AND TITUS

NCCS | New Covenant Commentary Series

The New Covenant Commentary Series (NCCS) is designed for ministers and students who require a commentary that interacts with the text and context of each New Testament book and pays specific attention to the impact of the text upon the faith and praxis of contemporary faith communities.

The NCCS has a number of distinguishing features. First, the contributors come from a diverse array of backgrounds in regards to their Christian denominations and countries of origin. Unlike many commentary series that tout themselves as international the NCCS can truly boast of a genuinely international cast of contributors with authors drawn from every continent of the world (except Antarctica) including countries such as the United States, Puerto Rico, Australia, the United Kingdom, Kenya, India, Singapore, and Korea. We intend the NCCS to engage in the task of biblical interpretation and theological reflection from the perspective of the global church. Second, the volumes in this series are not verse-by-verse commentaries, but they focus on larger units of text in order to explicate and interpret the story in the text as opposed to some often atomistic approaches. Third, a further aim of these volumes is to provide an occasion for authors to reflect on how the New Testament impacts the life, faith, ministry, and witness of the New Covenant Community today. This occurs periodically under the heading of "Fusing the Horizons and Forming the Community." Here authors provide windows into community formation (how the text shapes the mission and character of the believing community) and ministerial formation (how the text shapes the ministry of Christian leaders).

It is our hope that these volumes will represent serious engagements with the New Testament writings, done in the context of faith, in service of the church, and for the glorification of God.

Series Editors:
Michael F. Bird (Crossway College, Queensland, Australia)
Craig Keener (Asbury Theological Seminary, Wilmore, KY, USA)

Titles in this series:
Romans Craig Keener
Ephesians Lynn Cohick
Colossians and Philemon Michael F. Bird
Revelation Gordon Fee
John Jey Kanagaraj
1 Timothy Aída Besançon Spencer
1–2 Thessalonians Nijay Gupta
1–3 John Sam Ngewa
Luke Diane Chen
Matthew Scot McKnight
2 Corinthians David deSilva
James Pablo Jimenez
Galatians Jarvis Williams
1 Corinthians B. J. Oropeza

Forthcoming titles:
Philippians Linda Belleville
Acts Youngmo Cho and Hyung Dae Park
1 Peter Eric Greaux
2 Peter and Jude Andrew Mbuvi
Mark Kim Huat Tan
Hebrews Cynthia Westfall

2 TIMOTHY AND TITUS

A New Covenant Commentary

Aída Besançon Spencer

CASCADE *Books* • Eugene, Oregon

2 TIMOTHY AND TITUS
A New Covenant Commentary

New Covenant Commentary Series

Copyright © 2014 Aída Besançon Spencer. All rights reserved. Except for brief quotations in critical publications or reviews, no part of this book may be reproduced in any manner without prior written permission from the publisher. Write: Permissions, Wipf and Stock Publishers, 199 W. 8th Ave., Suite 3, Eugene, OR 97401.

Cascade Books
An Imprint of Wipf and Stock Publishers
199 W. 8th Ave., Suite 3
Eugene, OR 97401

www.wipfandstock.com

ISBN 13: 978-1-62564-253-0

Cataloging-in-Publication data:

Spencer, Aída Besançon

2 Timothy and Titus : a new covenant commentary / Aída Besançon Spencer.

xiv + 170 p. ; 23 cm. —Includes bibliographical references and index(es).

New Covenant Commentary Series

ISBN 13: 978-1-62564-253-0

1. Bible. Titus—Commentaries. 2. Bible. Timothy, 2nd—Commentaries. I. Title. II. Series.

BS2745 S69 2014

Manufactured in the U.S.A.

Paul and His Coworkers at His Last Battle at Rome
by William David Spencer and Aída Besançon Spencer,

Every army is like a single soldier.
Some of its bodily parts are functioning well.
Some are malfunctioning and harming the rest of the body.
Some are assigned to maintenance to keep the body militant functioning.
And the post-commander, like the brain, is multi-tasking—
accomplishing several goals at once.
So was the army of Christ, as commanded by the Field Marshall Paul at Rome.
This campaign was Paul's final battle.
At his side was his medic Luke and the platoon at Rome: Eubulus, Pudens, Linus,
Claudia, and the brothers and sisters—courageous and valiant each.
As any army or anybody, Paul's command had its problems and its strengths:
Demas, the deserter, the body's wandering eye, following after another general;
Alexander, a virus, doing great damage to the entire system;
Trophimus in the infirmary;
absent were Crescens and Titus;
off on a mission was Tychicus to secure the reinforcement—Timothy;
while maintaining other fronts were Erastus in Corinth and Prisca, Aquila,
Onesiphorus and his supply depot in Ephesus.
This was Paul's army of Christ, wounded, as was his own body,
as together they fought the good fight.
(February 3, 2013)

Contents

Abbreviations | ix

Introduction to Pastoral Letters | 1

Introduction to Titus | 3

Titus 1 | 6

   Fusing the Horizons: The Place of Education | 31

Titus 2 | 33

   Fusing the Horizons: The Importance of Holiness | 54

Titus 3 | 56

   Fusing the Horizons: The Place of Grace | 73

Introduction to 2 Timothy | 75

2 Timothy 1 | 79

2 Timothy 2 | 94

2 Timothy 3 | 117

   Fusing the Horizons: Why Study the Bible? | 131

2 Timothy 4 | 133

   Fusing the Horizons: Coworkers | 160

Bibliography | 161

Subject Index | 165

Abbreviations

SECONDARY REFERENCES

ANTC	Abingdon New Testament Commentaries
BA	La Biblia de las Américas
BBR	*Bulletin for Biblical Research*
BDAG	Bauer, Walter, et al. *A Greek-English Lexicon of the New Testament and Other Early Christian Literature*. 3rd ed. Chicago: University of Chicago Press, 2000.
CE	Halsey, William D., and Bernard Johnston, eds. *Collier's Encyclopedia*. 24 vols. New York: Macmillan, 1987.
CEB	Common English Bible
CEV	Contemporary English Version
DHH	Dios habla hoy
ESV	English Standard Version
CGTSC	Cambridge Greek Testament for Schools and Colleges
GW	God's Word Translation
HNTC	Harper's New Testament Commentary
ICC	International Critical Commentary
IDB	Buttrick, George Arthur, et. al. *The Interpreter's Dictionary of the Bible*. 5 vols. Nashville: Abingdon, 1962.
JB	Jerusalem Bible
JBL	*Journal of Biblical Literature*
JETS	*Journal of the Evangelical Theological Society*

x *Abbreviations*

KJV	King James Version
LCL	Loeb Classical Library
LEC	Library of Early Christianity
LSJ	Liddell, Henry George, and Robert Scott. *A Greek-English Lexicon*. Rev. Henry Stuart Jones. 9th ed. Oxford: Clarendon, 1968.
LXX	Septuagint
MM	Moulton, James Hope, and George Milligan. *The Vocabulary of the Greek Testament*. London: Hodder and Stoughton, 1930.
NASB	New American Standard Bible
NCBC	New Century Bible Commentary
NCCS	New Covenant Commentary Series
NewDocs	Horsley, G. H. R., and S. R. Llewelyn, eds. *New Documents Illustrating Earliest Christianity*. 9 vols. N.S.W., Australia: Ancient History Documentary Research Centre Macquarie University, 1976–1987.
NIBC	New International Biblical Commentary
NICNT	New International Commentary on the New Testament
NIRV	New International Reader's Version
NIV	New International Version
NLT	New Living Translation
NRSV	New Revised Standard Version
NT	New Testament
NTME	New Testament in Modern English
NTS	*New Testament Studies*
NVI	Nueva Versión Internacional
OCD	Hammond, N. G. L., and H. H. Scullard, eds. *Oxford Classical Dictionary*. 2nd ed. Oxford: Clarendon, 1970.
OT	Old Testament

OTP	Charlesworth, James H., ed. *Old Testament Pseudepigrapha*. 2 vols. New York: Doubleday, 1983, 1985.
RevExp	*Review and Expositor*
REB	Revised English Bible
RV	Reina-Valera 1995
TDNT	Kittel, Gerhard, and G. Friedrich, eds. *Theological Dictionary of the New Testament*. Trans G. W. Bromiley. 10 vols. Grand Rapids: Eerdmans, 1964–1976.
TEV	Today's English Version
Thayer	Thayer, Joseph Henry. *Thayer's Greek-English Lexicon of the New Testament*. Marshallton, DE: National Foundation for Christian Education, 1889.
ThTo	*Theology Today*
TLG	*Thesaurus linguae graecae*
TLNT	Spicq, Ceslas. *Theological Lexicon of the New Testament*. 3 vols. Trans. and ed. James D. Ernest. Peabody, MA: Hendrickson, 1994.
TNIV	Today's New International Version
UBS	*The Greek New Testament*. Ed. Barbara Aland et al. 4th rev. ed. Stuttgart: United Bible Societies, 2001.
WBC	Word Biblical Commentary
WYC	Wycliffe Bible
YLT	Young's Literal Translation

ANCIENT SOURCES

Apostolic Fathers
   1–2 Clem. 1–2 Clement
   Did. Didache
   Ign. Eph. Ignatius, *To the Ephesians*
   Mart. Pol. Martyrdom of Polycarp

Aratus
  Phaen. Phaenomena

Aristotle
  Pol. Politics
  Rhet. Rhetoric

Arrian
  Epict. diss. Epicteti dissertationes

Athenaeus
  Deipn. Deipnosophistae

Callimachus
  Hymn. Jov. Hymn to Jove or Zeus

Cicero
  Div. De divinatione

Clement of Alexandria
  Strom. Miscellanies

Diodorus
  Diodorus Diodorus of Sicily

Epictetus
  Diatr. Dissertationes
  Ench. Enchiridion

Eusebius
  Hist. eccl. Ecclesiastical History
  Praep. ev. Preparation for the Gospel

Hippocrates
  Artic. Joints
  Mochl. Instruments of Reduction
  Off. In the Surgery

Irenaeus
  Haer. Against Heresies

Josephus
  Ag. Ap. Against Apion
  Ant. Jewish Antiquities
  J. W. Jewish War

Lucian
> *Sacr.* Sacrifices
> *Philops.* The Lover of Lies

Mishnah (*m.*)
> *'Abot* Avot
> *Git.* Gittin
> *Ketub.* Ketubbot
> *Meg.* Megillah
> *Ned.* Nega'im
> *Qidd.* Qiddushin
> *Sanh.* Sanhedrin
> *Tehar.* Teharot

Philo
> *Embassy* On the Embassy to Gaius
> *Flaccus* Against Flaccus
> *Mos.* On the Life of Moses
> *Spec. Laws* On the Special Laws

Plato
> *Leg.* Laws

Polybius
> *Hist.* Histories

Pseudepigrapha
> *1 En.* 1 Enoch (Ethiopic Apocalypse)
> *Jub.* Jubilees
> *T. Sol.* Testament of Solomon

Strabo
> *Geogr.* Geography

Tacitus
> *Ann.* Annales

Xenophon
> *Oec.* Oeconomicus

Introduction to Pastoral Letters

When Luke the evangelist wrote his Gospel, he highlighted for Theophilus, his reader, some of the features he offered, while affirming the Gospels already written (Luke 1:1–4). Following the model of this wonderful historian, I, too, would like to affirm the many wonderful commentaries written on the Pastoral Epistles, which are Pastor Paul's instructions and admonitions to two young pastors. Like the other commentary writers of the New Covenant Commentary Series, I come from an international background, born and reared in Santo Domingo, Dominican Republic, and later in New Jersey in the United States, my mother from Puerto Rico and my father from The Netherlands. Like others in the series, I have focused on the flow of argument. My own translation is an attempt to illustrate the literal text as a basis for interpretation and stylistic analysis. I have studied the meaning of the text in light of its immediate and larger literary, biblical, historical, social, and cultural contexts. In particular, I have asked myself, how might these ancient communities have understood and received these teachings? To enrich my study, I traveled to Crete, Ephesus, Rome, and Greece, visiting many key ancient Greco-Roman sites. These were wonderful trips, which were accomplished with the help and companionship of my husband and son, Rev. Dr. William David Spencer and Mr. Stephen William Spencer.

In addition, I have always thought that scholarship would be advanced if more women were to study and publish on these letters that relate frequently to women and to church life. Thus, as a female Presbyterian minister ordained for over forty years (October 1973), I have paid consistent attention to any issues that relate to women and their role in the church. It is not, however, a commentary solely focused on "women's issues." As an active minister, who has taught New Testament theology for ministry for many years, I have also highlighted Paul's ministry strategies, his coworkers, and their community. My own initial training was in stylistics, and, thus, when appropriate, I have also highlighted Paul's rhetorical strategies.

Even though I have focused on the flow of argument, paragraphs and sentences are constructed from words and phrases. Therefore, in order to study the thoughts, I have also paid attention to semantics and grammar.

I have done a close reading of the text. Like Luke, I have attempted to do a thorough investigation, but one understandable to my readers. My husband, as a theologian and a grammarian, graciously read the entire commentary. I am a "scholar," but I am also a believer with the simple faith of a child (Luke 18:16–17). These words, although those of the Apostle Paul, are also God-breathed, I have, therefore, not read these letters as a skeptic, but as someone who is in love with God, who inspired the words and thoughts, and in sympathy with Paul, as a friend and colleague in ministry, who was mentoring other ministers in very difficult situations.

Introduction to Titus

SETTING: CRETE

Crete, in the Mediterranean Sea, 160 miles south of Athens, 200 miles north of Africa, is 160 miles long and 7 to 35 miles wide. It is a mountainous island with excellent shallow harbors. Ancient farmers grew wheat, barley, figs, olives, grapes, and tended to sheep and goats, and fish were plentiful.[1] In Roman times Crete was covered with forests, now the interior mountains have few forests.[2] Nevertheless, it has been called "the garden of the whole Universe," for its "beauty, pleasure and profit."[3]

Crete had a mixed culture with influence from Western Semites (Phoenicia, Syria, Israel), Egypt, Mesopotamia, Babylonia, Anatolia, Cyprus, and Greece. Jews lived in Crete as well. Ancient Cretans were known as a maritime people. Cretan archers were especially renowned and frequently hired as mercenaries. The society was organized very similar to Sparta's, a communal society set up to train citizen-soldiers.[4] Even the buildings were set up in a communal manner, with construction built around a central court. Streets would radiate out from the center of the palace.[5]

Minoan Crete had a predominance of female deities, including the Snake Goddess, protector of the household. But each new civilization brought its own deities. As in Ephesus, the goddess Artemis could be

---

1. Gordon 1987: 330; Vucinich and Vouras *CE* 7, 1987: 430; Branigan and Vickers 1980: 48–49. The author observed in a visit to Crete in May 2010 that olives, oranges, sheep, goats, and fish are still plentiful.

2. Strabo, *Geogr.* 10.4; Willetts 1965: 37–38. Crete was celebrated for its timber in Roman times (Hood 1971: 20).

3. William Lithgow, 1609, as cited by Hood 1971: 16.

4. *OCD* 1970: 298, 97.

5. Gordon 1987: 334; Branigan and Vickers 1980: 32.

found.⁶ Cretans claimed that Zeus was born in a cave in Crete and that Crete was the birthplace of many deities.⁷

Although females in Crete did not have all the political rights that men had, in Minoan Crete women were probably the social equals of men and participated in all activities including the dangerous sport of vaulting over charging bulls.⁸

ANALYTICAL OUTLINE OF TITUS

Paul's overall purpose is for Titus "to set straight what was remaining" at the church in Crete in order to further the faith of God's elect and their knowledge of the truth that accords with godliness.

I. Introduction: Paul writes Titus for the sake of the faith of God's elect and the knowledge of the truth that is in accordance with godliness (1:1–4).

II. Paul left Titus behind to set straight what was remaining by appointing godly elders and rebuking ungodly people (1:5–16).

    A. Paul left Titus in Crete to set straight what was remaining by appointing godly elders in every city (1:5–9).

    B. Sound teaching is necessary to correct the many who are deceptive and need to be rebuked (1:10–14).

    C. Although they claim to know God, their minds and consciences are defiled (1:15–16).

III. Paul wants Titus to teach what is consistent with healthy doctrine (2:1—3:11).

    A. Paul wants Titus to promote healthy teaching by encouraging godly behavior among the elders, youth, and slaves (2:1–15).

    B. Paul wants Titus to remind people to live godly lives in the world because they are justified by Christ's grace (3:1–8).

---

6. Branigan and Vickers 1980: 44, 82; Nilsson 1971: 400, 405. According to Nilsson (509), the Minoan Mistress of Wild Nature developed into the Great Mother of Asia Minor (with lions) and the virgin huntress of Greece. The Minoans "personified the Supreme Principle as a woman to whom was subordinate a young male" (401).

7. E.g., Aratus, *Phaen.* 30–34; Callimachus's *Hymn.* 1, *Hymn. Jov.* 6.33–34; Diodorus 5.64.2.

8. Gordon 1987: 332–33; Branigan and Vickers 1980: 41–43.

C. Paul wants Titus to have nothing to do with anyone who causes divisions (3:9–11).

IV. Conclusion: Paul wants Titus to come to him and, by helping Zenas and Apollos, teach people to devote themselves to good works (3:12–15).

A. Paul wants Titus to come to him (3:12).

B. Titus, by helping Zenas and Apollos, needs to teach people to keep busy in good works (3:13–14).

C. Final greetings: Christians greet Titus and ask Titus to greet Christians in Crete (3:15).

TITUS 1

ADDRESS (1:1–4)

All the components of the letter are present in microcosm in the introduction. In the letterhead, Paul has an introduction second in length only to that of Romans (46 vs. 71 Greek words). His self-description contains themes he will develop in the letter, such as "knowledge of the truth" and God and Jesus as "our Savior." Like most ancient letters, the first sentence presents the author, the reader, and the greeting (**Paul, God's slave, and Jesus Christ's apostle, Titus, grace and peace**). Paul adds, though, two lengthy prepositional phrases to describe his apostleship: (1) **according to faith of God's elect ones and knowledge of truth, the one according to godliness**; and (2) **upon hope of eternal life, which the truthful God promised before eternal time and revealed, in [God's] own time, his word in proclamation, which I myself was entrusted according to the command of God our Savior** (1:1–3). This is a dense synopsis of the Christian message. Paul reminds Titus first of the importance of one's calling resting upon **faith**, that God elects, that God's revelation is true, and it affects one's way of life (*eusebeia*). Paul then reminds Titus of the second basis of his apostleship: **hope of eternal life**. God, who is described as "truthful" did two actions in regard to "eternal life": **promised** and **revealed**. Both relate to time: eternal life was promised before eternal time, eternal life was revealed in God's **own time** by means of **proclamation**. Paul then reiterates that he was entrusted with this proclamation by command of God.

Paul normally describes himself as a "slave of *Christ*" (e.g., Rom 1:1; Phil 1:1; Gal 1:10). Here in contrast he calls himself a **slave of *God***. Possibly, his reason is that in this letter he will clarify that Jesus Christ is indeed "God." Later in the letter, as a "*slave* of God," he will also give directions to slaves of human masters (2:9–10).

The content of faith and its demonstration in one's lifestyle are important themes for this letter. Titus is a **genuine child according to the faith held in common** (1:4). A "healthy or sound" **faith** is important to have in contrast to those who have an unhealthy or unsound faith (1:14). Slaves need to demonstrate their "good" faith in their actions (2:10) and love is done in the sphere of faith (3:15).

Truth (1:1, 2) (or its opposite) is not a frequent word-family in Titus but it is important since it sets an overarching theme. God does not lie (1:2). Therefore, God's message is truth (1:1). Paul's testimony is also true (1:13). Heterodoxy leads people away from the truth (1:14).[1]

Eusebeia (**godliness**; 1:1) literally refers to "good reverence or worship." It is an important word-family in the Pastoral Letters,[2] where "godly living" is an important topic. Orthodoxy affects orthopraxy. One way to live is in a "godly manner" (2:12).

The object of **hope** is **eternal life**, both in 1:2 and 3:7. Thus, eternal life is something to which we aspire. That is why the *"now* age" (2:12) affects the *eternal* age. In 2:13, hope more specifically refers to the reappearance of Jesus Christ. **Eternal life** is a term frequently used in the Gospels.[3] *Aiōn* may be connected to *aēmi* (*"to breathe, blow,* as to denote properly *that which causes life, vital force"*).[4] Thus, "eternal life" may be considered to be "a life that is alive." Understanding that "life" is a central aspect of "eternal" helps us understand the "now," but "not yet" aspect of "eternal life" (1:2). In Titus and for Paul and for the lawyer and ruler who asked Jesus, "What must I do to inherit eternal life?" (Luke 10:25; 18:18), eternal life is something to obtain and to which one aspires (e.g., 1 Tim 6:12). Jesus and his disciple John bring out that it is also something one now has. Eternal life, according to Jesus' prayer, is to know the only true God and Jesus Christ whom he sent (John 17:3). The goal or end is eternal life, but also it is a free gift from God in Christ Jesus. In effect, when one decides to keep or lose one's life, one begins a trajectory in either the direction of eternal life or eternal punishment.[5]

In this introduction, we find clear examples of the archetypal uses of *chronos* and *kairos*. *Chronos* has to do with duration: God's **eternal time** (1:2). In contrast, *kairos* has to do with changeableness: human specific **time** (1:3).

---

1. For a letter that claims to be about truth, ironically some contemporary scholars claim that it was written neither by Paul nor to Titus nor were either of them in Crete: "The Pastoral Epistles practiced their deception with great success and influence for nearly two thousand years" (Marshall 2008: 799).
2. Thirteen of twenty-two NT occurrences, 59 percent. See also 1 Tim 4:8.
3. Twenty-five times vs. nine times by Paul, eight times elsewhere in the NT.
4. Thayer, 18, 20.
5. John 12:25; Matt 25:46; Rom 6:22–23; 2 Cor 2:15.

Sōtēr is a frequent and an interesting word in Titus.[6] Whenever *God* is referred to as **our Savior**, a second reference soon follows to *Christ Jesus* as "our Savior" (1:3–4; 2:10–13; 3:4–6). Thus, Paul emphasizes by juxtaposition that both persons of the Trinity are "our Savior." Moreover, in one passage Jesus Christ is even called "God" (2:13). The "Savior" commands, gives grace and peace (1:3–4), teaches (2:10), has glory (2:13), is kind, loving, and pours out salvation (3:4, 6). "Savior" is also an important political word during this era. Caesar was acclaimed as "savior" of the people. From AD 66–68 Nero was officially described as "lord and saviour of the world."[7] Although the emperor could command and have temporal glory,[8] in contrast to the eternal God, Nero certainly did not exhibit **grace**, **peace**, kindness, love, and salvation.

Titus, like Timothy, is described as a **genuine child** (1:4; 1 Tim 1:2). Possibly Jews at Crete might "criticize" Titus (2:15) because he was an uncircumcised Greek (Gal 2:3). Unlike Timothy, whose mother was Jewish but father was Gentile, Titus was not compelled by the leaders in Jerusalem to be circumcised (Acts 16:1–3). Thus, Paul uses **genuine** or "legitimate" as a word play. As a Gentile, Titus' faith, held in common with Jews, made him a "legitimate or genuine" child. Titus also demonstrated a "genuine" faith. Titus first appears from Antioch in Syria accompanying Paul with a relief visit to Jerusalem.[9] Titus is gifted in organization. He helped arrange the relief collection for the poor in Judea (2 Cor 2:13; 7:7; 8:17). As Paul's coworker and partner, he is "urged," but not "sent," to go to Corinth as Paul's representative (2 Cor 8:6, 17, 23; 12:18). At Corinth he functions as a peacemaker, also representing the Corinthians to Paul (2 Cor 7:7, 15). At Crete, Titus will again use his organizational and peacemaking gifts with the church to put in order what remained to be done (e.g., Titus 1:5).

---

6. Six of twenty-four NT instances, which comprise 25 percent of the NT references, although Titus is about 0.5 percent of the NT. In fact, ten or 41.6 percent of all NT references of *sōtēr* occur in the Pastoral Letters.

7. Hanson 1982: 186.

8. Once when Nero entered Rome, for example, he came in Augustus's chariot wearing a purple robe and a Greek cloak adorned with golden stars with the Olympic crown on his head (Suetonius, 6. *Nero* 25.1). Gaius Caligula and Nero took their divine status seriously (Alan Richardson, "Salvation, Savior," *IDB* 4:177).

9. Gal 2:1–3, which probably refers to the mission described in Acts 11:29–30, but could refer to the one mentioned in Acts 15:2–4.

SET STRAIGHT (1:5–16)

Paul connects the first section (1:5–16) to the introduction (**Because of this, I left you in Crete,** 1:5a). Because Paul **was entrusted** with the message revealed in God's own time—commanded by God (1:3), a message so important it was promised by God even before the start of time, a message which gives eternal life, by a God who does not lie (1:2)—therefore, identifying godly elders to promote these truths is crucial.

Paul Left Titus in Crete (1:5–9)

When did **Crete** (1:5) receive Christian influence? Titus and Paul traveled together in Syria, Asia Minor, Macedonia, and Achaia, according to Acts, Galatians, and 2 Corinthians. This letter is the only reference to both of them having been in Crete. The New Testament has two references to Crete outside of the Letter to Titus. One reference is to Pentecost (May-June) when devout Jews from Crete were present in Jerusalem, hearing Jesus' disciples proclaim God's wonder in the Cretan language (Acts 2:1–11). The Cretans spoke a dialect of Greek.[10] The second reference is in Acts 27. As Paul, Aristarchus, and Luke set sail to Rome, they travel by Crete's Cape Salmone, arriving at Fair Havens near Lasea (Acts 27:7–8). Because sailing was now dangerous (until Pentecost), the owner of the ship preferred to sail to Phoenix in Crete to winter there (Acts 27:12). Instead, the storm winds drove the ship as far as Malta (Acts 28:1), near Sicily.

Jews had been living in **Crete** for many years. In the second century BC, Roman Consul Lucius sent King Ptolemy a letter expressing that Jews were allies of the Romans. A copy of the letter was sent to Jews in Gortyn, Crete (not too far from Fair Havens) (1 Macc 15:15–23).[11] Cretans may have been mentioned in the Old Testament as early as Genesis 10:14, descendants of Ham, Noah's son ("Caphtorites, from whom the Philistines were descended"; also 1 Chr 1:12). Even though the Philistines were enemies of the Jews (1 Sam 30:14), Kerethites were part of David's loyal guards.[12] The Philistines are described as the "remnant of the isle of Caphtor" (Jer

---

10. Diogenes Laertius, *Lives of Eminent Philosphers* 1.10.112.

11. Josephus, whose wife was a Jew from Crete, *Life* 76 [427], mentions Cretan Jews during the time of Herod: *J.W.* 2.7 [103]; *Ant.* 17.12 [327].

12. 2 Sam 8:18; 15:18; 20:7, 23; 1 Kgs 1:38, 44.

47:4). Caphtor is a Hebrew name for Crete. Caphtorites and Kerethites were names used for descendants from Crete.

Thus, we cannot be sure when the Christian community began in **Crete**, but, most likely some Jews returned to it from Jerusalem after Pentecost to live as disciples of the Messiah Jesus. However, the church needed better organization, doctrine, and moral standards.

Paul regularly works with a team of coworkers, picking them up as he comes to their city, and leaving them behind to handle specific problems.[13] Paul now describes the twofold purpose of Titus' ministry: (1) **that you yourself might set straight further the things remaining**; (2) **and you might set up in each city elders, as I myself directed to you** (1:5). *Epidiorthoō* (**set straight**), like *orthotomeō* ("to cut straight"; 2 Tim 2:15) is built on the root *orthos* ("straight"). Even as the physically crippled man Paul healed at Lystra was able to stand straight (Acts 14:10), those spiritually "crippled" need to "stand" straight (Heb 12:12–13). *Diorthōsis* ("making straight") could refer to restoring a broken or misshapen limb.[14] Thus, the implication is that some restoring or making straight had been done when Paul was in Crete, but it had not been completed, and that Titus himself had to make the effort to finish it. One way to **set straight** is by appointing elders. However, the church at Crete had more than leadership that was not "straight." It also had ungodliness and worldly passion (2:11), including dissipation, pleasing only oneself, quick tempers, bullying, shameful gain, empty and deceptive talk, turning to lies from the truth, corruption, unfaithfulness, disobedience, slander, quarreling about the law, and divisiveness. The elders could help, but ultimately every believer had to decide if he or she wanted to walk straight. And, while Titus was there, he had to encourage good choices by his teaching and exhortation (2:15; 3:14).

What did the **elders** do (1:5)? Their function is only suggested in the letter. Their role had similarities to Titus'. The same verb (**set up**; *kathistēmi*) is used elsewhere in the New Testament of those placed in charge of small or large households, such as a slave or manager who feeds and oversees the other workers and makes investments,[15] judges over disputers,[16] exemplified

---

13. For example, in Paul's second missionary journey, Timothy joins Paul and Silas at Lystra (Acts 16:1–5), Luke joins them at Troas (Acts 16:8–10), then Luke stays behind to minister in Philippi (Acts 16:12–17; 20:5–6), while Timothy and Silas stay behind to minister in Beroea (Acts 17:14–16; 18:5).

14. Thayer, 152; Hippocrates *Off.* 16.

15. Matt 24:45–49; 25:21–23; Luke 12:42–44.

16. Luke 12:14; Acts 7:26–27, 35.

by Joseph as ruler over a household and all of Egypt (Acts 7:10). In addition, the function of steward is explicitly mentioned in Titus 1:7 (*oikonomos*). The establishment of elders is modeled by Moses, who chose trustworthy and honest judges over groups of a thousand, hundred, fifty, and ten to judge the minor cases while he handled the difficult cases (Exod 18:13–26). These judges were chosen by the tribes themselves and were trained by Moses (Deut 1:9–18). Later, the Lord commands Moses to gather seventy of these judges so that they too would be filled with the Spirit as Moses was and share his leadership burdens. In addition, the Spirit came upon Eldad and Medad, who prophesied in the camp (Num 11:16–17, 24, 26).

In Greco-Roman times, Jewish **elders** had authority in religious and civic matters. They handled city administration and jurisdiction. The council of elders (and chief priests in Jerusalem [or Sanhedrin]) decided cases of orthodoxy and heterodoxy with the power of possible excommunication.[17] In a village, one of the elders might be chosen to be "ruler of the synagogue" to oversee the worship service and the synagogue building and represent the congregation to Roman officials.[18] *Presbyteros* (**elders**), like *presbeia* ("a delegation"), could represent a group or a person, to ask for a favor, peace, or the resolution of differences.[19] Thus, a synonym for "elders" was "ambassadors," people who sought reconciliation.[20]

The Jewish Christians appeared to have adapted the Jewish leadership format. Christian **elders** first appear in Acts. Elders in Jerusalem receive the gifts collected by Barnabas and Saul (Paul) for the starving Christians in Judea (Acts 11:29–30). As in Crete, at the second visit to new churches in Asia Minor, Paul and Barnabas oversaw the election of elders in every church (Acts 14:23). The apostles and elders in Jerusalem would decide questions of heterodoxy versus orthodoxy (Acts 15:2–23; 16:4). The whole church would consent to their decision. Even as the apostles, Christian elders have the responsibility to pray for healing (Jas 5:14; Mark 6:13).

In Titus, **overseer** (*episkopos*; 1:7) is a synonym for **elder** (*presbyteros*; 1:5; also Acts 20:17, 28; 1 Pet 5:1–2). *Episkopos* etymologically signifies "to

---

17. Matt 21:23; 26:3–4, 47, 57; 27:1, 12; John 9:22; 12:42; 16:2; Acts 4:5–9; 25:15; *m. Sanh*; Schürer, 1979: 2:431–35; Levine 2000: chap. 5.

18. Acts 13:15; Luke 13:14. Sometimes women were "rulers of the synagogue" and elders (Brooten 1982: chaps. 3, 4; Levine 2000: 482, 486).

19. E.g., Luke 7:2–4; 14:32; 19:14.

20. 2 Cor 5:19–20 *katalassō*.

look upon or over."[21] In Acts 20:28, "to oversee" includes the function of overseeing doctrine and is synonymous with shepherding (also 1 Pet 5:2).

As in Acts (14:23; 20:17), every church in each city should have more than one **elder** (1:5). In Crete, historically, the cities were notorious for their disputes with one another. Willetts summarizes their relationship as "almost perpetual warfare."[22] The two most powerful city states, Knossos in the north and Gortyn in the south, were repeatedly in conflict.[23] But, finally, in 67 BC, Crete became a Roman province and Gortyn its capital.[24] Thus, Paul, by directing Titus to set up elders in **every city**, was beginning where the people were, blending the Christian organization with the indigenous one.

Paul does not clarify how Titus was to go about the process of **setting up elders**, except to make specific their moral qualities. However, Moses certainly had encouraged the Hebrew tribes to select their own leaders (Deut 1:13), and Paul appears to allow the local Christians to select their elders.[25] What Paul did *not* require is instructive. Paul did not require that the elders be Jewish, or circumcised, as the circumcision party might have required. Paul did *not* require that the elders be aristocrats, as the Minoans might have required.[26] Paul did not require that the elders be free citizens, as the Romans or Greeks required.[27] Paul did not require that the elders be wealthy, men of leisure, as the rabbis required (*m. Meg.* 1:3; 4:3). There is no mention of ethnic or class or political or economic status. The term **elder** probably implied a certain age. Some early rabbis said thirty was the age for

21. Thayer, 242. Robertson (*Word Pictures*, 1930: 3:217) suggests "elder" was the Jewish name and "overseer" the Greek name for the same office.

22. Willetts 1965: 152.

23. "After Cnossus, the city of the Gortynians seems to have ranked second in power; for when these two co-operated they held in subjection all the rest of the inhabitants, and when they had a quarrel there was dissension throughout the island" (Strabo, *Geogr.* 10.4 [478]).

24. Willetts 1965: 152–57.

25. Thayer, 668; LSJ, 1986. Acts 14:23, *cheirotoneō*, literally means "to vote by stretching out the hand." According to John Calvin, Paul and Barnabas "suffer the matter to be decided by the consent of them all. Therefore, in ordaining pastors the people had their free election, but lest there should any tumult arise, Paul and Barnabas sit as chief moderators" (*Calvin's Commentaries John-Acts*: 1168).

26. Among the Minoans in Crete, only the aristocrats (not the serfs) could carry arms and exercise in the gym. At "manhood," after years of training, Cretan youths wore the mature citizen warrior's dress (Willetts 1965: 87, 95–96, 117).

27. The political leadership in Greece was done by adult free male citizens (Willetts 1965: 149).

authority, sixty was the age to be an elder (*m. 'Abot* 5:21). Sixty was also the age for a widow to enter the church's order of prayer (1 Tim 5:9).

Paul now adds the first set of qualifications for "elders" (**if any are not open to attack, a one-woman man, having faithful children, not in accusation of wildness or disobedience;** 1:6), to be further developed in a second longer sentence (**For it is necessary [for] the overseer to be not open to attack as God's steward, not self-pleasing, not prone to anger, not given to getting drunk, not pugnacious, not fond of shameful gain, but hospitable, loving what is good, wise, righteous, holy, self-controlled, holding fast the faithful word according to the teaching . . . ;** 1:7–9). Paul uses the same basic qualifications in 1 Timothy 3, but Titus has some different emphases.

Moral Qualities for an Elder Compared and Set in Sequence

Titus 1:6–9	1 Timothy 3:2–7
1. and 4. not open to attack	1. not open to attack
2. one-woman man	2. one-woman man
3. faithful children	13. children in submission
5. not self-pleasing	
6. not prone to anger	
7. not given to getting drunk	3. and 8. not given to getting drunk
8. not pugnacious	9. not pugnacious
9. not fond of shameful gain	12. not greedy
10. hospitable	6. hospitable
11. loving what is good	
12. wise	4. wise
13. righteous	
14. holy	
15. self-controlled	
16. holding fast the faithful word	7. able to teach
	Qualities not in Titus
	5. respectable/modest
	10. gentle
	11. peaceable
	14. not newly converted
	15. good witness from outside

Despite the close initial similarity between Titus 1:7 and 1 Timothy 3:2, the characteristics for godly **elders** are set in different sequences. Each list has some moral qualities not in the other list (but certainly not contradictory to the other list). The first characteristic for leaders (elder and widow [1 Tim 3:2; 5:7; Titus 1:6]) is that someone be chosen who is **not open to attack**, who cannot be discredited, someone against whom a justifiable charge could not be brought (*anenklētos*) from within the church (e.g., circumcision party, 1:10) or from outside the church (e.g., 2:5, 8) or eventually from God (2:13). Even before overt Roman persecution (AD 61–64), Nero's actions had become more violent than earlier in his reign. In AD 59, for example, Nero had his mother Agrippina murdered. In AD 62, senator Seneca retired and Burrus, the serious Prefect of the Praetorians, died. Both had been positive influences on Nero. Nero then divorced his wife Octavia and had her murdered. In AD 62, after the law of *maiestas minuta* was revived, wealthy nobles were executed simply on suspicion. In other words, before the fire in Rome in AD 64, changes in the Roman political situation were evident. Nero clearly became a volatile, vicious ruler.[28]

In Titus (1:6) as in 1 Timothy (3:2; 5:7) having an elder who is (or was) devoted to his spouse (**a one-woman man**) would be a dramatic contrast to many in the larger society.[29] In Crete, as in the rest of the Roman and Greek society, sexual relations between a married free man and a slave or even the wife of a serf were not fined as "adultery." According to the ancient Cretan Gortyn Code, even rape against a household slave received only a penalty of one to twenty-four obols depending on the circumstances (while against a free person was 1,200 obols).[30]

Elders are described as **having faithful children, not in accusation of wildness or disobedience** (1:6). **Faithful children** may refer either to children with belief in Jesus (in other words, "Christian" children)[31] or to children who were trustworthy, for example, as the "trustworthy" word.[32] But, how can a parent be held responsible for the faith of a child if every child has free choice?[33] On the other hand, the modifying phrase "not in

---

28. *OCD*,729, 976.
29. See 1 Tim 3:2 for further details (Spencer 2013). E.g., Xenophon, *Oec.* 10.12.
30. Willetts 1965:94.
31. 1 Tim 4:3, 10, 12; 5:16; 2 Tim 2:2, 13.
32. Titus 1:9; 3:8; 1 Tim 1:15; 3:1; 4:9; 2 Tim 2:11.
33. Ngewa (2009: 68) agrees: the "focus is not so much on what the children have chosen, as on what their father and mother have done" (referring to 1 Tim 3:4).

accusation of wildness or disobedience" (Titus 1:6) may very likely modify the "children" (**wildness** and **disobedience** being the antithesis of **faithful** or "trustworthy"). When children cannot be relied upon to obey the parent, they are "unfaithful." They are incorrigible (*asōtos, asōtia*). These children are leading abandoned, dissolute lives.[34] The same adjective is used for what happens as a result of drunkenness (Eph 5:18), the wild living of Gentiles (1 Pet 4:3-4), the Gentile immorality and disobedience of the law of followers of Bacchys in the temple of Jupiter (2 Macc 6:2-7). This is the life once led by the prodigal son (Luke 15:13). Children who live such a wild life dishonor their parents (Prov 28:7). They will not be subject to control of the parents (Heb 2:8). They are consistently disobedient, without any law (*anypotakta*; 1 Tim 1:9).[35]

To what age is a parent responsible for a child? Ancients, as many today, tended to classify people by whether they were minors[36] or whether they had or had not yet reached puberty.[37] Adulthood or mature citizenship was marked by new clothing in Crete.[38] However, in the New Testament, **children** (*teknon*) is a generic term that can refer to the unborn (Rev 12:4-5), babies under two years of age (Matt 2:16-18), twelve year olds (Luke 2:48), those mature enough to work but are living with their parents (Matt 21:28; Luke 15:31), and as a term of endearment for an adult coworker.[39] Thus, Paul uses a general term in Titus. In addition, adult "children" often continued to live within the household of the parents. The child was responsible to the *paterfamilias* even in adulthood.[40]

When the Christians are trying not to give opportunity for **charges** (*kategoria*) by the church or the larger society (1:6; 2:5, 8), for elders to have such wild children would be dangerous for the church. The impact would be especially harmful in such communal settings as Crete and other ancient Greek societies. Such wild living had already affected "whole households" (Titus 1:11).

---

34. BDAG, 148; Thayer, 82.

35. BDAG, 91; Thayer, 52.

36. E.g., *nēpios*, Gal 4:1, 3, vs. *huios*, Gal 4:7. The Cretans defined a "runner" (*dromeus*) as over twenty as opposed to an *apodromos* (Willetts 1965: 113).

37. Willetts 1965: 113. *m.'Abot* 5:21 says at thirteen a child is responsible to fulfill the law.

38. Willetts 1965:117.

39. Matt 21:28; Luke 15:31; Phil 2:22; 2 Tim 1:2.

40. Witherington 2007: 336.

An additional important reason for believers with **wild children** not to take on the responsibility of oversight of the church was to allow them the time to reach out to their children. The Old Testament has continual references to the importance of parents educating their children, for example, at Passover,[41] reminding their children of what God did in their midst (Deut 4:9–10; Ps 78:3–8) and who God is (Deut 6:4–7). Similar exhortations can be found in the New Testament (e.g., Eph 6:4; 1 Thess 2:11–12). The church needed children who were cooperative members of a mini-nation, the household.

In ancient Greece and Rome, the household, with more of an extended family, is larger than in many contemporary North American and European households. A household would include all persons economically dependent on a master—children, even adult sons, slaves, freedpersons, clients, spouses of all these persons, including the master's spouse.[42] Aristotle explains that the household (*oikia*), the "partnership" for "everyday purposes," in its "perfect form," consists of slaves and free persons, "master and slave, husband and wife, father and children" (*Politics* I.1.6–7; I.2.1). The household might include twenty to thirty people.[43] An ancient household would be an extended family with all the workers in the family business who lived in one housing complex.[44]

In the Cretan society the household was of considerable importance.[45] One Minoan palace would sustain hundreds of people.[46] The relatives and followers would construct their houses radiating out from the palace at the center.[47] The Cretans were particularly communal. Meals and sleeping quarters were communal, one for the young men, another for the young women. Even mature men ate together. Contributions from the harvest were made by serfs toward worship of the gods, upkeep of public services, and to meals for citizens. Even marriage was collective: the young men were required to marry at the same age.[48]

---

41. Deut 11:19; 31:12–13; Josh 8:35; Exod 12:26–27; 13:8, 14–15.
42. Lampe 1993: 20.
43. Lampe 1993: 27.
44. E.g., Stephana's household chose to enter the "business" of ministry (1 Cor 16:15) (Spencer, 2005: 69–77).
45. Willetts 1965: 48.
46. Hawkes 1968: 52, 55, 58.
47. Gordon 1987: 334.
48. According to the Cretan Gortyn Code, the father had power over the children and

An **accusation** (*katēgoria, katēgoreō*) then was a formal affair. For example, Paul refers to formal accusations against elders in 1 Timothy 5:19, reminding the church that two or three witnesses were needed, alluding to Deuteronomy 19:15. In the New Testament, such accusations before the Jewish religious leaders or Roman political leaders could lead to excommunication from the synagogue and death.[49] *Katēgoreō* and *katēgoria* refer especially to an accusation before judges.[50] Thus, an elder should not be recommended for leadership if that elder or a child living in the household is under a serious accusation process.

The overseer is God's steward (1:7). A "steward" (*oikonomos*) was the manager of a household. The owner entrusted the management of affairs to the *oikonomos*: the oversight of the property, receiving and paying bills, planning expenditures, apportioning food, and overseeing minors.[51] They had to be trustworthy.[52] Erastus, for example, was a city "manager" (Rom 16:23). Overseers or elders were managers of church life. The owner of their property is "God" (Titus 1:7).

Paul enumerates five failings to avoid that would make God's steward trustworthy (**not self-pleasing, not prone to anger, not given to getting drunk, not pugnacious, not fond of shameful gain;** 1:7) and seven qualities to cultivate to make God's steward trustworthy (**but be hospitable, loving what is good, wise, righteous, holy, self-controlled, holding fast the faithful word according to the teaching;** 1:8–9). God's manager must be willing to please God, not only oneself (**not self-pleasing;** *authadēs*).[53] If a manager is **prone to anger** without cause,[54] that will result in unnecessary conflict (Prov 29:22). Jesus spoke against anger without a good cause, as from envy, which can be a precondition to murder. Anger is a violent emotion that can lead to a violent action. It disparages the listener. The opposite is reconciliation or peacemaking.[55] Anger is also infectious. Simply being

---

the property. Strabo, *Geogr.* 10.4.16, 20; Plato, *Leg.* I.625C-626A; Aristotle, *Pol.* II.ii.10 (1264a); II. vi.21 (1271a); II. vii.3 (1272a); Willetts 1965: 86–87, 111, 113–14, 117, 119.

49. E.g., Matt 12:10; 27:12; John 18:29; Acts 22:30; 24:2, 8, 13, 19; 25:5, 11, 16.

50. LSJ, 926–27.

51. BDAG, 697; Thayer, 440–41; Luke 12:42–44; 16:1–7; Gal 4:2; Xenophon, *Oec.* I, V, IX.

52. *Pistos*, 1 Cor 4:1–2; Matt 25:21, 23.

53. Xenophon mentions the importance of loyalty for a steward (*Oec.* XII [5]).

54. God can express a just anger, with good cause (e.g., Rev 11:18; Matt 18:34; 22:7).

55. Matt 5:21–26; Luke 15:28–32; cf. 1 Tim 3:3, *amachos*.

a companion to a person given to anger can encourage one to be irascible too (Prov 22:24-25).[56]

The components of *aischrokerdēs* (1:7) occur later in Titus (1:11, *aischros kerdos*) to describe those of the circumcision party who overturn whole households because of **shameful gain**. *Aischrokerdēs* is also used for "deacons" in 1 Timothy 3:8. *Aphilargyros* (the quality for an overseer in 1 Tim 3:3 and any believer in Heb 13:5) clearly refers to "not loving money."[57] *Aischrokerdēs* is a broader term.[58] Josephus uses *aischrokerdeia* for deceitful financial gain (*Life* 13 [75]). Polybius sees the love for "shameful gain" (*aischrokerdeia*) and lust for wealth to prevail among the Cretans. They are "the only people in the world in whose eyes no gain is disgraceful" (*Hist.* 6.46.3-4). Because the state allows them to acquire as much land as they want, he accuses them of having an "ingrained lust of wealth" that causes "constant broils both public and private, and in murders and civil wars" (*Hist.* 6.46.9; 47.5). Thus, Paul's requirement for an elder/overseer *not* to desire "shameful gain" would especially be significant in Crete. In contrast, for God's stewards to be trustworthy, they must not shamelessly and deceitfully seek their own gain or profit.

Sitting long drinking wine (**not given to getting drunk**; *paroinos*)[59] and fighting (**not pugnacious**; *plēktēs*, 1:7) are related words, because sometimes excessive drinking can lessen inhibitions that cover more hidden aggressive emotions, especially if a person is prone to **anger** anyway (*orgilos*). If the overseer begins with a foundation of pleasing oneself, instead of God, and to this foundation is added a tendency to be angry without good cause, impelled by intoxication and readiness to fight, no wonder the end would be shameless self-gain (*aischrokerdēs*).

In contrast, the trustworthy household manager is **hospitable** (*philoxenos*), **loving what is good** (*philagathos*) (not intoxicants or self-gain), is **wise** (*sōphrōn*), **righteous** (*dikaios, dikaia*), **holy** (*hosios, hosia*), and certainly **self-controlled** (1:8). Some of these positive qualities for an overseer/

56. See 1 Tim 3:2-3 for explanation of *paroinos* ("given to getting drunk"), *plēktēs* ("not pugnacious"), *philoxenos* ("hospitable"), and *sōphrōn* ("wise") (Spencer 2013).

57. Literally, "not [a] loving [*philos*] silver [*argyros*]."

58. Literally, "shameful gain" (*aischros* + *kerdos*) or "sordidly greedy of gain." The verb *kerdainō* can refer to financial profit (e.g., Jas 4:13).

59. A typical Minoan touch in harvest festival vases is "the celebrant who has had too much to drink and has fallen almost flat on his face" (Gordon 1987: 333). The Cretans claimed that Dionysus, the wine god, was born in Crete (*Diodorys* 5. 75. 4-5). Xenophon points out that drink makes estate managers "forget everything they ought to do" (*Oec.* 12.11).

elder also appear in other ancient literature. Philo concludes that the lawgiver should especially have four virtues: love of humanity (*philanthrōpos*), love of justice (*philodikaios*), love of good (*philagathos*), and hatred of evil (*misoponēros*).[60]

Two additional key characteristics of God are righteousness and holiness. As early as the Pentateuch, Moses summarizes God's character as great: "God is trustworthy (*pistos*) and has no unrighteousness; **righteous** (*dikaios*) and holy (*hosios*) is the Lord" (Deut 32:4), and, as late as Revelation, an angel describes God as "righteous, the One who is and the One who was, the Holy One" (Rev 16:5). Jesus too is described as "holy and righteous" (Acts 3:14).[61] In the first century, *dikaios* could refer to people who observe societal rules.[62] In the Bible, it refers to people who observe God's rules, like Noah, a "righteous human," pleasing to God (Gen 6:10) or Zechariah and Elizabeth "righteous before God, walking blamelessly in all the commandments and regulations of the Lord" (Luke 1:6).

The opposite of **righteous** (1:8) is lawless and disobedient, godless, sinful, and unholy (Titus 2:12; 1 Tim 1:9), as the wild and disobedient child (Titus 1:6). Righteousness is a characteristic people may have and yet will pursue but never perfect (1 Tim 6:11; 2 Tim 3:16). Human works of righteousness cannot save; only Jesus, the perfect Righteous One, can die for the unrighteous to bring them to God (Titus 3:5-7; 1 Pet 3:18). Nevertheless, the new believer is instructed to live according to God's likeness in "true righteousness and holiness" (Eph 4:24).

How is anyone to avoid self-pleasure, anger, drunkenness, fights, shameful gain but to pursue hospitality, loving what is good, acting wisely, righteously, and in a holy manner? Self-control is the key. **Self-control** (1:8), to have power over oneself,[63] is one of the fruits of the Spirit, which is made possible by crucifying the flesh with its passions while being guided by the Spirit (Gal 5:23-25). It is a characteristic of winning athletes (1 Cor 9:25). The persons with power over themselves are guided by holding

---

60. Philo, *Mos.* 2.2 (9); Minos, the founder of Crete, imitated Rhadamanthys, "a man most *just* . . . who is reputed to have been the first to civilize the island by establishing laws . . . and by setting up constitutions." In ancient times, according to Strabo, Crete had "good laws," but later "it changed very much for the worse" when it began piracy (Strabo, *Geogr.* 10.4.8-9 [C476-C477]; Plato, *Leg.* I.624-25A, 631B); *TLNT* 3:438. See also Titus 1:8.

61. See also Acts 7:52; 22:14.

62. LSJ, 429; Thayer, 148; *TLNT* 1:320.

63. Thayer, 167.

firmly to the trustworthy message they were taught (Titus 1:9). This is the godly truth proclaimed by Paul (not the circumcision party)—his healthy teaching (Titus 1:1–3, 10; 2:1).

Overseers/elders must be able to do two things: (1) encourage and (2) reprove: **in order that (s)he may also be able to encourage healthy teaching and to reprove those who are opposing** (1:9).[64] While they encourage **healthy teaching**, they also discourage those who undermine healthy teaching. Both **encouragement** and **reproving** will come up again in the letter for the elder and for Titus (1:13; 2:6, 15). Here explicitly Titus is reminded that there are some people at Crete who oppose (*antilegō*) healthy teaching.[65] They are not obedient to the truth. Paul had been opposed before by some of his Jewish compatriots (Acts 13:45; 28:19), as had been John the Baptist (Luke 2:34).[66] Therefore, the overseers/elders are to be people who will work with Titus while he is there (Titus 3:12) to facilitate true teaching.

Sound Teaching (1:10–14)

Paul left Titus behind to set straight what was remaining to be done by appointing godly elders in every city (1:5–9). Why was this necessary? **For there are many disobedient, empty talkers, and deceivers, especially the ones from the circumcision, who it is necessary to silence, who overturn whole households teaching what is not necessary because of shameful gain** (1:10–11). Paul begins by listing three negative qualities that many people have at Crete: **disobedience** (*anypotaktos*), **empty talk** (*mataiologos*), and **deception** (*phrenapatēs*) (1:10). Children (1:6), and certainly the elders themselves, should *not* be people unable to subject themselves to healthy teaching (*anypotaktos*, 1:9; "knowledge of truth," 1:1). Does **empty talk** refer simply to someone who is verbose ("a windbag"),[67] or is it a stronger term? *Mataiologia* (*mataios*, **empty;** and *logia/legō*, **to speak**)[68] is synonymous with heterodoxy, myths, and endless genealogies that promote speculations, teaching what is wrong in contrast to God's "household management" whose goal is love from a pure heart and a good conscience and

---

64. Xenophon also understands "overseers" to be guardians of the laws . . . commending the law-abiding and punishing law-breakers (*Oec.* 9.14).

65. See Titus 1:13.

66. God had been opposed (Rom 10:21; Jude 11) and, of course, even Jesus' own people rejected him (John 1:11).

67. BDAG, 621.

68. Ibid.; Thayer, 392.

sincere faith (1 Tim 1:3–7; Titus 1:7). *Mataios* in Titus describes the lack of value in discussing "foolish arguments and genealogies and contentions and battles pertaining to the law" (3:9). *Mataios* is used in the New Testament to describe the pagan gods, like Zeus, who do not have the ability and force to create the world (Acts 14:15) and the way Gentiles who believe in such gods live and think.[69] *Mataios* can also refer to lack of truth or value or force,[70] as faith without the historic resurrection has no value (1 Cor 15:17; also 1 Cor 3:20; Jas 1:26). In Titus 1:10, Paul describes those people whose words have no value most likely because their content is not in accordance with truth. Possibly, they go through a sequence of steps. First, they do not subject themselves to healthy teaching and teachers (*anypotaktos*), then their words become heterodox (*mataiologos*), and, finally, they deceive others (*phrenapatēs*).

Eve is an illustration of someone who sinned because of **deception**, unlike Adam who sinned knowingly (1 Tim 2:14; 2 Cor 11:3). In Ephesians, Paul warns his readers not to be deceived because of "empty words" (Eph 5:6). Deception is based on untruthful information. For example, the serpent misled Eve by suggesting to her that God had told her not to eat from *any* tree in the garden, that she would *not* die, and that eating the fruit would make her like God (Gen 3:1, 4–5). The serpent made God's commands (Gen 2:16–17) more strict and as well contradicted them. The same process was likely true of the opponents at Crete, and especially "the ones from the circumcision" (Titus 1:10). The Cretan mercenaries were so well known for their art of deception, the ancients had a saying, "to play the Cretan," which meant to take every precaution and to examine a situation from every angle in order to deceive and vanquish one's opponent (Polybius, *Hist.* 8.19.5).

The deviation from the truth at Crete has many similarities with the one at Ephesus. What is implied in Ephesus is explicit in Crete: the presence of some people from the circumcision party.

---

69. Eph 4:17; Rom 1:21; 1 Pet 1:18. 2 Pet 2:10–19 describes such a lifestyle as one that indulges in irrational passions of the flesh, such as sexual immorality and greed, and despises authority.

70. Thayer, 393.

Heterodoxy Compared[71]

Titus	1 Timothy
Wild pagan; impure vs. holy, 1:6–8, 15–16; 2:3, 5, 11	Unholy, impure, demonic, godless, 1:5, 9; 2:10; 4:1, 7; 5:15; 6:6, 20
Disobedience, 1:6, 10, 16; 3:3	Disobedience, 1:9
Empty talk, 1:10	Empty talk, 1:6; 5:13; 6:20
Deception, 1:10, 12	Deception, 2:14; 4:1–2
Shameful gain, 1:11	Using godliness as a means of gain, 6:5
Myths, 1:14	Myths, 1:4; 4:7
Mind and conscience defiled, 1:15	Conscience, 1:19–20; 4:2; corrupted minds, 6:5
Profess to know God, 1:16; turn away from truth, 1:5, 14; 3:3	Turn away, 1:6; 6:20–21 Heterodoxy, 1:3; 2:4; 6:3, 5, 20
Unacceptable for God's works, 1:16; 3:8, 14	Acceptable to God, 5:4, 10; 6:18
Controversies (foolish), 3:9	Controversy, 6:4
Genealogies, 3:9	Genealogies (endless), 1:4
Contentions and quarrels about law, 3:4, 9–11	Speculation, disputes, evil conjectures, irritations, misuse of law, 1:8; 2:8; 6:4–5, 20
Slanderers? 2:3; 3:2	Slander, 1:13, 20; 5:13; 6:4
Necessary needs, 3:14	Living luxuriously; love of money, 5:6; 6:10, 17
Human commands, 1:14–15	Ascetic-forbid marriage and foods, 4:3
Idle bellies; passion, 1:12; 2:11; 3:3	
Teach good; harmful, 1:12; 2:3;	Want to teach, 1:7
Jewish myths, 1:14 Circumcision party, 1:10	Old-women's myths; widow problems, 4:7; 5:3–16

71. See also chart 2 Tim 2:16–18, p. 108.

In 1 Timothy, Paul discusses the law and the misuse of the law (1:8–10), as he does in Titus (3:9–10). However, in Titus, the **circumcision** party is explicitly mentioned and the Jewish aspect of the myths (1:10, 14). In contrast, in 1 Timothy, the speculative aspect of the myths is described as "old-women's myths" (4:7). In Ephesus, difficulties with younger widows are mentioned (1 Tim 5:3–16), but not in Crete. Heterodoxy and the desire to teach are more explicit in Ephesus (1 Tim 1:3, 6–7; 6:3, 5, 20). Nevertheless, both churches are dealing with controversies and quarrels that relate to genealogies and myths (Titus 1:14; 3:9; 1 Tim 1:4; 4:7).

Circumcision (*peritomē*; 1:10) is a symbol of the old covenant and obedience to Moses' law.[72] It can serve as a synecdoche to refer to Jews in general[73] or to Jewish Christians in particular.[74] But Paul argues that real circumcision is of the heart, not physical and external (Rom 2:28–29; Col 2:11). He points out that Abraham was circumcised as a symbol of imputed righteousness after he believed in God (Rom 4:11). Thus, when some Jewish believers insisted on circumcision and obedience to all of Moses' laws and some rabbinic laws, they became a party critical of Paul and Peter.[75] Exactly what is the Cretan circumcision party teaching? Are they requiring Gentiles to be circumcised (Gal 5:2–4; 6:12–15; Phil 3:2–5)? Are they requiring Gentiles and Jews to eat only kosher food and celebrate all Old Testament holidays?[76] Even non-Jews in ancient times were aware of Jewish food prohibitions.[77] Paul does not elaborate, although at Crete and Ephesus the teaching had to do with "Jewish myths and human commandments" that veered followers away from God's truth (Titus 1:14). Whatever was happening in Crete, however, was motivated by "shameful gain" (1:11). Those in the circumcision party were out to please themselves by shamelessly and deceitfully seeking their own profit (1:7).

To silence (*epistomizō*; 1:11) has very different connotations from "silence" (*hēsychia, hēsychios*) in 1 Timothy 2:2, 11–12. *Epistomizō* literally

---

72. E.g., John 7:22–23; Acts 7:8; Rom 2:25—3:1; 4:10–12; 1 Cor 7:19; Gal 5:6, 11; 6:15; Phil 3:4–5.

73. Rom 4:12; Gal 2:7–9; Eph 2:11; Phil 3:3; Col 3:11.

74. Acts 10:45; Rom 3:30; 4:9; Col 4:11.

75. Acts 11:2–3; Gal 2:12–13; 5:2–4; John 18:28–29; *m. Tehar.* 7.2, 5–6.

76. Acts 11:2–3; 10:12–14; Deut 14:3–21; Gal 2:12–13; Col 2:16; 1 Tim 4:3; Rom 14:14–23; Heb 13:9.

77. E.g., Epictetus, *Disc.* 1.22.11.

refers to stopping up or bridling the mouth, a punishment.[78] For example, Varus, the ruler of Syria, "punished" or "silenced" some Jews who had revolted against Caesar.[79] Likewise, one of the functions of the elders was to reprove opposition (Titus 1:9, 13).

Paul then cites a **Cretan** as support against the wrong teachings in Crete: **Someone said from out of their own, a prophet from among them: Cretans always are liars, evil beasts, idle bellies. This testimony is true** (1: 12–13a). Clement of Alexandria (AD 150–212) cites Epimenides' poem *Peri Chrēsmoi* in *Oracula* as the source of the quotation (*Strom.* 1.14.59). Epimenides, son of Phaestius, who lived 600–500 BC, born in Knossos, Crete, was a legendary seer who was said to have lived 157 or 299 years (*Diogenes Laertius* 1.10.109, 111). Cicero cites him as an illustration of those who prophesy while in a frenzy (*Div.* 1.18.34). Ancient writers give him credit, because he had "superhuman foresight," for a number of miraculous acts, such as stopping pestilence in Athens. Even some Cretans sacrificed to him as a god.[80] If indeed Paul is quoting Epimenides, Paul is simply saying that his testimony about the general nature of Cretans (in ancient times) was true and applicable in this case (Titus 1:13).[81]

The first three words of Paul's quotation are cited by Callimachus of Cyrene (circa 310 BC), an epic poet and contemporary of Ptolemy Philadelphus, **Cretans always are liars** (*Hymn. Jov.* line 8). This idea was so proverbial in ancient times that the Greek *krētizō*, "to play the Cretan," for many meant simply "to lie."[82] Even though some ancients might agree with the Cretan myth that many gods had their origin in Crete (Diodorus 5.46. 3), many did not appreciate the Cretan version that Zeus was buried in a tomb in Crete. Callimachus doubts that Zeus was born in Crete rather than Arcadia because the Cretans are known for their lying. He especially doubts their legend that Zeus was buried in Crete because Zeus is "forever" (line 9). Lucian cites Cretans as an illustration of "cities and whole peoples" who tell lies "unanimously and officially": "The Cretans exhibit the tomb of Zeus

78. Thayer, 243; BDAG, 382; LSJ, 661.

79. Josephus, *Ant.* 17.10.1 (251). For other examples, see *TLNT* 2:61–62.

80. *Diogenes Laertius* 1.10.110–111, 114; Plato, *Leg.* I.642D-E; Aristotle, *Rhet.* III.17.10.

81. In Romans, Paul asserts that all humans can learn about God from creation (1:19–21). Even Jesus' adversary, the high priest Caiaphas, could prophesy accurately about Jesus' substitutionary death (John 11:49–53). Thus, even nonbelievers can observe truths about Jesus. Christ "enlightens everyone" (John 1:9).

82. LSJ, 995.

and are not ashamed of it" (*Philops.* 3).⁸³ The Jews who were overturning whole households might have been promoting their Cretan heritage. And, they did have many things to be proud of, as the earlier advanced Minoan civilization. Also, the Cretans were famous for their past laws. In Plato's dialogue about ideal governments, he includes a representative of Crete (Clinias, along with a representative of Sparta-Megillus of Lacedaemon, and, of course, himself as the "Athenian Stranger"). Cretans claimed that Zeus gave his laws directly to King Minos.⁸⁴ The laws of the Cretans were held in "superlatively high repute among all the Hellenes."⁸⁵ Nevertheless, there was an underside to Crete.

To what is Paul referring when he agrees with the accusation of **evil beasts** (*thērion*) and **idle bellies** (*gastēr* [1:12])? For ancient Greeks, *thēr* referred to a **beast** of prey, such as a lion or a monster.⁸⁶ A *thērion* (a "little animal") often referred to a "wild animal," including even elephants.⁸⁷ In the Bible, *thērion* is used as early as Genesis 1 to refer to animals that were not four-footed animals (cattle) or reptiles or birds.⁸⁸ They were brought for protection by pairs into the ark (Gen 6:20; 7:14). Some were unclean.⁸⁹ Sometimes the word referred to all wild animals (Lev 17:13; Jas 3:7). The snake was one example (Gen 3:2; Acts 28:4–5). Thus, *thērion* generally referred to animals, especially wild animals. The adjective **evil** limits the type of animal. This would be a harmful animal. God mentions four means of judgment: sword, famine, pestilence, and *evil* beasts/animals (Ezek 14:21). Thus, an ***evil* beast** is an animal harmful to humans or domesticated animals.⁹⁰ Sometimes, people are described as living like "wild animals," or being treated as animals.⁹¹ Paul's reference, of course, is clearly a negative metaphor. Probably he would understand "evil beasts" in its Old Testament

---

83. Lucian repeats this illustration in *Sacr.* 10.

84. Plato, *Leg.* I.624A, 630B; Diodorus 5.78. 3.

85. Plato, *Leg.* I.631B; Polybius, *Hist.* 6.7.43.1. The Cretans also claimed to have discovered the use of fire and the metals copper and iron, the domestication of sheep, the making of honey, the art of shooting with the bow, the making of swords and helmets, and the war-dance (*Diodorus* 5.64.5; 65.3–4; 74.5).

86. LSJ, 799.

87. LSJ, 800; 1 Macc 6:35–37; 11:56.

88. E.g., Gen 1:24–25, 30; 7:21; 8:1, 17, 19.

89. Acts 11:6; Lev 11:27; Deut 28:26.

90. Lev 26:6, 22; Deut 7:22; 32:24; Isa 35:9; Ezek 5:17; 14:15; 34:25, 28; 2 Macc 9:15.

91. Judas Maccabeus lived in the mountains feeding on wild herbs as a wild animal might (2 Macc 5:27; 10:6). Some Jewish martyrs were dragged like beasts (3 Macc 4:9).

context, comparing these false teachers to destructive animals who destroy people by attacking them and destroying their healthy faith.

Plato, in his dialogue about the ideal government, mentions how the common meals and gymnasia in Crete (though beneficial in many ways) also could be quite harmful, corrupting "the pleasures of love which are natural not to humans only but also natural to **beasts**" (*thērion*). He mentions that these state structures encouraged pleasures "contrary to nature when male mates with male or female with female, and that those first guilty of such enormities were impelled by their slavery to pleasure. And we all accuse the Cretans of concocting the story about Ganymede" (*Leg.* I.636B–C). In this myth, Zeus, disguised as an eagle, takes Ganymede, a handsome youth, tending his flock, away with him. Plato appears to allude to a Cretan custom where a young man, with the aid of his friends, abducts another young man. He is given presents and taken away where for two months they feast and hunt. The abducted man is honored as "those who were chosen as stand-bys," the abductor is called "lover."[92] However, not all in the ancient world would see this practice as admirable—certainly Plato did not (at least in this referral). Paul would not.[93]

The second descriptive phrase would also remind the reader of eating, since *gastēr* refers to the **belly** or "paunch," the belly, especially "as craving food," or "the womb."[94] Elsewhere in the New Testament, *gastēr* only refers to the wombs of pregnant women.[95] *Argē, argos* is used in 1 Tim 5:13 for the young widows who do not pray but instead are **idle**, not having productive ways to spend their time. This is the same adjective that James uses to describe faith without action. It is "fallow" (2:20 vs. 1:21 "implanted"). Jesus uses it for laborers who have no work to do (Matt 20:3). Therefore, the phrase literally refers to "inactive bellies" or "stomachs that do not work" (people who eat but do not use their energy for work) or "wombs that do not bear children." Consequently, **evil beasts, idle bellies** could allude to the pleasure-seeking Cretan lifestyle. Polybius describes the Cretan "point of view" to be one of only self-interest (*Hist.* 8.16.5–8). No wonder these opponents were seeking their own shameful gain (1:7, 11).

How is it possible that those in the **circumcision** party could be known for pleasure-seeking? Paul apparently thought it possible when

---

92. Strabo, *Geogr.* 10.4.21 (C483–84); Willetts 1965: 116.
93. E.g., 1 Cor 6:9.
94. LSJ, 339
95. Matt 1:18, 23; 24:19; 1 Thess 5:3; Rev 12:2.

he challenged some Jews who thought they were teachers to the ignorant: "Will you not teach yourself? While you preach against stealing, do you steal? You that forbid adultery, do you commit adultery? You that abhor idols, do you rob temples? You that boast in the law, do you dishonor God by breaking the law? For, as it is written, 'The name of God is blasphemed among the Gentiles because of you'" (Rom 2:21–24; NRSV). He also claimed that those who required circumcision were avoiding persecution for the cross of Christ (Gal 6:12). They remove "the offense of the cross" (Gal 5:11). Sometimes those who insist on "self-abasement" (Col 2:18) are the very same people who indulge their flesh. Paul warns that regulations appear to help in promoting piety, but "they lack any value in restraining sensual indulgence" (Col 2:23; TNIV).

Because many, especially of the circumcision party, are disobedient to God's truth, talk without teaching God's truth, and deceive people, Titus needs to: **rebuke them rigorously, in order that they may be healthy in the faith, not paying attention to Jewish myths and human commandments, turning for themselves away (being turned away) from the truth** (1:13b–14). People can err either on the side of harsh narrow-mindedness or lax permissiveness. The promotion of truth necessitates a balance between compassion and integrity. In Titus, the goal is health, healthy faith and healthy teaching (1:9, 13; 2:1–2, 8). Good **health** is a reoccurring and helpful metaphor in the Pastorals.[96] God warned the Israelites that "I am the Lord who heals" those who obey his statutes (Exod 15:26). Jesus explained that he ate with sinners because, like a physician, his intention was to heal the sick (Luke 5:30–31). Good health necessitates honest diagnosis and a rigorous program of avoiding unhealthy habits and foods and promoting healthy habits and foods. In the same way, spiritual health requires individuals (Titus) and groups of people (elders/overseers) who are vigilant to do something about teachings that turn people away from the truth. Frequently *elenchō* (**rebuke**) is balanced off by *parakaleō* ("encourage") because a good physician promotes health and discourages sickness (e.g., 1:9). *Elenchō* has to do with bringing deeds and thoughts out in the open for clarity and truth (e.g., John 3:20; Eph 5:11, 13). The secrets of the heart are disclosed by prophetic teaching (1 Cor 14:24–25). Titus and the elders are assisted by prophets (1 Cor 14:24–25), the law (Jas 2:9), and the Holy Spirit (John 16:8–11). But the intention is not malicious; rather, conviction

---

96. Two-thirds of the NT uses of *hygiainō* occur in the Pastoral Letters (four of eight in Titus). 1 Tim 1:10; 6:3; 2 Tim 1:13; 4:3; Titus 1:9, 13; 2:1, 2, 8 (*hygiēs*).

of sin is done out of a relationship of love, like a parent's love for a child: to build up, not simply to tear down.[97] The process helps to maintain a right attitude: to win over the Christian brother or sister.[98] Jesus explains that the first confrontation should be private, then two or three witnesses should be included (Matt 18:15–16; also Deut 19:15). Then, the leadership should evaluate the situation, and, finally, the whole congregation should be a witness (Deut 19:16–20; 1 Tim 5:20). Only after all these stages should the person be "silenced" or treated as an outsider (Titus 1:11; Matt 18:17).

The use of *apotomōs* (**rigorously**) indicates that the problems at Crete are serious and persistent. They are serious because they cause people to turn away from the knowledge of the truth that gives eternal life (Titus 1:14, 1–2). They are persistent because a gentle explanation is not enough. But Titus has already shown he has the qualities of compassion and integrity when working with the Christians at Corinth who also had serious and persistent spiritual problems (2 Cor 7:13–16; 8:16–17).

The opposite of healthy or sound faith is **paying attention to Jewish myths and human commandments** (1:14). *Mythos* (**myth**) could simply refer to a "tale, story, narrative," but, in this context, Paul treats it as "fiction," "legend," of which the opposite is *logos* or "historic truth."[99] The Bible contrasts it with God's *oikonomia*, God's principles (1 Tim 1:4), and the truth (2 Tim 4:4; 2 Pet 1:16). The secular Cretan had many myths about which they were proud, such as about Zeus.[100] They used the myths as bases for their actions, as "sound" Jews use God's written revelation as a basis for actions. Myth, thus, became a "didactic literary genre."[101] Therefore, possibly the Cretan "Jewish-Christian opponents were creating speculative doctrines based on stories of ancient OT heroes and using them to lend the weight of antiquity to certain questionable practices that Paul regarded as ungodly."[102] In a similar fashion, Jesus criticized the Pharisees who, abandoning God's command, held on to human tradition (Mark 7:8).

Scholars who agree Paul wrote the Pastoral Letters have suggested that these **Jewish** false teachers could have been similar to (a) Essenes, (b)

---

97. Heb 12:5–6; Rev 3:19; 2 Cor 13:10.
98. See also Gal 6:1–2.
99. LSJ, 1151; *TLNT* 2:528–33.
100. See, e.g., Titus 1:12–13.
101. *TLNT* 2:531.
102. Towner 2006: 705.

Hellenistic Jews, or (c) proto-gnostics.[103] Many Essenes did not marry, were ascetic, had food and Sabbath restrictions, were hierarchical, and thought matter was evil.[104] The Book of Jubilees (circa 160–50 BC) is a proto-Essene document[105] that illustrates many of the false Jewish teachers' concerns. It is a paraphrase or commentary (midrash) of parts of Genesis and Exodus. However, in contrast to Genesis, its main focus is the law. Those who "search out the Law" will be persecuted (1:12) and when children begin again "to search the law" God's blessed time will have arrived (Jub 23:26; cf. Titus 3:9; Gal 4:21; 5:18). Jubilees highlights the importance of observing the Sabbath (Jub 2:24–33; 50:1–13; vs. Col 2:16), observing the moon and time (6:32–38; 49:10), and not eating blood (6:11–14; 7:27–33; 21:18–20; vs. Col 2:16). Circumcision is also indispensable (15:25–34; 16:25). Uncircumcised men cannot be forgiven. It is an "eternal error."[106] Hebrew is "the tongue of creation" (Jub 12:26; vs. 2 Cor 11:22). The author shows a fascination with angels (Jub 2:2, 18; 15:27; cf. Col 2:18). Perfection is possible (e.g., Abraham 23:10; Jacob 35:12; cf. Titus 3:5; Phil 3:8–9). True Israelites are to keep separate from Gentiles and not even eat with them (Jub 22:16; 30:7; vs. Gal 2:12–13).[107]

Certainly, we cannot determine the particular books used at Crete or Ephesus, but Jubilees exemplifies the type of thinking that would be similar to the **Judaizers** in Crete and Ephesus.[108]

Some second-century gnostics such as the Encratites abstained from marriage and animal food.[109] Full-blown Gnosticism was a second-century phenomenon, but some proto-gnostics lived in the first century, such as Simon Magus and Cerinthus. Simon, a Samaritan, who in Acts already

---

103. E.g., Lock 1924: 47; Towner 2006: 110; Fee 1988: 41, 211.

104. Josephus, *J.W.* 2.8 (119–159).

105. O. S. Wintermute, "Jubilees," *OTP* 2:43–46.

106. *Jub.* 15:34; cf. Titus 1:10; Phil 3:2–5; Gal 2:3; 5:2–3; 6:12–15; Rom 2:28–29.

107. See also 1 En. 20:1–7; 69:1–15; 71:3, 10; 72:1—75:9; 79:1–6; 82:5; 92:2; 108:2, 9, 15; 109:15.

108. Hegesippus (AD 180) mentions that the Essenes did not believe in Jesus as Messiah and some of the Apocrypha was "fabricated by certain heretics of his own day" (Eusebius, *Hist. eccl.* 4.22 [7–9]). Ebionites, who rejected Paul's writings (they used only Matthew's Gospel or the Gospel according to the Hebrews) because they thought Paul was "apostate from the law," according to Irenaeus, "circumcise themselves and continue in the practices which are prescribed by the law and by the Judaic standard of living" (*Haer.* 1.26.2).

109. Irenaeus, *Haer.* 1.28.

demonstrated his interest in "shameful gain" (Titus 1:11; Acts 8:18–20), was considered by Irenaeus the person "from whom all heresies got their start."[110] Holding to elements of reincarnation, docetism, and syncretism (*Haer.* 1.23.2, 4), Simon saw himself as "Father on high" who gave birth to "Thought" (Helen), who gave birth to Angels and Powers, who kept her from returning to her "Father on high" (*Haer.* 1.23.2). According to Irenaeus, the "mystic priests of these people live licentious lives and practice magic" (*Haer.* 1.23.4). Cerinthus, unlike Simon, appeared to be **Jewish** and was "enslaved to lusts and pleasure" (Euseb. *Hist. eccl.* 3.28 [2]; 7.25 [3]). He thought the world was not created by the first God, thereby appearing to treat matter as evil (Irenaeus, *Haer.* 1.26.1; cf. 1 Tim 4:3–5). Jesus died, but not "Christ" (*Haer.* 1.26.1). Thus, the Simonians might illustrate the focus on genealogies, and Cerinthians a low view of matter, but neither illustrated the Jewish quarrels about the law.

Minds and Consciences Are Defiled (1:15–16)

These teachers who claim to know God were seeing things that were clean or pure and treating them as unclean or impure because their own minds and consciences were soiled: **All things are pure to the pure ones; but to the defiled and unbelieving nothing is pure, but also their mind and conscience are defiled. They profess to know God, but they are denying his works, being abominable and disobedient and unacceptable for every good work** (1:15–16). Paul uses imagery from the Old Testament sacrificial system, as Hebrews explains: "The law requires that nearly everything be *cleansed* with blood, and without the shedding of blood there is no forgiveness" (Heb 9:22; TNIV). *Katharos, -a, -on, katharizō* (**pure**) can refer to "clear" or "clean,"[111] but it also refers to ritual purity, such as a purified cup (Matt 23:25–26), or "clean" food,[112] or a body free of leprosy.[113] The opposite is **defiled**.[114] The circumcision party (Titus 1:10) would be concerned for ritual **purity**, which would be met by such things

---

110. *Haer.* 1.23.2. Yamauchi concludes that there is "unanimous testimony" among the Church Fathers "that Simon is the first individual who was designated a Gnostic, and that Simonianism is the earliest form of Gnosticism recognized by the patristic sources" (1973: 59–60).

111. E.g., Rev 21:18, 21; Matt 27:59, gold or linen.

112. Acts 10:15; Mark 7:19; Rom 14:20.

113. Matt 8:2; 10:8; 11:5.

114. *Mainō*, e.g., John 18:28.

as circumcision, kosher food and drink, and festival observation (e.g., Col 2:16–23). In contrast, Jesus' blood given in behalf of sin results in genuinely purified or "cleaned" people, evidenced by their enthusiasm to do good (Titus 2:14). The focus, then, is taken away from external to internal purity. Thus, those who have been purified by Jesus' atoning death now see all through purified inner selves. As Jesus explained, "For it is from within, from the human heart, that evil intentions come" (Mark 7:21–23; NRSV). In the same way, as Jesus challenged the Pharisees and scribes who were concerned for the ritual external purity of the drinking and eating utensils while they remained internally greedy and self-indulgent (Matt 23:25–26), Paul challenged the circumcision party who chastised ritual impurity in the church while inwardly *they* were defiled. They denied God's works by not doing them.

They are then described by three adjectives: *bdelyktos* (**abominable**), *apeithēs* (**disobedient**), and *adokimos* (**unacceptable**) (1:16). *Bdelyktos* is a strong word: "He that pronounces the unjust just, and the just unjust, is unclean (*akathartos*) and **abominable** (*bdelyktos*) with God" (Prov 17:15 LXX). Its noun form is used to describe the sacrilege at the temple in Jerusalem in 168 BC by worshipers of Zeus (1 Macc 1:54, 59). For those who are concerned for the law, to be called an "abomination," a term employed for what is most abhorrent to God, would be shocking. But, they were people who could not be persuaded, and thus were disobedient to God's truth (Acts 26:19). *Apeithēs* is the negation of *peithos* ("persuasive"). Paul will later describe himself as formerly *apeithēs* (Titus 3:3). And, finally, they are *adokimos* ("not approved" or "accepted"). As an athlete prepares to enter and win a race, a Christian should prepare to do good actions that merit God's approval (1 Cor 9:24–27). But false teachings do not lead to good actions. The false teachers are **unacceptable**, they have failed the test (2 Cor 13:5)!

Fusing the Horizons: The Place of Education

What is the value of education? Education prevents deception and clarifies what we should believe and do. Orthodoxy affects orthopraxy. But, are orthodox people like a cement block? Do they become fixed, immovable, merciless, without life? Or, are the orthodox like a healthy body, which can move easily, be flexible, compassionate, alive? Paul uses the latter image in the Pastoral Letters.

Many across the globe are attracted to the awesomeness of the Triune God and the good news. However, they are not always discipled, educated, and helped to mature. Sometimes it is the fault of the new believer. They think they now own a card that they can show God and others: "The bearer of this card will receive grace no matter what they say or do." Sometimes it is the fault of the evangelist: "I bring them in. God takes care of them from now on." However, such attitudes make the new believer like a newborn who is cast out into the street to live on its own resources. Sometimes it is the fault of the church: "Just come to services to worship, bring your body, bring your money, take your seat." The new believers may grow a bit, but they remain infants their whole lives. Sometimes the church does not have enough people to disciple the new believers. They may be busy with other matters or simply disorganized. The Pastoral Letters reiterate the importance of educating people in the truth, even as God had insisted on education in the old covenant. God's law was regularly to be taught in the home by the adults and in the community by the priests and before the whole assembly by the religious leaders (e.g., Deut 31:12–13a).

TITUS 2

TEACH WHAT IS CONSISTENT WITH HEALTHY DOCTRINE (2:1—3:11)

But you are speaking what is appropriate to healthy teaching (2:1). But (*de*) is a strong adversative here. Titus is emphasized.[1] He, unlike the opponents (1:9), should be speaking what is appropriate to **healthy teaching**,[2] described in 2:1—3:8, not the unhealthy teaching described earlier (1:10-16). Chapter 2 begins the second major section of the letter. The first major section is more negative, dealing with setting straight what was remaining to be done (1:5-16). This next major section is more positive, dealing with teaching what is consistent with healthy doctrine (2:1—3:11). The first subsection deals with specific groups in the churches, the second subsection deals with the churches as a whole, and the third subsection deals with Titus specifically.

Godly Behavior among the Elders, Youth, and Slaves (2:1-15)

Paul recommends Titus speak to five groups: male and female elders, female and male youth, and slaves: **(Encourage) elders** (males) **to be sober, honorable, wise, healthy in faith, in love, in perseverance; (encourage) elders** (females), **likewise, to be in demeanor holy, not slanderous, and not enslaved to much wine, teaching what is good, in order that they exhort the young** (females) **to be loving their husbands, loving their children, wise, pure, working at home, good, being subject to their own husbands, in order that God's word not be blasphemed** (2:2-5).

What is the relationship between the male (*presbytēs* [2:2]) and female (*presbytis* [2:3]) **elders** to the "elders" of chapter one (*presbyteros* [1:5])? All terms go back to the root *presbys* (an old person or elder). *Presbyteros* is the comparative of *presbys*,[3] literally, "the older one" or "elder of two," as in Luke 15:25. *Presbytēs* and *presbytis* are the masculine and feminine prose forms of *presbys*. Do the forms in Titus 2 refer to church leadership posi-

1. "You" begins the sentence.
2. See Titus 1:13.
3. LSJ, 1462; Thayer, 535.

tions (male and female "elders") or simply to age ("old men," "old women")? Many English translations render the latter.[4] However, the former is also possible. Why? First, in ancient times deference was given to elders simply because of their age.[5] Second, in the same way as *presbyteros* could refer to leadership positions or to age,[6] *presbytēs* could refer to age or to leadership positions. Although the Bible does have several references where *presbytēs* refers simply to age,[7] other references clearly refer to ambassadors or envoys, as the "elders" of the ruler from Babylon who visited Hezekiah (2 Chr 32:31; LXX) and elders representing the Jews to Sparta and to Rome (1 Macc 14:22; 15:17; LXX). Even the envoys from Rome are called "elders" (2 Macc 11:34; LXX). Elders (*presbytēs*) are also mentioned at the city gate where judgments were made in Israel (Job 29:7–8; Lam 5:14; LXX). When Paul calls himself *presbytēs,* some translators render it "ambassador" (REB, TEV), while others "old man"/ "aged" (NRSV, NIV, TNIV, KJV) (Phlm 9).

The feminine *presbytis* occurs only in Titus 2:3 in the Bible. Were women ever called "elder" implying a leadership position in ancient times? One heroic "aged" (*gēraia*) mother of seven sons was called by the author of 4 Maccabees an "elder" (*presbytis*) even though a woman (4 Macc 16:14).[8] At Crete, a female, Sophia of Gortyn, is described on a plaque as "elder (*presbytera*) and ruler of the synagogue."[9] A woman, Mannine of Venosa, thirty-eight-years-old, is described as an "elder" in a cemetery in Italy. Brooten found six or seven Jewish women "elders" spread over a wide

---

4. E.g., NRSV, NIV, TNIV, REB, TEV, CEV, NASB, JB have "older men/women." KJV has "aged men" and "aged women" (2:2–3). The Spanish versions do not differentiate between Titus 1:5–6 and 2:2, 3, rendering them all "anciano/a" (RV, DHH, BA, NVI). Kroeger agrees (2002: 757) that *presbytēs* is best understood as a church officer, a "female presbyter."

5. E.g., Lev 19:32; Deut 28:50; Isa 9:14–15; Wis 2:10.

6. See notes on Titus 1:5.

7. E.g., Abraham, Gen 25:8; Jacob, Gen 43:27; Eli, 1 Sam 2:22; 4:18; Zechariah, Luke 1:18.

8. See translation by H. Anderson, *OTP* 2:561.

9. First through fourth century AD, Brooten 1982: 41. Levine confirms that women have been identified as elders and rulers of the synagogue (officials) in the area of Asia Minor and its immediate surroundings: Smyrna, Crete, Myndos, Thrace, Venosa, Tripolitania, Rome, Malta (10 percent of total names mentioned; 2000: 482–83, 487). Horsely (1987) has found numerous examples of female elders. Moreover, even the term *presbytera* has been used for women elders in 1 Tim 5:2. All this data contradicts Mounce's pronouncement that "there was no position of 'women elders' in the Pauline churches or in the second century (2000: 270).

geographical area.[10] In the early years after the New Testament, female **elders** had leadership in the church.

If *presbytēs* and *presbytis* in Titus 2 refer to leadership positions, how do they relate to the qualifications in 1:6–9? In the same way as Paul describes the ministers/deacons in 1 Timothy 3:8–10 in a general way first and then goes on to describe the female and male distinctive qualities (3:11, 12), also in Titus, Paul first describes the general qualities of an **elder**/overseer (1:6–9) and then goes on to highlight qualities on which the men (2:2) and the women (2:3) need to work. Another way to understand the passage is that, in the same way as everyone is encouraged to seek an overseeing office (*episcopēs*) in 1 Timothy 3:1, but then the distinctive qualities of overseer (*episcopos*) and minister/deacon (*diakonos*) are delineated in 3:2–13, so the elders, youth, and slaves are encouraged to seek positive qualities that would make them eligible to serve as Christian leaders.

Comparison of Qualities in Titus 2:2-10 with Those Needed for Elder and Minister/Deacon

Male elders (*presbytēs* [2:2])	Female elders (*presbytis* [2:3])
1. sober (elder, Titus 1:7; 1 Tim 3:2, 3; minister/deacon, 1 Tim 3:8, 11)	1. in demeanor holy (elder, Titus 1:8)
2. honorable (minister/deacon, 1 Tim 3:8)	2. not slanderous (minister/deacon 1 Tim 3:11)
3. wise (elder, Titus 1:8; 1 Tim 3:2)	3. not enslaved to much wine (elder, Titus 1:7; 1 Tim 3:2, 3; minister/deacon 1 Tim 3:8, 11)
4. healthy in: a. faith (elder, Titus 1:9; minister/deacon, 1 Tim 3:11)	4. teaching what is good (elder, Titus 1:8; 1 Tim 3:2)
b. love	
c. perseverance (elder, Titus 1:7; 1 Tim 3:3)	

---

10. Not until the Synod of Laodicea (AD 343–81) is the order of female elders forbidden by some (Brooten 1982: 43, 45). It forbade any more *presbytides* (canon 11). *Herm. Vis.* used *presbytis* and *presbytera* as synonyms for the church (Vision 1 [2:2], Vision 2 [5:3; 8:1]). See 1 Tim 5:5–6. See also Kroeger 2002: 757.

Qualities for **elders**/overseers are evident throughout Titus 2:2–10: self-controlled limiting of consumption of intoxicating substances (elders), honor, wisdom (male elders, young women and men), faithfulness (male elders and slaves), love (male elders and young women), perseverance, holiness (female elders and young women), ability to teach (female elders), household-oriented, not being self-pleasing, not being disobedient, and not seeking selfish financial gain. Yet the male and female elders have distinctive aspects of their Christian walk to which they had to pay attention. Only women in these lists are challenged not to be slanderous (Titus 2:3; 1 Tim 3:11).

Paul highlights six qualities important for the male **elder: to be sober, honorable, wise, healthy in faith, in love, in perseverance** (2:2). A recurring topic at Crete and Ephesus is the necessity not to become intoxicated, but rather to remain **sober**.[11] If one is sober, then the second quality is more likely—to be **honorable** or godly. *Semnos* has been translated by such diverse terms as "honorable, serious, dignified, and holy."[12] It describes the ideal minister/deacon (male and female, 1 Tim 3:8, 11), children (1 Tim 3:4), male elder (Titus 2:2), teaching (Titus 2:7), and all Christians (1 Tim 2:2). The noun, like its verb form (*sebō*)[13] properly refers to God or the gods.[14] Thus, *semnos* can refer to the feeling of awe or reverence before God. In the New Testament, *semnos* is always used in a positive sense. Luke uses it in Acts to describe the Gentile converts to Judaism, such as Lydia (16:14) and Titius Justus (18:7), the "God-fearers" (13:43; 17:4, 17), and to the respectable, august, or honorable women of Pisidian Antioch (13:50). Thus, *semnos* appears to be an aspect of God that humans should have. More than "serious," it is "august." It is a synonym for "godliness" (1 Tim 2:2) and "uncorrupted" (Titus 2:7). We are to think of whatever is honorable or godly or awesome (Phil 4:8) so that we can become honorable, godly, and awesome ourselves. This is true for all Christians, and certainly Christian leaders.

Wisdom permeates every aspect of leadership. Even though it is twelfth on the list for an elder in Titus as opposed to fourth on the list for

---

11. See discussion on "sober" in Titus 1:7 and 1 Tim 3:2–3 (Spencer 2013).

12. Phil 4:8, "honorable" (NRSV); Titus 2:7, "seriousness" (NIV); Titus 2:2, "serious" (NRSV); 1 Tim 2:2, "dignity" (NRSV) and "holiness" (NIV).

13. LSJ, 1591; Thayer, 573.

14. E.g., Acts 18:13; Matt 15:9; Acts 19:27 Artemis; Aristotle, *Rhet*. II.xxiii.12 "awesome goddesses."

an elder in Ephesus,[15] nevertheless, Paul repeats it as an important quality for male elders and young women and men. Although one would expect this word-family to be more frequent in the New Testament, it occurs only sixteen times, ten of which are in the Pastoral Letters.[16] The basic idea in wisdom is soundness or wholeness of mind, as the opposite of lunacy.[17] In Attic especially, it refers to having control over the sensual desires, having moderation and self-control. The elder who keeps away from intoxication and dwells on godly attributes (Titus 2:2) will then be able to have a mature mind directed by self-control.[18] In the New Testament, this quality is necessary for all, male and female, young and old. It is a prerequisite to prayer (1 Pet 4:7). Unfortunately, some translators will chose an aspect of wisdom to highlight when addressing particular groups of people. Mature men are to be "prudent" (Titus 2:2; NRSV) and "reasonable" (Acts 26:25; NIV), whereas women are to have "propriety, decency, modesty" (1 Tim 2:9, 15; NRSV, NIV) and the young are to have "self-control, self-discipline" (Titus 2:5-6; 2 Tim 1:7; NRSV, NIV). Of course, context affects the aspect of a word a translator might want to emphasize, but the sex or age should not limit meaning because then readers fail to see the continuity of virtue desired for all men and women, younger and older, indicated by the use of the same word-family for all.

If *sōphrōn* has to do with soundness of mind, *hygiainō* has to do with soundness of body. Both have to do with good health. The male elder has "to be in good health" when it comes to faith, love, and perseverance (2:2). **Healthy** or "sound" **faith** has already been mentioned as a goal in this letter for all.[19] The three attributes of faith, **love**, and **perseverance** occur together once in each Pastoral Letter, referring in Titus to the elders (2:2), in 1 Timothy to Timothy (6:11), and in 2 Timothy to Paul (3:10). Faith and love are two of three qualities that persist longer than any spiritual gift (1 Cor 13:8-13). The content of faith has been summarized in 1 Tim 3:16. But

---

15. See Titus 1:8 and 1 Tim 3:2 (Spencer 2013).

16. 62.5 percent of the total references, six (37.5 percent) in Titus to *sōphrōn*, *sōphronismos*, *sōphroneō*, *sōphronizō*, *sōphronōs*, and *sōphrosynē*.

17. E.g., Mark 5:15; Luke 8:35; 2 Cor 5:13.

18. *Sōphroneō* comes from *sōs* (safe and sound, alive and well or whole) and *phrēn* (the midriff, the seat of the passions, and seat of the mental faculties, especially will and purpose; LSJ, 1750-52, 1954). Thus, *sōs* and *phrēn* combine into "wisdom" (*sōphrōn*), wholeness of mind and passion, where one can do the good that one wills to do; BDAG, 987.

19. See Titus 1:13.

since God is truth *and* love, love is necessary to work together with faith. Now, as well, the elder needs to persevere in faith and love with a constancy that persists through testing, cares, riches, pleasures, and persecution (Luke 8:13–15; 21:12–19).

The list for the female **elders** is connected with the list for the male elders by "likewise": **(encourage) elders (females), likewise, to be in demeanor holy, not slanderous, and not enslaved to much wine, teaching what is good** (2:3). Thus, although Paul highlights distinctive qualities for each, yet their function as elders is similar. In 1 Timothy the **likewise** indicates that the women are to pray as the men (2:8–9), the ministers/deacons need leadership qualities similar to the overseer's (3:8), and the female ministers/deacons need leadership qualities similar to those of the male ministers/deacons (3:11). The **likewise** also indicates that Titus is to encourage the female elders as much as he does the male elders.

Paul places the prepositional phrase **in demeanor** first (2:3), therefore highlighting it. *Katastēma*, occurring only here in the Bible, refers to an external bodily or mental state.[20] For instance, some elephants were driven to a maniacal state by external inducements (3 Macc 5:45). Or, Alexandra, mother of Queen Mariamne, wife of King Herod, changed her behavior from boldly supportive of her daughter to critical of her (Josephus, *Ant.* 15.7 [232–34]). But Paul does not advise the women elders to display criticism or a maniacal state—rather a steady behavior of holiness.

The neuter form, *hieron*, is always used in the New Testament literally for the temple in Jerusalem (e.g., Matt 21:23). If indeed all believers are members of God's "holy priesthood,"[21] then certainly women elders also need to act appropriately to a priestly vocation, in other words, in a **holy** or reverent manner. *Hieroprepēs* signifies "appropriate to a sacred place." It is a synonym for *semnos* (Titus 2:2).

The opposite of a **holy demeanor**, which is fleshed out in **teaching what is good** (2:3), is being **slanderous** (*diabolos*) and **enslaved to much wine**. Normally *diabolos* (with the article) refers to *the* devil. Jesus told some religious leaders that the devil "was a murderer from the beginning and does not stand in the truth, because there is no truth in him. When he lies, he speaks according to his own nature, for he is a liar and the father of lies" (John 8:44; NRSV). In Ephesians, the devil's schemes work against

---

20. LSJ, 914.

21. *Hierateuma* and *hiereus* (1 Pet 2:5; Exod 19:6; Isa 61:6; Rev 1:6; 5:10). Lock 1924: 140.

truth, righteousness, peace, and faith (Eph 6:11, 14–16). He is called "that ancient serpent," "the deceiver of the whole world" (Rev 12:9).

The devil's character is implied by aspects of the Letter to Titus. The devil would encourage wildness, disobedience, attack, self-pleasure, anger (cf. Eph 4:26–27), drinking, fighting, shameful gain, opposition, deception, lying, evil, idleness, false teachings, envy, hate, and lawlessness.[22] In contrast, Paul encourages faith, truth, godliness, eternal life, grace, peace, salvation, goodness, wisdom, righteousness, holiness, self-control, honor, love, and perseverance (1:1–4, 8; 2:2–3). Thus, when Paul calls for women elders not to **slander**, he is calling for them not to act in a diabolical way.[23] The verb *diaballō* highlights one aspect of the devil's character—lying about another person, thereby breaking the ninth commandment, "You shall not bear false witness against your neighbor" (Exod 20:16; NRSV). **Slander**, from a biblical perspective, is a larger concept, referring to deception and lying that promotes the devil's kingdom, which would affect the implementation of many of the Ten Commandments, including having gods before the Lord, promoting murder (of character at least), and, as well, bearing false witness (Exod 20:3, 13, 16).

The Pastoral Letters use a couple of synonyms that relate to drinking: *nēphalios* (Titus 2:2; 1 Tim 3:2, 11) and *paroinos* (Titus 1:7; 1 Tim 3:3). In Titus, the male elders are encouraged to be "sober" (*nēphalios*), while female elders are encouraged not to be **enslaved to much wine** (Titus 2:3).[24]

Instead of wasting their time being drunk, the female elders are to **teach** (2:3). *Didaskalos* is the same root word used in 1 Tim 2:12. The difference is that in Crete the women are encouraged to **teach what is good** (*kalodidaskalos*), whereas the women at Ephesus were forbidden from teaching what is bad.[25] The elder/overseer was to *love* what is good (*philagathos*, 1:8). The next step would be to *teach* what is good (2:3).

What is the purpose of teaching what is good? Paul answers with two adverbial clauses, one stresses the positive (**in order that they exhort the young** (females) **to be loving their husbands, loving their children,**

---

22. Titus 1:6–7, 9, 11–12, 14, 16; 2:8, 14; 3:3.

23. Thus, Judas is called "a devil" when he betrays Jesus (John 6:70–71) and Elymas Bar-Jesus of Cyprus, a false prophet, "a child of the devil" (Acts 13:10), an enemy of righteousness, full of deceit and trickery, perverting the Lord's right ways.

24. Athenaeus writes, "That womankind is fond of wine is common report," and yet Roman "women are forbidden to drink wine" in Italy, but they can drink *passum*, a sweet wine made of raisins, also made in Crete (*Deipn.* 10.440).

25. See 1 Tim 1:3, 7; 5:13–14.

wise, pure, working at home, good, being subject to their own husbands) and the second avoids the negative (**in order that God's word not be blasphemed**) (2:4–5). The first purpose of the teaching is to help the younger women become wise. **Exhort** (*sōphronizō*) literally is to cause one to become wise or to recall or bring people to their senses.[26] At first glance, for the young women to be exhorted to **love their husbands** and children seems to apply to a domestic role limited to the female sex. However, the male elders also are encouraged to be "healthy" "in love" (2:2). In contrast to Crete, where the wives are challenged to love their husbands (2:4), in Ephesians 5, the husbands are challenged to love their wives (Eph 5:25, 28, 33). The situation of women varied among the differing ancient cultures. Cretan marriage was a public, state-controlled ceremony, involving those who belonged to the same age-grade and same social class.[27] However, the wives usually did not join the husbands' homes until later when the young women had learned how to manage household affairs.[28] Most marriages were arranged. For example, in Xenophon's *Oeconomics*, the husband says to the wife, "I took you and your parents gave you to me" to obtain "the best partner of home and children" (*Oec.* 7.11). Thus, love for one's husband had to be learned. Paul places responsibility for the training on the female elders. Neither Titus nor the husbands teach the women (cf. Xenophon, *Oec.* 7.8–9), nor the mothers, as we might expect. Paul wanted Christian models for the younger women.

A Christian's responsibility to one's family is very important. One's spouse and children are one's closest neighbor ("Love your neighbor as yourself," Matt 22:39). Similarly, elders are to be a "one-woman man, having faithful children, not in accusation of wildness or disobedience" (Titus 1:6; and 1 Tim 3:2, 4–5).[29] Love is the greatest motivator both for the one loving and the one being loved.

If one is sound of mind (**wise**, *sōphrōn*, 2:5) with self-control (also needed by elders/overseers [1:8; 1 Tim 3:2]), then one result will be purity. Purity is important for elders too (1:8; 2:2). Five different synonyms for "holy/**pure**" are used in Titus for leaders (*hosios* [1:8], *semnos* [2:2],

---

26. BDAG, 986; LSJ, 1751; Thayer, 613; e.g., Josephus, *J.W.* 2.18 (493). See Titus 2:2.

27. An exception would be a minor who was allowed to marry an heiress who could be even as young as twelve to safeguard the household's interests.

28. Spartans could not live with their wives until the men were 30 years of age (Strabo, *Geogr.* 10.4.20 [C482]; Willetts 1965: 112–14).

29. See also minister/deacon, 1 Tim 3:12; and widow, 1 Tim 5:9 (Spencer 2013).

hieroprepēs [2:3], and, for the youth, leaders-in-training, (*hagnē* [2:5] and *aphthoria* [2:7]). *Hagnē* (adjective) and the verb (*hagnizō*) go back to the Old Testament to the vow of separation with *purity* to the Lord. Men or women could make this vow for a certain time by abstaining from all products made from the vine, not cutting their hair, not coming near a dead body, and, finally, bringing offerings to the temple (Num 6:2–21). Or, Levites would purify themselves by washing their garments (Num 8:21). Certain symbolic acts were done to demonstrate one's devotion to God. The same adjective is used for Jesus (1 John 3:3), Timothy (1 Tim 5:22), Paul,[30] a wise teacher or a godly minister (Jas 3:17; 2 Cor 6:6), and betrothed virgins (2 Cor 11:2; 4 Macc 18:7). The young women in Crete who received the charge to be pure could be married, but they could also be betrothed, getting prepared for marriage. Peter also uses *hagnē* to describe the ideal conduct of wives who are trying to win over their unbelieving husbands (1 Pet 3:1–2). There is a lot of similarity between the situation of the wives in 1 Peter and those in Titus. Both are called to be pure in conduct (1 Pet 3:1–2; Titus 2:5), good, submissive to their husbands in order to "win over" someone (in 1 Peter the husband, in Titus maybe the husband but definitely a larger group).

How a Wife Can Win over Nonbelievers

1 Peter 3:1–6[31]	Titus 2:5
won over without a word	in order that God's word may not be blasphemed
being subject to own husbands	being subject to own husbands
pure conduct	pure
do good	good

Thus, a key component in these instructions is evangelism. Evangelism is an important element of the whole letter of Titus (and 1 Peter) and an important motivator for the behavior of all leaders. The elders/overseers must not be "open to attack" (1:6–7) and children "not in accusation of wildness or disobedience" (1:6). Titus models good behavior for the leadership to follow so the opponent cannot say "evil" concerning them (2:8). Since the goal of the elders' exhortation is for **God's word not to be blasphemed**

---

30. Paul did the rite of purification in Acts 21:24, 26; 24:18.
31. See further Spencer 2000: 107–19

(2:5), one would expect that the qualities exhorted in the young women would be positively viewed by the larger society. For instance, Xenophon's ideal wife says her mother told her, her duty is to be **wise** (*sōphroneō*; *Oec.* 7.14).

Hypotassō (verb) and its noun (*hypotagē*; **submit**) are used in the Pastoral Letters for wives to husbands (2:5), slaves to masters (2:9), the ruled to ruling authorities (3:1), students to teachers (1 Tim 2:11), and children to parents (1 Tim 3:4). The New Testament never commands one adult human to **subject** another adult human.[32]

In contrast to some in the larger society, Paul has Titus address his words to females directly (2:3), whereas Aristotle, for example, addresses his to male masters (*Pol.* I.ii.2 [1253b]). Aristotle uses the language of one human ruling another in the household (*archō*, *Pol.* I. ii. 8, 12 [1254a-b]), which Paul does not. Although *hypotassō* can be used for hierarchical relationships, it can also be used for mutual or equal authorities, as prophets who are **subject** to other prophets, allowing each other to speak and evaluate each other's message (1 Cor 14:29–33), Christians to Christians (Eph 5:21), the Son and the Father (1 Cor 15:27–28), the people served and those serving in ministry (Corinthians and Stephana's household, 1 Cor 16:15–18). Wives, along with other Christians, are exhorted to be supportive presences in actions and words. They are respectively to cooperate with their husbands, treating them as valuable.[33] This is particularly important (and challenging) in a society where the father or husband was the *paterfamilias* or chief priest who held the power of life and death over the entire household.[34]

Paul encouraged the young women to work in the **household** (*oikourgos*; 2:5). In contrast to postindustrial societies, in ancient times all people worked in the household, as Xenophon explains, husband and wife are "partners (*koinōnos*) in the household (*oikos*)." Xenophon goes on to explain that men work outdoors, while women work indoors (*Oec.* 7.30), however, the outdoors and the indoors are all part of the household. In contrast, the model of an ideal biblical, capable wife works *both* outdoors

---

32. Only the case of parent to child is unclear. Although the parent is to have "children in submission" (1 Tim 3:4) yet they are not to "provoke" their children to anger (Eph 6:4). The only use of the active voice in the NT of *hypotassō* is of God the Father or God the Christ to all of creation at the end or beginning of time (Phil 3:21; 1 Cor 15:27; Heb 2:8; Ps 8:6).

33. Spencer 2000: 110; 1 Pet 2:13, 17; 3:1.

34. Spencer 2000: 109; Willetts 1965: 87.

and indoors (Prov 31:13–27).³⁵ According to Xenophon, the landed Greek wife is responsible to supervise and care for all the household workers, manage the budget, oversee the making of clothes and the quality of the raw food, teach spinning and housekeeping to the workers, and organize storage of supplies.³⁶ A Jewish wife was required to grind flour, bake bread, wash clothes, cook food, nurse their child, make ready the husband's bed, and work in wool unless she could afford household workers to help (*m. Ketub.* 5:5). Moreover, women would often participate in a joint business with their husbands (e.g., Prisca and Aquila—tentmakers, Acts 18:3). The women were rulers of the household (1 Tim 5:14) and thus could not be idle (1 Tim 5:13). The rabbis agreed "idleness leads to unchastity" and "idleness leads to lowness of spirit" (*m. Ketub.* 5:5). Their basis may be King Lemuel's mother, who said: the capable wife "does not eat the bread of idleness" (Prov 31:27).

Early Christians, like Christians today, were concerned that God's revelation not be treated in a disrespectful way. **Blaspheme** (2:5) can be used for disrespectful language about God (e.g., Rev 13:6) or about other human beings.³⁷ With respect to the young women being loving toward husband and children, wise, pure, active, good, and respectful to husbands (Titus 2:5), Paul was trying to stem opposition to the faith.

Paul now finally clarifies what action Titus is to do: **encourage: the younger ones** (probably males),³⁸ **likewise, to be wise concerning all, showing yourself a model of good works, in the teaching—pure, honorable, beyond reproach, with a healthy message, in order that the opponent might be ashamed, not having evil to say concerning us** (2:6–8). If the female elders are compared to the male elders by the use of **likewise** (2:3), now the male **youth** are compared to the female youth (2:6). The young men, like the young women, as well as the elders, are to be **wise**³⁹ **concerning all** (2:7). **Concerning all** appears to summarize all the previous lists: young men, in every area of your life implement everything that applies to you which I have already stated to the others. If the elder women

---

35. The Shulammite also is a vineyard keeper (Song 1:6) and, as well, Rachel was a shepherd (Gen 29:9).

36. *Oec.* 7.33–41; 8.18–19; 9.6.

37. BDAG, 178. E.g., Acts 13:45; 18:6. See also 1 Tim 1:13 (Spencer 2013).

38. The masculine plural can also serve as the generic, but since younger women were earlier mentioned (2:5), younger males are probably intended in 2:6.

39. 2:6, 2, 5; 1:8. See Titus 2:2.

are models for the younger women, Titus is a comparable **model** for the younger men. They are like "brothers" (1 Tim 5:1). Education by model is a most effective means of communication, especially to those who are one's equal.[40]

Comparison of the Models of Timothy and Titus

1 Timothy 4:12 To all believers	Titus 2:7–8 To believing younger men
in word	good works
in conduct	in the teaching—pure
in love	honorable
in faith	beyond reproach in healthy message
in purity	

The women at Ephesus were having more difficulty with heterodoxy, thus, Timothy has to be a **model** for all believers, whereas at Crete, the elder women can share the educational burden with Titus. The first priority for Titus is orthopraxy (right action), in contrast to Timothy's priority which is orthodoxy (right doctrine). The opponents in Crete were confessing knowledge of God but their actions did not demonstrate their beliefs (1:16). Thus, Titus first had to work on acting like a Christian. Titus' good actions do not save him (3:5), but they are the goal and evidence of salvation (2:14; 3:1, 8, 14). The second priority for Titus is **teaching**. Doctrine is important in both Crete and Ephesus at this time. As elders must teach healthy doctrine (1:9), so must Titus (2:1, 7). The unhealthy teaching of the opponents was overturning whole households (1:11). It was destructive. In contrast, Titus' teaching was not to be destructive (*phtheirō*), rather, indestructible or uncorrupted, sound (2:7, *aphthoria*).[41] Then, Titus was to be **honorable** (*semnotēs*, 2:7), as the male elders (2:2). And, finally, even as his actions are to be good, so must Titus' words be **healthy** (sound) and without basis for any to condemn (**beyond reproach**, *akatagnōstos*; 2:8). Not being open to

---

40. See 1 Tim 4:12. Elsewhere, models are Paul and Timothy as friends of the cross of Christ (Phil 3:17); the church at Thessalonica for receiving the word with joy inspired by the Holy Spirit in spite of persecution (1 Thess 1:7); Paul, Silvanus, and Timothy for working and not being idle (2 Thess 3:9). Paul himself is a model (*hypotypōsis*) in 1 Tim 1:16.

41. BDAG, 156.

attack has been an important quality for leaders in Crete because there are opponents there (1:6, 7, 9) and God's word could be criticized (2:5). Earlier the elder is encouraged to be able to reprove those who oppose (1:9). Now, Titus' actions, teaching, honor, and words might be so effective as to **shame and silence** (*entrepō*; 2:8) the opponent. Although Crete had a number of opponents (1:9), Titus can win them one by one (**the opponent**; 2:8). An opponent is like a strong wind that could turn over one's boat (*enantios*; Matt 14:24; Acts 27:4). The goal is not to be "turned" oneself but to make the opponent "turn about" or be shamed and show respect to oneself.

The final group that Titus needs to encourage to do what is appropriate to healthy teaching is slaves: **slaves—to their own masters, to be subject in all, to be well-pleasing, not opposing, not misappropriating for themselves, but demonstrating for themselves every good trust, in order that they might honor the teaching, the one of our Savior God, in all** (2:9). The household and the larger Cretan society had free citizens, serfs, and slaves. The Cretan Gortyn Code refers to *woikeus*, a person attached to the household (*oikos*), and a *dolos*, a "serf" or "slave." *Dolos* could refer to the household *woikeus* or commercial chattel slave (slaves who were bought and sold like other commodities; e.g., Rev 18:13). Legal marriage was not allowed between chattel slaves but the serf family could marry, divorce, and own property. Free citizens could pay a debt by becoming slaves, pledging themselves voluntarily (*katakeimenos*; e.g., 1 Cor 7:23), or being condemned to bondage (*nenikamenos*; e.g., Matt 18:23–25). Serfs had similar rights to a free citizen except they were restricted from military aspects such as gymnastic exercises and possession of arms and required to pay tribute to a landlord. Their status was between that of a full citizen and chattel slave. Serfs in Crete, unlike other ancient areas, did not successfully revolt. A slave was not recognized by the law as a responsible person in his own right and could own no property. Cretans called urban slaves *chrysonetoi* ("persons bought for gold"). Some people were enslaved as prisoners of war (Aristotle, *Pol.* I.II.18 [1255a]; 2 Macc 8:10–11). When Cretan piracy increased in Hellenistic times, kidnapping people increased because slave trading was a profitable business.[42] However, piracy was largely terminated by the Romans by the first century AD.[43] Paul's directions in Titus could be addressed to people, then, in a variety of situations, from serfs to house

---

42. See 1 Tim 1:10 (Spencer 2013); and Deut 24:7.

43. Willetts 1965: 87, 96–97, 99–102, 143–44, 150; Aristotle, *Pol.* I.ii.6 (1254a); II.ii.12 (1264a); II.vi.3 (1269b); *1 Clem.* 55:2; Strabo, *Geogr.* 10.4.9, 16 (C477, C480).

slaves to chattel slaves, from those voluntarily in their positions to those unjustly placed in their positions.

In striking contrast to Aristotle who writes from the master's perspective (*Pol.* I.ii.2–4 [1253b]), 1 Timothy 6:1–2 and Titus 2:9–10 only address **slaves**, whereas Ephesians 6:5–9 and Colossians 3:22–4:1 address slaves *and* masters,[44] and 1 Peter 2:16–25 addresses *free* and slave. Both 1 Timothy 6:1 and Titus 2:9 limit the topic to the slaves' **own masters**, whereas, since 1 Peter 2:18 is addressed to "household slaves," Peter assumes that the submission is limited to one's own master. Only Titus and 1 Timothy call the masters *despotēs*, as opposed to *kyrios*. Only Titus and Colossians describe the obedience/submission to be **in all**/everything. Titus has a number of unique commands, to the slave not to be opposing nor misappropriating, but instead showing good faith or trustworthiness.

Like the younger women, the slaves are to **subject** or submit themselves (2:9). First Peter 2:17 orients the attitude of free and slave and helps define *hypotassō* in 1 Peter 2:18 in the same way that Ephesians 5:21, mutual submission (*hypotassō*) orients the attitude of all Christians to one another and helps define *hypotassō* in Ephesians 5:22–24.[45] First Peter 2:17 challenges all believers to "honor (*timaō*) everyone, love the family of believers, fear God, honor the emperor." Thus, slaves, as all Christians, are to honor others, including their masters, and cooperate with them.[46] Slaves, like women, were in a challenging position. Slaves could hold many responsible positions in the household. They could serve as the manager of the household.[47] They could plow fields, tend sheep, cook meals, invest and develop the master's property, collect the rent, represent the landowner or ruler, be the master's "apostle" or messenger,[48] and yet their duties and authority were temporary as opposed to the authority of an heir (John 8:35) and they had to carry out their master's orders (Luke 15:22–23; Gal 4:1–2). As Paul explains: "To their own master they stand or fall" (Rom 14:4; TNIV). Thus, Paul exhorts slaves to get free if they can and he exhorts free people to try not to become a slave (1 Cor 7:21, 23). In other words, for some people

---

44. In contrast to the NT, the *Didache* addresses first the masters, then the slaves (4:10–11).

45. See Spencer 2009: 85–87.

46. See Titus 2:5.

47. See Titus 1:7.

48. Matt 8:9; 21:33–36; 22:2–4, 8–10; 25:14; Luke 17:7–8; John 4:51; 13:16; Acts 10:7–8.

slavery offered opportunities, but ultimately it was a limiting position because the slave is not free.

Thus, in the New Testament, **slavery** is both a positive and a negative image. Voluntary slavery to a gentle master is the positive image for Christians who are disciples or "slaves" of Jesus Christ.[49] It is also an exemplary image for humble leadership.[50] Many believers are called or call themselves "slaves" of God.[51] However, when people become disciples of Jesus, no matter their previous status, now they are "beloved" brothers and sisters and friends (Phlm 16; John 15:14–15), equal to one another (1 Cor 12:13; Gal 3:28; Col 3:11). They are infused by the Holy Spirit to become prophets (Acts 2:18). The free become slaves and the slaves become free (1 Cor 7:21–22). These were revolutionary ideas. Yet, Paul does not want to create sudden massive societal revolts. He wants gradual change. Thus, Christians are exhorted how to behave in their current societal position (1 Cor 7:17, 21). Societal change is possible, but acting in a Christ-like manner immediately is most important.

Slavery, because of its limitations, can also have negative connotations. For instance, in Titus, female elders are not to be **enslaved** to an intoxicating substance such as wine (2:3). Believers in general are not to be enslaved to passions and pleasures (3:3). Elsewhere, the New Testament describes sin as causing slavery or lack of freedom.[52] The law can also enslave (Rom 7:6; Gal 5:1). Pagan gods can enslave (Gal 4:8–9). Household **slavery** in the ancient world was very similar to indentured service. Paul wanted to promote hard work and trustworthiness (Titus 2:10), but also teach that believers should be moving to freedom both spiritually and societally.

Many of the qualities needed for an elder (1:6–9) are reiterated in the later lists.[53] The opposite of pleasing oneself (*authadēs*; Titus 1:7) is pleasing others (*euarestos*; 2:9). *Euarestos* (**well-pleasing**)[54] is a positive term in biblical literature. For example, Enoch is repeatedly described as so well-pleasing

---

49. Rom 12:11; 14:18; 16:18; 1 Thess 1:9; Rev 1:1; 2:20; 7:3; 19:2, 5; 22:3.

50. Matt 20:26–28; Phil 2:7; 2 Cor 4:5; 2 Tim 2:24; Gal 5:13.

51. E.g., Mary (Luke 1:38, 48), Moses (Rev 15:3), Simeon (Luke 2:29), Paul (Titus 1:1; Rom 1:1; Phil 1:1; Gal 1:10; Acts 16:17), Timothy (Phil 2:22), James (Jas 1:1), Peter (2 Pet 1:1), Jude (Jude 1), Epaphras (Col 4:12).

52. John 8:34; Gal 5:13; Rom 6:6, 16–20; 7:25; 2 Pet 2:19.

53. See Titus 2:2–10.

54. Thayer, 257. See also verb *euaresteō*.

to God that God "took him."⁵⁵ Christians are to aim to "please" God.⁵⁶ Faith and good deeds please God (Heb 11:6; 13:16). Jesus always pleased the Father when on earth (*arestos*; John 8:29). Joseph when he was enslaved (not voluntarily) to the Egyptian Potiphar still was so "well-pleasing" to his master that Joseph was placed as manager over Potiphar's household (Gen 39:4). Paul wants the Christian slave to follow Joseph's example. The opposite of being well-pleasing is being **opposing** (*antilegō*; Titus 2:9). *Antilegō* is also used to describe the opponents to healthy teaching.⁵⁷ Certainly the Christian slave does not want to be included in this group.

The misuse of money is a continual theme at Crete and Ephesus. The circumcision party was affected by it (1:11). The overseers/elders are to avoid shameful gain⁵⁸ and now, as well, Christian slaves are not to **misappropriate** funds (*nosphizō*; 2:10). Even as Ananias and Sapphira "set apart" secretly (and with intent to deceive)⁵⁹ part of the proceeds of the sale of their land (Acts 5:2–3), slaves who managed a master's property could be tempted to do the same. Jamaicans call this the *Quashie*, the sense that the slave deserves to take secretly what has not been given.⁶⁰ Although one can defend taking what one thinks is one's due, the danger is that one becomes used to stealing and, for Paul, one does not promote Christians as demonstrating themselves to be trustworthy good people (2:10). Instead, the Christian slave should aim to honor the teaching of the Savior God. *Kosmeō* (**honor**) has a basic sense of put in order, arrange, decorate, make attractive.⁶¹ For the slave who works in the household and could be the house steward or manager (*oikonomos*; 1:7), Paul uses a metaphor, comparing the gospel with decorating a house. In the same way as someone might organize, decorate, and make attractive a house (Matt 12:44; Luke 11:25),⁶² so too by cooperating with the master, being well-pleasing, not opposing,

---

55. Gen 5:22–24; Sir 44:16 LXX; Heb 11:5.

56. Gen 48:15; Rom 12:1; 2 Cor 5:9; Eph 5:10; Phil 4:18; Heb 13:21; 1 John 3:22 (*arestos*).

57. See Titus 1:9.

58. See Titus 1:7.

59. BDAG, 679; Thayer, 429.

60. See, e.g., Campbell 1987: 22–23.

61. Thayer, 356. See also *kosmos*.

62. Also graves can be decorated (Matt 23:29), lamps can be arranged (Matt 25:7), gifts can be put in order (Luke 21:5), women can decorate themselves (1 Pet 3:5; Rev 21:2), a city can be arranged (Rev 21:19), and in a deceitful way passions can look attractive (Titus 2:12).

not stealing, but showing oneself trustworthy, the Christian slave "makes attractive" or **honors** the teachings of God, encouraging salvation for the slave, the master, and for others.

All the principles for the slaves, as well as all the other groups, are for the final purpose of encouraging salvation for all humans: **For God's grace illuminated with saving power all humans, instructing us, in order that, having denied for ourselves the ungodliness and the alluring passions, wisely and uprightly and in a godly manner we might live in the now age, waiting for the blessed hope and appearing of the glory of the great God and our Savior Jesus Christ, who gave himself in behalf of us, in order that he might ransom us from every lawlessness and he might purify for himself a chosen people, an enthusiast of good works** (2:11–14). Paul wants Titus to "set straight what was remaining" at the church in Crete, first, by appointing godly elders and rebuking ungodly people (1:5–16) and, second, by teaching what is consistent with healthy doctrine (2:1—3:11). Paul wants Titus to promote healthy teaching by encouraging godly behavior among the elders, youth, and slaves (2:1–15) so God's word is not slandered. And now Paul digs down to the positive foundational principle: **God's grace illuminated with saving power all humans.**[63] As the sun and the stars **illuminate** (*epiphainō*) the darkness (Acts 27:20), so too **God's grace** illuminates those living in spiritual darkness because of their sins (Luke 1:76–79). Paul (like John the Baptist [Luke 3:3–6]) may be alluding to Isaiah 40:1–6 in Titus 2:11–13. These passages include reference to the forgiveness of sins (Isa 40:1–2; Luke 3:3; Titus 2:14), making "straight" (Isa 40:3–4; Titus 2:12; 1:5; Luke 3:4), the salvific nature of God's work (Isa 40:5; Luke 3:6; Titus 2:11), and the appearance of God's glory (Isa 40:5–10; Titus 2:13) to all humans (Isa 40:5; Luke 3:6; Titus 2:11). Humans have seen the appearance of God's grace in order that they be **instructed**. *Paideuō* (2:12) has to do with the daily instruction and supervision of conduct of a minor.[64] The Cretans too were "minors" in the faith and needed to become more mature. **Grace** is the name of their pedagogue or tutor or governess. The limitations (or "laws") in Titus are not ends in themselves but means to a better life.

They should live in five ways: **having denied, wisely, uprightly, in a godly manner, waiting** (2:12–13). Negative behavior needs to end before positive behavior begins (e.g., Eph 4:22–24; Col 3:5–17). Often **deny**

---

63. "Saving power" is a helpful translation by Towner 2006: 745.
64. Spencer 1985:68; used also of the law in Gal 3:24.

refers to what a believer is *not* to do, for example, denying God by one's actions (Titus 1:16; 1 Tim 5:8), or denying rather than confessing one's belief in Jesus (2 Tim 2:12; Matt 10:33). **Denying** (*arneomai*) basically refers to saying "no" (e.g., Matt 26:70). But in Titus 2:12 **deny** refers to what a believer should do, as in Jesus' teaching to deny oneself and take up one's cross (Luke 9:23). Believers must say "no" to two synonyms: **ungodliness** (*asebeia*) and **alluring passions** (Titus 2:12). **Ungodliness** is the negation of worship (*sebomai*).[65] Godless chatter results in *godless* doctrine and behavior (2 Tim 2:16–18). The Lord will judge ungodliness (Rom 1:18; Jude 15). However, since Jesus died for the ungodly (Rom 5:6), no one need remain in that state.

Kosmeō has positive connotations in Titus 2:10 where the Christian slave "makes attractive" God's teachings. However, the adjective (*kosmikos*; **alluring**) has negative connotations in 2:12. **Passions** (*epithymia*) basically refer to strong feelings (*thymos*) turned "upon" (*epi*) something.[66] In the New Testament largely the term has negative connotations, except where it refers to the desire to be with Christ or to be with other believers (Phil 1:23; 1 Thess 2:17). But, it can also signify an inward strong feeling that can be the cause of temptation and sin (Rom 1:24; Jas 1:14–15) if the emotion opposes God's will (1 Pet 4:2; 1 John 2:17). The negative nature of *epithymia* in the New Testament is understandable because it is in the same word-family (*epithymeō*) used in the tenth commandment, not to "covet" or desire what belongs to one's neighbor, whether spouse, property, workers, or animals.[67] These desires may appear attractive to the person, but they do not result in good actions pleasing to Jesus (Titus 2:14).

The opposite of **ungodliness** and **alluring passions** are wisdom, and righteousness, and godliness. **Wisdom** has already been mentioned as a positive attribute for male elders (2:2), young women (2:4–5), and young men (2:6).[68] **Righteousness** is also a positive attribute for elders.[69] A sound mind (**wise**) would choose to please God by observing God's commandments (becoming **upright**), thereby resulting in a worshipful (**godly**) way of living (2:12; 1:1).

---

65. Synonyms of *asebeia* are unrighteousness and sinfulness (1 Tim 1:9; Rom 1:18; 1 Pet 4:18; Jude 15).

66. Thayer, 238, 293; LSJ, 810.

67. Rom 7:7; Exod 20:17; Deut 5:21.

68. See Titus 2:2.

69. See Titus 1:8.

While Christians refuse to keep behaving as non-Christians and instead live in ways pleasing to God, they **wait** expectantly. Such faithful living should affect their perspective toward the past and the present and the future (2:12–13). *Prosdechomai* can signify "looking forward" to an event, such as God's kingdom (Mark 15:43), or the resurrection (Acts 24:15), or to a person, so as to "welcome" them (Luke 12:36).[70] Jesus would eat with sinners to "welcome" them into the kingdom (Luke 15:2). Paul wanted his readers to welcome Phoebe and Epaphroditus (Rom 16:2; Phil 2:29). In the same way as devoted slaves would look forward to serve their master, Christians should look forward to serve their Master, Jesus Christ. The way to **wait** for Christ is to avoid behavior that displeases Jesus and proactively live in ways pleasing to Christ (Titus 2:12). In this way, the **now age** affects the age to come (2:12–13).

God's grace illuminated humans with saving power because of the incarnation and return of Jesus Christ. Only God can save humans eternally. That is why humans should be living in a way to welcome Jesus' second appearing (Acts 1:11). We have seen[71] how both God (1:3; 2:10; 3:4) and Jesus Christ (1:4; 2:13; 3:6) are called **savior**. In 2:13, Jesus is called **God** and **Savior**.[72] By a Gentile, such a title might be possible, but a devout monotheistic Jew as Paul would have undergone a great transformation to affirm one God in three Persons. As the Jewish philosopher Philo explains: the "most grievous" of all sins for Jews is "when the created and corruptible nature" of humanity was made to appear "uncreated and incorruptible... since sooner could God change into a human than a human into God" (*Embassy* 16 [118]).[73]

Jesus is our **Savior** because **he gave himself in behalf of us** (2:14). Titus 2:14 alludes to Jesus' words about himself to his disciples: "The Son of Humanity did not come to be served but to serve and *to give* his life

---

70. Examples are Joseph of Arimathea, Simeon, and Anna, who looked forward to God's work in the world (Mark 15:43; Luke 2:25, 38; 23:51).

71. See Titus 1:3–4.

72. According to Granville Sharp's grammar rule, when "the copulative *kai* connects two nouns of the same case, if the article precedes the first noun and is not repeated before the second noun, the latter always refers to the same person that is expressed or described by the first noun" (Metzger 1953: 79). A similar phrase occurs in 2 Pet 1:1. Jesus is also explicitly named as **God** in Matt 1:23; Mark 2:7; Luke 9:42–43; John 1:1, 18; 5:17–18; 8:56–59; 10:30; 20:28; Rom 9:5; Phil 2:5–6; Col 2:8–9; 2 Thess 1:12; 1 Tim 3:15–16; Heb 1:8; 1 John 5:20. See also Harris 1992.

73. See 1 Tim 3:16.

a ransom for many" (Mark 10:45; Matt 20:28). In these passages (and in 1 Tim 2:6) **give** (*didōmi*) and **ransom** (*lytron, lytroō*) occur together. In Titus, Paul brings out the personal nature of Christ's sacrificial gift (**in behalf of** us) and explains the twofold purpose of the gift: **in order that he might ransom us from every lawlessness and he might purify for himself a chosen people** (2:14). **Ransom**, a significant Old Testament concept, can signify being "delivered" from enemies in a broad sense, as God "ransomed" the Israelites from the Egyptians.[74] In this basic sense, it refers to being saved from death.[75] At Passover, instead of the firstborn of the Hebrews being killed along with the firstborn of the Egyptians, the Hebrew firstborn are "ransomed" by the Levites, money, and sheep.[76] Humans can be "redeemed" from indentured slavery.[77] Humans can also be "redeemed" from iniquities (Ps 129:8) and Hades (Pss 48:15; 102:4; Hos 13:14). Those redeemed become God's possession (Isa 43:1–3). When Jesus **ransoms** humans, he "delivers" them from difficulties, dies instead of them, "frees" them from spiritual slavery and judgment, and thereby **cleanses** them from sins eternally (Titus 2:14; Heb 9:7–22). One of the "difficulties" is the empty or **lawless** way of life (Titus 2:14; 1 Pet 1:18–19). Thus, people are not ransomed simply for their own benefit but that they might change their way of living, becoming one of God's people, **enthusiastic** to act in ways pleasing to God.

Paul concludes this section (2:1–14) with a charge to Titus, summarizing: **These things say and encourage and reprove with all command; let no one despise you** (2:15). Paul sets in a polysyndeton three parallel verbs which are all equally important (**say, encourage, reprove**).[78] Each word is increasingly intensive. *Laleō* (**say**) at its root refers to the forming of words with the mouth (onomatopoetically *la-la*).[79] Paul uses *laleō* for "speaking in tongues" but also for speaking prophecy.[80] He uses it for strange or infantile

---

74. Exod 6:6; 15:13, 16; Deut 7:8; 9:26; 13:5; 15:15; 21:8; Neh 1:10; Pss 7:2; 24:22; 31:7; 43:26; 76:15; 77:42; 105:10; 106:2; 135:24; 143:10; Jer 15:21; 27:34; Mic 6:4; 1 Macc 4:11.

75. See also Num 35:31–32; Prov 6:35; 13:8.

76. Exod 13:11–15; 34:20; Num 3:12–13, 40–51; 18:15–17.

77. Lev 25:47–55; Isa 52:3; Lam 3:58.

78. In this polysyndeton, the same conjunction *kai* is used between each verb. It lends rhetorical emphasis by slowing up the rhythm, producing an effect of extensiveness and abundance, emphasizing the verbs between the conjunctions (Spencer 1998b: 204–5).

79. Thayer, 368.

80. E.g., 1 Cor 12:30; 13:1; 14:2–3, 6, 13, 18–19, 23, 27, 29, 39.

sounds (1 Cor 14:11; 13:11) and for authoritative revelation from God.[81] In Titus 2:1, 15, Paul wants Titus to **speak** the true teaching from God about mature Christian qualities (2:2–10) and the nature of God (2:11–14).

Parakaleō (**encourage**) and *elenchō* (**reprove**, 2:15) are used earlier in Titus (1:9) in contrast to each other. *Parakaleō* literally signifies "to call to one's side."[82] Its use in legal situations can form a helpful basis for understanding its other uses. In legal situations, *parakaleō* can mean to "*summon one's friends to attend one* in a trial, . . . *call* them *as witnesses*, . . . *summon a defendant into court*" or simply "*appeal to*."[83] First, as a defendant appeals to friends for help, God and Christians can appeal to (as opposed to command) people to do an act.[84] The appeal can be to do something good,[85] or to watch out for wrong teaching and behavior (Rom 16:17), or to change behavior.[86] Second, as a witness supports a friend, God and Christians can help others in difficult times.[87] Third, when a witness supports a friend, the friend feels the support. In the same way, change of behavior or good news or education can **encourage** the friend.[88] Both Titus and Timothy are to teach and **encourage**.[89] In Titus 2:15, the first meaning of *parakaleō* ("appeal") would fit well in a context where healthy teaching is needed.

Elenchō (**reprove**, 2:15) in the New Testament predominantly has to do with bringing sin out to the open. For example, Jesus explains, "For all who do evil hate the light and do not come to the light, so that their deeds may not be *exposed*."[90] It can be part of an attempt to become reconciled (Matt 18:15). It can also result in destructive retaliation (Luke 3:19–20); therefore its basis should be love. Its goal is repentance.[91] All Persons of the Trinity convict people of sin.[92] Authentic preaching also should result in conviction of sin (1 Cor 14:24). Although *parakaleō* ("appeal to") is not

---

81. Rom 15:18; 1 Cor 2:13; 9:8; 12:3; 1 Thess 2:2, 4.
82. Thayer, 482.
83. LSJ, 1311.
84. 1 Cor 16:12, 15; 2 Cor 2:8; 8:6; 9:5; 12:8, 18; 1 Tim 1:3; 2:1; Phlm 8–10.
85. Titus 2:6; Rom 12:1; 15:30; 1 Cor 4:16; Eph 4:1; 1 Thess 2:12; 3:2; 4:1, 10; 5:11.
86. 1Cor 1:10; 2 Cor 5:20; 6:1; 10:1–2; 13:11; Phil 4:2; 1 Thess 5:14; 2 Thess 3:12.
87. 2 Cor 1:3–6; 2:7; 7:6.
88. Titus 1:9; 2 Cor 7:7, 13; Eph 6:22; Col 2:2; 4:8; 1 Thess 3:7; 4:18; 2 Thess 2:16–17.
89. Titus 2:15; 1 Tim 4:13; 6:2; 2 Tim 4:2.
90. John 3:20; NRSV. See also John 8:46; 16:8; Eph 5:11–14; 1 Tim 5:20; Jas 2:9; Jude 15.
91. Rev 3:19; Heb 12:5–11.
92. John 16:7–8; Heb 12:5; Rev 3:19.

done as a command, *elenchō*, or the conviction of sin once discovered, commands change (Titus 2:15).

Thus, Titus is first to communicate true teaching, then appeal to listeners to follow it, and, finally, if people are still resistant, to exhort them to stop sinning. Paul concludes with a brief command to Titus: **let no one despise you** (2:15), or express a negative opinion against Titus' leadership. The same negative connotations can be found in other Jewish literature: for instance, to *dishonor* and affront parents because of being ashamed of them or thinking oneself wiser.[93] We do not know how old Titus was. Paul does not accentuate his youth (as he did with Timothy).[94] Why would the church at Crete "disregard" or **despise** Titus? One reason may be simply because, at times, those who do evil hate the one who shines the "light," as Jesus warned (John 3:20). Another additional reason might be that Titus is a Gentile[95] ministering among Jews and those attracted by legalistic Judaism.[96] Already some Jews had complained about Titus (Gal 2:3–5).[97] But, Paul, whose calling was to preach the gospel to the Gentiles, recalling Titus to his freedom in Christ (Gal 2:3–7), commands him not to let anyone disregard his leadership (Titus 2:15).

Fusing the Horizons: The Importance of Holiness

At the turn of the first century, an elder called Clement[98] wrote a sermon to his listeners exhorting them to change because their behavior was dragging the

---

93. 4 Macc 6:9; 14:1; Josephus, *Ant.* 4.8.24 (260).

94. Yet see 2:6–8. Paul uses the same root verb, *phroneō*, with a different prefix, *kata*, in 1 Tim 4:12.

95. See Titus 1:4.

96. Titus 1:10–14; 3:9–10.

97. Gentiles were not allowed to enter the inner courts of the temple in Jerusalem. If they did enter, "death without appeal is the sentence" (Philo, *Embassy* 31 [212]; Acts 21:28; *m. Kelim* 1:8). Devout Jews were not to marry Gentiles (*m. Git.* 9:2; Josephus, *Ant.* 18.9 [345]). Jews also considered Gentiles to be impure. If they entered a home, they rendered it unclean (*m. Tehar.* 7:6; John 18:28). Rabbi Eleazar ben Azariah concluded: "Hateful is the uncircumcision, whereby the wicked are held up to shame, as it is written, *For all the nations are uncircumcised*" (*m. Ned.* 3:11). Aside from food restrictions, no wonder Peter said that Jews "can not associate with or approach" a Gentile (Acts 10:10–14, 28; Deut 14:3–21) and even he and Barnabas kept separate from Gentiles for fear of the circumcision party (Gal 2:11–13).

98. This "Clement" is most likely not the same author as 1 Clement (Holmes 2007:

name of Christ through the mud. Alluding to Isaiah 52:5, he wrote: "The Lord says, 'My name is continually blasphemed among all the nations,' . . . Why is it blasphemed? Because you do not do what I desire. For when the pagans hear from our mouths the oracles of God, they marvel at their beauty and greatness. But when they discover that our actions are not worthy of the words we speak, they turn from wonder to blasphemy, saying that it is a myth and a delusion" (*2 Clem.* 13:2–3). Sadly, today the church is not that different.[99] When my husband and I applied for our first calls after completing seminary, we discovered that the male chaplains that preceded us at both colleges had had sexual liaisons with female students. One secular institution was so upset, it was about to prohibit the Christian ministries board from sending any more Protestant chaplains. The only way the ministries board was able to send another chaplain was by sending them a female, which in this case was myself. Being a female in itself was not the key, but being a female who was intent on demonstrating her faith in her lifestyle was. We preserved our witness at this institution, but how much irreparable harm was done previously? What did others think of religious persons abusing their authority? What happened to the women who were sexually abused? Did they ever forgive God? What about the chaplains' wives and children? Did they blame God? What about all the people who heard about these sins? Have they come to understand what true Christianity is all about? This is where Paul's Letter to Titus is so helpful. As a wise mentor, Paul is counseling Titus to clarify the place of good deeds in the lives of those who have received God's grace. Actions express one's genuine beliefs, educate others, reflect God's purposes for our lives and help others, as well as oneself.

In both the old and the new covenants, God desires holy behavior. The behavior, in itself, does not save us, but good behavior has its positive role to play.

132–35).

99. While showing that many Christians are living "just like the rest of the world," Sider (and others) demonstrate that people with a "biblical worldview demonstrate genuinely different behavior" than others (2005: 128).

TITUS 3

LIVE GODLY LIVES IN THE WORLD (3:1-8)

Paul next reminds Titus of general exhortations about how to conduct oneself in the world. He begins with a command: **Remind them to be submissive to rulers, authorities, to obey (a ruler), to be ready for every good work, to slander no one, to be peaceable, gentle, showing all humility to all people** (3:1-2). Paul wants Titus to **remind**[1] the church in Crete to do three basic actions: to be proactive, maintain good character, and refrain from some action.

Paul, who has been imprisoned unjustly by the Roman authorities, warned by Jesus that his followers would be persecuted as their Master has been (John 15:20), yet also repeatedly implores believers to cooperate with or **be submissive to** governing authorities (3:1).[2] In Romans 13, Paul reminds believers that all power ultimately comes from God (v. 1) and those in authority are supposed to encourage good conduct (v. 3).[3] In 1 Timothy (2:1-4) and Titus (3:1-2), Paul encourages believers to evangelize these rulers by cooperating with them and praying for them, which in the end would make believers' lives better.[4] When in Rome, despite the disreputable behavior of the Emperor Nero, Paul did establish positive relation-

---

1. *Hypomimnēskō* is also used for Timothy (2 Tim 2:14).

2. *Hypotassō* (**to be submissive**, 3:1; see Titus 2:9) basically has to do with cooperation with others, in this case, those governing oneself. The following verb, *peitharcheō*, is a stronger verb, which appears to function as an appositive intensifying *hypotassō*, signifying **to obey** one in authority (LSJ, 1353). *Archais exousiais* may be rendered as an asyndeton, **rulers, authorities** (Robertson 1931: 606) or the second noun can serve as an adjective modifying the first noun (**authoritative rulers**). The meaning is similar either way. *Archē* foundationally has the idea of "beginning" (e.g., Matt 19:4) or the "first one" in preeminence (Col 1:18). *Exousia* refers to having the power to determine or cause (e.g., God in Acts 1:7 or humans in Acts 5:4; 8:19; 9:14; 1 Cor 7:37; 2 Cor 10:8). The two nouns occur together often as synonyms (e.g., Luke 20:20; 1 Cor 15:24). They can refer to human governing authorities that can persecute believers for their faith (Luke 12:11; 20:20) or spiritual powers, such as angelic ones (Jude 6; Eph 1:20-21; 3:10; 6:12; Col 2:15).

3. See also 1 Cor 15:24; 2 Cor 13:10; Col 2:10.

4. See also Jer 29:7; Towner 2006: 769.

ships with Caesar's household and the Praetorium Guard (Phil 1:13; 4:22). At Ephesus, Paul was assisted by the Asiarchs, leaders in the province, and the city clerk, the chief executive officer (Acts 19:31, 35).[5]

Then, the Cretans are to **be**, in other words, maintain good character. They are **to be ready** (or prepared, *hetoimos*) **for every good work** (3:1),[6] in contrast to some besieged Jews, who were "ready (or prepared) for *battle*" (1 Macc. 12:50). Titus 3:1 may be an allusion to Isaiah 40:3-4,[7] John the Baptist's call to the nation of Israel: "*Prepare* the way of the Lord, *make straight* his paths" (Luke 3:4). John's listeners were to prepare for the Lord by making "straight" their own behavior (Luke 3:7-14). Here the church is to prepare (**be ready**) for the Lord (Titus 2:11-13) by being prepared themselves to do any good action as necessary. They were to be "soldiers" ready to fight with wholesome weapons. Or, as Paul will exhort Timothy, vessels, cleansed, ready to be used (2 Tim 2:21). Paul has already reminded Titus that Jesus died so that he "might purify for himself" enthusiastic people of good works (Titus 2:14).[8]

Now he will elaborate some features of good action (3:2). While the Christians might be slandered by others, they are not to lie, deceive, or speak falsely of anyone.[9] Instead, they are to **be** people who are **peaceable** (*amachos*) and **gentle** (*epieikēs*, 3:2), not "pugnacious" (Titus 1:7; 1 Tim 3:3). These same qualities are necessary for all Christians (Titus 3:2). To reinforce his point, Paul uses a synonym for "gentleness" (*prautēs*; **show humility**) and explicitly mentions it should be demonstrated to **all people** (3:2). *Praus* (noun) is a key characteristic of Jesus: "I am *gentle* (*meek*) and humble in heart" (Matt 11:29).[10] A **gentle** person gives rest and loads light burdens (Matt 11:30). Paul exhorts the Corinthians by these two qualities of Jesus: "humility and gentleness" (2 Cor 10:1), fruits of the Spirit (Gal 5:23).[11] This is the way to correct sinners (1 Cor 4:21; Gal 6:1) and opponents (2 Tim 2:25; 1 Pet 3:16). Gentleness might be shown with the use of a

---

5. Bruce 1990: 418, 420; Strabo, *Geogr.* 14.1.42 (C649); Kearsley 1994, 2:364-76.

6. Paul emphasizes the prepositional phrase "for every good work" by placing it first, in contrast to Clement who reorganizes the phrase into normal Greek word order (*1 Clem.* 2:7). According to the *TLG* (8 April 2010), no one before Paul used this same combination of three words (**ready for every good work**).

7. See also Titus 2:11-13.

8. See also Eph 2:10.

9. For **slander**, see Titus 2:3, 5; 3:2.

10. The synonym *epieikēs* also is used to describe God (Ps 85:5).

11. Also see Eph 4:2; Col. 3:12. See also Jas 3:13, 17.

"soft" voice or a reasonable, fair, mild, not angry or contentious, manner.¹²
In the Old and New Testaments, we learn that the "meek shall inherit the earth" (Ps 36:11; Matt 5:5). In Psalm 36, the "meek" are those who may be envious of the worldly success of sinners and even may be unjustly treated by evil-doers, but, if the "meek" persist in doing the good that God requires, they will be rewarded by God and will live in peace. Moses was known as more "meek" than all the people living on the earth during his lifetime (Num 12:3). Thus, when Paul calls the church at Crete to exhibit **humility**, he is exhorting them to be gentle, humble, noncontentious, good, and to rely on the Lord's care.

How might the Cretans react to such commands? Cretans were known for their military upbringing. During the Hellenistic period, "Cretan mercenaries became as familiar as Cretan pirates."¹³ The cities in Crete were in "almost perpetual warfare."¹⁴ Polybius remarked that the Cretans "are involved in constant broils both public and private, and in murders and civil wars" (Polybius, *Hist.* 6.46.9). They might well understand the necessity to obey their military superiors (Titus 3:1). However, the emphasis on gentleness and peacemaking (3:2) would be more difficult to act on. Would the aristocracy be able to be gentle with the peasantry and slaves? Now the Christian Cretans would have to redirect their values to those of peacemaking.

Paul explains his rationale for cooperating with ruling authorities in Titus 3:3–7: **For we once also ourselves were foolish, disobedient, being led astray, enslaved to passions and manifold pleasures, living in wickedness and envy, hated, hating one another** (3:3).¹⁵ *Anoētos* (**foolish**) has the basic idea of slow to understand, as humans who are thinking like cattle to which human words are unintelligible (Ps 48: 12, 20; 4 Macc 5:8–9). This state can come from lack of education (Rom 1:14) or from being deceived or lack of belief (Gal 3:1; Luke 24:25). The New Testament speaks of those who obey (or are persuaded by) the good news (the word) as opposed to those who **disobey** (or are not persuaded).¹⁶ *Apeithēs* is a synonym for

---

12. LSJ, 632, 1459.
13. Willetts 1965: 145.
14. Willetts 1965: 152.

15. Paul uses asyndeton (the omission of conjunctions between a series of two or more words, phrases, or clauses) to list a series of negative qualities, emphasizing **we** by including the pronoun (Spencer 1998b: 188).

16. **Disobedient** (*apeithēs*) literally is "not persuadable" (1 Pet 2:8; 3:20; 4:17).

anoētos, a nonbeliever, as in John 3:36: "Whoever believes in the Son has eternal life; whoever *disobeys* the Son will not see life."[17] It is a characteristic of those in the Cretan circumcision party (Titus 1:16). *Planaō (planē,* **led astray**) has a basic idea of someone who wanders about aimlessly or roams hither and thither, without a sense of proper direction,[18] as Joseph did looking for his brothers (Gen 37:15) or as sheep might wander (Matt 18:12). Metaphorically, it can refer to those who "wander" away from the truth (Jas 5:19) or leave the straight road and go astray (2 Pet 2:15).

Possibly with these words (3:3a) Paul alludes to his previous state as a Jew who had rejected Jesus as Messiah and therefore persecuted Christians.[19] He was **foolish** or lacked understanding (*anoētos*). He was **disobedient** (*apeithēs*) to the truth. He was **led astray** or deceived (*planaō*) by the teaching he had gotten. But, he turned his life around when he chose to be *obedient* to Jesus in the vision on the road to Damascus (Acts 26:19).

The next phrase (**enslaved to passions** [*epithymia*] **and manifold pleasures** [*ēdonē*]; 3:3) hearkens back to earlier references in the letter. Female elders are encouraged not to be enslaved **to** much wine (2:3). God's grace teaches believers to "deny" alluring passions.[20] In the same way that addictive intoxicating substances, such as wine and beer, can enslave us, other objects can elicit strong feelings and passions from us, enslaving us as well. The wrong kind of pleasures can keep people from persevering in the Christian life. People can receive God's word, but as time goes on are overwhelmed by worries and riches and "pleasures of life," thereby not maturing (Luke 8:14). **Pleasures** (*ēdonē*) may be similar to the coveting aspect of **passions** (*epithymia*). Because someone wants something, the person will quarrel and fight for it and even pray for it. But pleasures are a wrong basis for prayer (Jas 4:1–3). Pleasures can result in wild and self-indulgent debauchery (2 Pet 2:13).[21] Thus, an important aspect of **humility** (3:2) is being satisfied with what one has.

Next, the Cretans are to remember that they used to live **in wickedness** (*kakia*) **and envy** (3:3). *Kakia* can refer in a general way to evil intentions

---

17. See also Acts 14:2; 19:9; Rom 1:30; 11:28–32; 10:21; 15:31; Eph 2:2; 5:6; Heb 11:31; 1 Pet 3:1.
18. BDAG, 821; Thayer, 514.
19. 1 Tim 1:13; Acts 9:1; 26:9–11.
20. See Titus 2:12.
21. See Titus 1:6; *asōtia.*

and actions,[22] or it can serve as a synonym for a specific type of evil, a ramification of a life not serving the Creator.[23] Paul is not referring to one sinful act, but to a way of **life** (*diagō*, 3:3).

Finally, the result of their former way of life is being **hated and hating one another**. Paul uses two synonyms for **hatred** (*stygētos* and *miseō*; 3:3). A *Stygian* was "of the nether world," pertaining to the River Styx, a river of the underworld, whose waters were thought poisonous.[24] For instance, high priest Jason, who had an unhappy end to his life, accused by King Aretas, fleeing from city to city, pursued by all, an enemy of his country and countrymen, was "*hated* as a forsaker of the laws" (2 Macc 5:8). Beginning with lack of understanding, one chooses not to believe, is led astray, becoming enslaved to passions and pleasures. Such dissolute, addictive masters lead to a way of life that is wicked and full of jealousy, bringing out hatred against oneself and hatred of one another (3:3). All this contrasts with God's compassionate love, God's way of life (3:4). Paul's point is: be empathetic as you deal with those in the world because you used to act like they do now.

But, what happened to former hateful unbelievers such as Paul and the Cretans? They did not change their lives by themselves. Rather, two characteristics of the Savior God appeared in their lives: **And when the kindness and the love for humanity of our Savior God showed itself, not out of works, the ones in righteousness, which we ourselves prepared, but according to his mercy, he saved us through washing of rebirth and renewal by means of the Holy Spirit, who poured out upon us richly through Jesus Christ our Savior, in order that, having been justified by that grace, we might become heirs according to hope of eternal life** (3:4–7). In this one sentence, we have a compact summary of the good news. The main clause is **he saved us** (3:5), but Paul places before it an extended adverbial clause, the subject of which is God's two attributes (*chrēstotēs, philanthrōpia*). God's actions are driven by his attributes, similar to human foolishness which drives human actions. *Chrēstotēs* (**kindness**, 3:4) and its adjective *chrēstos* are used many times in the Bible to describe God's nature.[25] In Titus 3:2, 4, Paul has picked up several words used by Jesus: "I am *gentle* (*praus*) and humble in heart, and you will find rest for

---

22. BDAG, 500. Acts 8:19–22; 1 Cor 14:20; 1 Pet 2:16.

23. Rom 1:25, 29–31; 1 Cor 5:8; Eph 4:31; Col 3:8; Jas 1:21. In 1 Pet 2:1 *phthonos* ("envy") is also used as a synonym.

24. LSJ, 1657; OCD, 1019.

25. Luke 6:35; Rom 2:4; 11:22; Pss 24:7, 8; 33:8; 85:5; 99:5; 105:1; 144:7, 9.

your souls; for my yoke is *comfortable* (*chrēstos*), and my burden is light" (Matt 11:29–30). Jesus' yoke is helpful and comfortable.²⁶ In a similar way, God's "milk" is wholesome, healthy, and good (1 Pet 2:3).²⁷ Thus, when God is *chrēstotēs*, God is forgiving toward humans, bringing them health and wholesomeness.²⁸

The second characteristic (*philanthrōpia*, **love for humanity**, 3:4) of the **Savior God** is a synonym to the first characteristic (*chrēstotēs*; **kindness**). In both of the New Testament examples of **love for humanity**, compassion is shown. For instance, the centurion Julius was empathetic to Paul's needs when he allowed him, even though he was a prisoner, to visit his friends at Sidon so they might provide for him (Acts 27:3). The Malta natives were also empathetic with Paul, Aristarchus, and Luke when they kindled a fire for them in the cold, rainy weather (Acts 28:2).²⁹

These two aspects of God's nature, God's forgiving and empathetic nature, led to their **salvation**. It was not their own deeds, even their righteous ones, that saved them.³⁰ If God's mercy (*eleos*) saves, what then is the value of good deeds or actions? In Titus, four valuable aspects of good actions are mentioned. First, they are a way believers "confess" publicly their belief in God (1:16). Second, they are part of the educational process, along with the verbal aspect (2:7). Third, God redeems humans from a sinful life in order that they might be enthusiastic to do good actions.³¹ This aspect is reminiscent of the many Old Testament covenants. For example, the Lord reminds Moses that "I bore you on eagle's wings" out of Egypt and now, if the people "obey my voice and keep my covenant, you shall be my treasured possession out of all the peoples . . . you shall be for me a priestly kingdom and a holy nation" (Exod 19:4–6; NRSV). What the New Testament calls "good actions" would be comparable to keeping God's covenant. Fourth,

---

26. With a yoke, two animals could work together, using their broad shoulders, enabling them to pull a plow (*IDB* 4: 924).

27. Or, old wine (as opposed to new wine) is better, tastier, lighter, less alcoholic (Luke 5:39).

28. See Titus 1:13; 2:8 *hygiainō*. See also Luke 6:35; Rom 2:4; 11:22; Gal 5:22; Eph 2:7; 4:32; Col 3:12.

29. See also 2 Macc 6:22; 14:9; 3 Macc 3:15; Wis 12:19. Possibly, then, when Paul encourages younger widows "to love their husbands" (*philandros*; 2:4), he may be calling for wives to be compassionate.

30. See also 2 Tim 1:9.

31. Titus 2:14; 3:1. See also 2 Tim 2:21; 3:16–17; John 15:16.

these good actions are good for people, for themselves, and for others (Titus 3:1, 8, 14).

Dikaioō (verb), *dikaiosynē* (noun, 3:5), *dikaios* (adjective), and *dikaiōs* (adverb) each occur once in Titus. The root word is *dikē*,[32] which signifies "right, justice." It can refer to a judicial hearing or decision, a trial, and to the execution of the sentence,[33] as when Aristotle describes those who play a part in "judicial justice," who judge claims (*Pol.* IV.III.13 [1291a]). Paul uses the word-family frequently to refer to **righteous** as a synonym for "holy."[34] For instance, it is a characteristic of an overseer and a right way to live (Titus 1:8; 2:12). It would certainly include the idea of justice, but as well holiness. God is holy and those who approach God in an unacceptable way die (Lev 16:2, 13). For example, on the Day of Atonement all sins were placed on a goat who was released outside the city and, thereafter, the Jews, cleansed from sins, were now "clean" before the Lord.[35] Jesus permanently took on the sins of the world to purify those who believe in him.[36] Because of Jesus' death, the unrighteous who had no inheritance but now believe in Jesus have been declared righteous heirs of God's kingdom by the righteous Judge.[37]

How then did God **save** them? They were *not* saved by their own good deeds. Rather, they were saved according to God's attribute of **mercy** (3:5). Mercy hearkens back to God's compassionate character (3:4). There were two agents of salvation: **washing of rebirth** and **renewal by means of the Holy Spirit** (3:5). *Palingenesia* (**rebirth**) appears to refer to the same experience as Jesus explains to Nicodemus: one must be born from above to see God's kingdom (John 3:3, 7). **Washing** is an important image in the Bible. It can refer to literal everyday bathing.[38] But for the Jews washing was a regular procedure for priests[39] and others who may have become unclean from touching a dead body[40] or having had a skin disease.[41] Priests would

---

32. Kohlenberger 1995: 216–19.
33. LSJ, 430; Thayer, 151. E.g., Acts 28:4.
34. See Titus 1:8.
35. Lev 16:20–22, 30; Heb 13:12.
36. 1 Pet 2:24; Heb 9:12–14, 28.
37. 2 Tim 4:8; Titus 3:7; Heb 9:15–18.
38. E.g., John 13:10; Exod 2:5; 2 Sam 11:2; 12:20.
39. Heb 10:21–22; Exod 29:4; 40:12; Lev 8:6; 16:4, 24, 26, 28; Num 19:7–8, 19.
40. Acts 9:37; Lev 11:40; 17:15–16.
41. Lev 14:8–9; 15:5–27; 22:6; Deut 23:11; Job 2:5.

bathe in preparation for entering God's sanctuary. Newborn babies also were washed (Ezek 16:4, 9). Thus, washing became an apt metaphor for not sinning, as in "*Wash* you, be clean; remove your iniquities from your souls before mine eyes; cease from your iniquities" (Isa 1:16). In Titus 3:5, Paul reminds his readers that simply being reborn washes or purifies one from sin. This idea was previously explained in Titus 2:14: Jesus died in order that people might be ransomed and cleansed.

The second agent of salvation is the **Holy Spirit** (3:5). The Holy Spirit makes people **new** (*anakainōsis*).[42] The Holy Spirit gives life. When God sends forth the Holy Spirit, life is created and the earth is made new again (Ps 103:30). Despite difficulties experienced through ministry that may affect Christians' outer nature, their "inner nature is *being renewed* day by day" (2 Cor 4:16; NRSV). Paul uses the imagery of **pouring** (*ekcheō*; 3:6) to describe the experience of being made new by the Holy Spirit. This verb continues the imagery of **washing** (3:5), because water can be poured out to fill a container. The same verb for "pouring" was used to describe the entering of the Holy Spirit into the disciples at Pentecost (Acts 2:17–18, 33) and the manner in which God's love enters human hearts (Rom 5:5).[43] Similarly, the Holy Spirit "fills" humans bringing birth (Luke 1:35) and rebirth (Titus 3:5).

The subtle mystery of the Triune God is included in Titus.[44] Either **God** as a whole or God the Father is the **Savior** who is described as kind and loving and merciful. Rebirth is accomplished by the agency of the **Holy Spirit**, who is **poured out** generously (3:4–5). This "pouring" is accomplished by the agent, **Jesus Christ** (who is also our **Savior** [3:6]), who made people righteous by means of God's grace (3:7). All three Persons of the Trinity are merciful and generous and work together to accomplish the same goal: that **we might become heirs** (3:7).

The theme of **inheritance** is a frequent and important one in the Old and New Testaments. Abraham set out from Chaldea to receive an inheritance for himself and his descendants.[45] His expectation and anticipation[46]

---

42. BDAG, 64; Thayer, 38.

43. The Spirit is first mentioned in the beginning of the Bible when the Spirit of God hovers over the waters (Gen 1:2). Living water is a symbol of the Holy Spirit (John 7:38–39). Water, essential for life, is a symbol of blessing (Mal 3:10; Joel 2:23–28).

44. Jerome mentions that this present section has "the clearest manifestation of the Trinity" (Jerome 2010: 339).

45. Heb 11:8; Gen 11:31–12:5; Josh 24:2–13.

46. Subjunctive verb, "might become," is in the mood of expectation and anticipation

were to receive the inheritance. God was the One who promised the inheritance, but Abraham had to trust the Lord.[47] God is still the One who promises inheritances (Titus 1:2). But God's inheritance is not earthly; as a matter of fact, earthly possessions can make it harder for the believer to inherit.[48] Only the humble will inherit (Matt 5:5; Titus 3:2). The inheritance is eternal life, which begins now, but continues forever.[49] It is God's "imperishable and undefiled and unfading" inheritance kept safely in heaven for the final resurrection (1 Cor 15:50–54; 1 Pet 1:4). However, the wicked do not inherit God's kingdom, but only the sanctified, those who "overcome."[50]

How might this promise be received by the ancient Cretans? Paul elsewhere has promised that Abraham's offspring, the **heirs** of God's promised kingdom, are Jew and Greek, foreigner and citizen, slave and free, male and female (Gal 3:28–29; Col 3:11). What might strike an original reader is that the promise of becoming heirs is for *all* people and for *all* time. Ancient Crete had numerous social classes. The ruling citizen class (a minority), of course, had the landed wealth. The household owned the family estate (*klēros*). There were free people who owned property and free people without political rights. The resident aliens had to live in special quarters of the city. The serfs originally did not own houses on the estate, but eventually they might inherit if the free citizens had no living relatives.[51] Slaves normally were not heirs.[52] They were part of the inheritance! But, they could be set free and adopted as heirs.[53] Women and non-citizens had no political rights. In Athens, a daughter could inherit when she had no brothers, similar to the Hebrew practice.[54] In Crete, daughters did inherit but smaller portions than the brothers. Daughters who were sole heirs had to marry next of kin.[55] Paul had described all believers as formerly slaves.

(Titus 3:7; Robertson 1934: 927–28).

47. Rom 4:13–14; Acts 7:5; Heb 6:17.
48. Mark 10:17–22; Luke 12:13–15.
49. See Titus 1:2.
50. Rev 21:7; Matt 25:34; Acts 20:32; 1 Cor 6:9–10; Gal 5:19–21; Eph 5:5.
51. Willetts 1965: 83, 85, 87, 93, 96–97, 99–101, 105.
52. See Gal 4:1–7; Col 3:23–24.
53. Gen 21:10; Willetts 1965: 83–84, 89, 102.
54. Spencer 1985: 69–70; Willetts 1965: 85, 90, 93; Fantham 1994: 80.
55. Willetts 1965: 84, 89–92.

But now they were all adopted and reborn as wealthy **heirs** looking to the realization of their glorious inheritance (3:3, 5–7). What a marvelous vision for then and for now!

Paul then summarizes a key principle in this section of his letter and a key theme in the whole letter: **The word is trustworthy; and, concerning these things, I desire you to maintain strongly, in order that the ones having believed in God may be careful to stand forth[56] with good deeds; these things are good and helpful to humans** (3:8). *Pistos ho logos* (**the word is trustworthy**) precedes five key teachings in the Pastoral Letters.[57] *Logos* (**word**) in the Pastoral letters can refer to God's revelation[58] and teachings of faith,[59] but also human teachings,[60] even heterodox ones.[61] In this context, modified by *pistos* (**trustworthy**), Paul refers to authoritative, accurate teachings or revelations from God expressed in a pithy saying or summary statement that can be passed on to others as fully reliable. Josephus also uses this phrase to describe an accurate report or news (*Ant.* 19.1.16 [132]). Paul emphasizes that Titus should promote this teaching strongly.[62] Although good deeds do not save anyone,[63] they are helpful for believers (3:8).

Avoid Anyone Who Causes Division (3:9–11)

In the second major section of the letter (2:1—3:11), Paul encourages Titus (a) to promote healthy teaching by encouraging godly behavior among the elders, youth, and slaves (2:1–15); (b) to remind people to live godly lives in

---

56. *Proistēmi*, literally, "set over" (LSJ, 1482; Thayer, 539), normally refers to leadership. See 1 Tim 5:17 (Spencer 2013). However, this use in Titus 3:8 (and 3:14) may be similar to the use in Isa 43:24 when God tells the Israelites that they *stood* before God in their sins. In contrast, Christians should "stand forth marked by *good deeds*" (3:8).

57. See 1 Tim 1:15 (Spencer 2013).

58. 1 Tim 4:5; 6:3; 2 Tim 2:9, 15; 4:2, 15; Titus 1:3; 2:5.

59. 1 Tim 4:6; 5:17; 2 Tim 1:13; Titus 1:9; 2:8.

60. 1 Tim 4:12.

61. 2 Tim 2:17.

62. Scholars are unsure whether the pithy teaching is 3:4(5)–7 (Robertson 1931: 607; Lock 1924: 155; Fee 1988: 206–7; Mounce 2000: 451 or 3:8b (Towner 2006: 144). My own preference is 3:8b because the saying follows a conjunction as in 1 Tim 1:15 and 4:9; in the other four sayings, the saying most likely follows the phrase *pistos ho logos* and 3:8b is more pithy than 3:4–7.

63. See Titus 3:5.

the world because they are justified by God's grace (3:1-8); and, now, (c) to have nothing to do with anyone who causes division (3:9-11). Most of the letter contains instructions for the church. Previously, Paul had exhorted Titus to be a model of good deeds to other young men (2:7-8), not to let others despise him in his role as minister (2:15),[64] and rebuke others (1:13). Now he warns Titus himself: **But foolish arguments and genealogies and contentions and battles pertaining to the law, avoid; for they are useless and without value** (3:9).

Genealogia (**genealogy**; 3:9) refers to a collection of words (*logeia*) about "persons in a family" (*genea*) or "tracing a pedigree."[65] Ancestry was very important to Jews, determining many things, such as eligibility for inheritance or for the priesthood. A priest had to trace his fiancee's descent four generations to make sure she was qualified to marry him (*m. Qidd.* 4:4). Marriage records were sent to the public registries in Jerusalem. They kept the records of succession of high priests for 2,000 years (*Ag. Ap.* 1.7 [30-36]). Knowing or talking about one's ancestry, in itself, cannot be wrong, because both Matthew (1:1-17) and Luke (3:23-38) accentuate the importance of ancestry as a basis for Jesus' representative nature and eligibility for ministry. In Titus 3:9, the adjective **foolish** precedes and modifies the four nouns that follow (**arguments, genealogies, contentions, battles**). These are discussions about ancestry that lead to spiritual error.[66] The Greeks loved to recount stories of mythic ancestry. Legalistic Jews might be proud of their "pure" ancestry. The current Herodian ruler in Judea (Marcus Iulius Agrippa [Acts 25-26]) himself was of mixed ancestry (Jewish and Idumaean). He would not be considered "pure." One's own genealogy or that of one's leaders might be concerns raised in Crete. However, Paul had already reminded the Christians that God intends all of them to become eligible as **heirs** (3:7).

In the New Testament *zētēsis* and *zētēma* (**arguments**) can refer to an official or judicial inquiry.[67] *Zētēsis, zētēma*, and *zēteuō* connote an inquiry[68] that is vigorous, a dispute or argument searching for the truth, or simply resolution, such as when some disciples argued over whether John the Baptist and Jesus were in competition (John 3:25) or whether circumci-

---

64. The closing, 3:12ff., is also personal.
65. LSJ, 342-43, 1055.
66. See Titus 1:11, 14.
67. Acts 23:29; 25:19-20; 26:3.
68. LSJ, 756.

sion was necessary for salvation (Acts 15:1-2). Sometimes a verbal dispute can have physical ramifications (Acts 18:12-17). Arguments in themselves are not wrong, but **foolish** ones are (Titus 3:9). **Foolish** can refer to error that is consciously chosen or to innocence. Those who hear Jesus' words but do not act on them deceive themselves and will suffer the ramifications for their actions (Matt 7:26-27; 25:2-13). Those religious leaders who make judgments that value what is less important also will be judged (Matt 23:13-26). These are arguments about topics that lead to spiritual error.

Eris (**contentions**) and *machē* (**battles**) are synonyms for *zētēsis* (**arguments**; 3:9).[69] In 3:9, they seem to be in intensifying sequence. *Eris* personified is a goddess who "excites to war."[70] *Eris* can be a result of not acknowledging God and a synonym for jealousy (Rom 1:28-29; 13:13). It describes the fighting in Corinth when the church divided over who was the best leader.[71] In secular Greek, *eris* referred mostly to "battle-strife."[72] *Machē* refers to the **battle** or combat of armies.[73] Paul uses it for external conflict (2 Cor 7:5). Thus, arguments necessitating resolution (*zētēsis*) become jealous contentions that incite people (*eris*) to full battles (*machē*). And in the mix are the questions of genealogy and the law.

All of these divisive topics, equally, Titus is to **avoid**. Titus is to *turn himself around away from* **arguments and genealogies and contentions and battles pertaining to the law** that lead to error (3:9).[74] He is not to participate; he is not to encourage others because: they **are useless** (*anōphelēs*), do not profit anyone[75] and they are **without value**, a waste of time (*mataios*). The circumcision party wastes its time in such words.[76] The opposite is love that comes from a pure heart and a good conscience and sincere faith (1 Tim 1:5). Paul warns Titus (and Timothy in 2 Tim 2:16) not to get involved in disputes that do not lead to truth.

Instead, Titus should warn (at least twice) people who create divisions with such arguments (3:9-10). And, after such warnings, then he should

---

69. See also 1 Tim 6:4 (Spencer 2013) and 2 Tim 2:23.

70. LSJ, 689.

71. Paul, Apollos, Cephas, or Christ in 1 Cor 1:11-12.

72. LSJ, 689.

73. LSJ, 1085. See also Jas 4:1.

74. Paul holds the imperative verb to the end of the clause emphasizing all that Titus is to avoid. The polysyndeton, repetition of **and**, amplifies the list.

75. Thayer, 52, 469, 683; BDAG, 92-93.

76. See Titus 1:10.

himself **reject** these people[77]: **A divisive person, after one and a second admonition, reject, knowing that such a person is completely turned away and sins, being self-condemned** (3:10–11). Eusebius cites Titus 3:10 word-for-word as a basis for Polycarp not acknowledging Marcion's teachings as orthodox and for the apostles and their disciples not "even to join in conversation with any of those who mutilate the truth" (*Hist. eccl.* 4.14.7). Paul describes someone who pushes people to choose sides in arguments that will not be edifying.[78]

On what two bases can Titus reject such people? They are **completely turned away** (*ekstrephō*) and they **sin** (3:11). *Ekstrephō* metaphorically can have positive or negative connotations. For example, Jesus challenges his adult disciples to **turn back** and become like children (Matt 18:3). Stephen describes his ancestors as having "turned back" to Egypt when they asked for the Egyptian gods (Acts 7:39). Since the perfect tense presents a "completed state or condition,"[79] sometimes in the past these people turned away from the truth and have remained in this state. They are similar to those in Moses' time who had turned from the living God to worship foreign gods. They are "twisted."[80] (But Titus still had to warn them.) In the end, they condemn themselves by their choosing not to change.

Conclusion (3:12–15)

With these words, Paul concludes the body of his letter and moves now to concluding directions to Titus. Paul wants Titus to come to him and, by helping Zenas and Apollos, teach people to devote themselves to good works (3:12–15).

Titus, Come (3:12)

Paul has left Titus behind in Crete to complete their work (1:5). Soon Paul will enable Titus to join him at Nicopolis in Greece by sending a coworker to take his place: **Whenever I will send Artemas to you or Tychicus, make every effort to come to me into Nicopolis, for there I decided to spend**

---

77. See 1 Tim 4:7; 5:11 (Spencer 2013); 2 Tim 2:23; Heb 12:25.
78. Titus 3:9; Gal 5:19–21; 2 Pet 2:1.
79. Robertson 1934: 893.
80. Deut 32:20; NLT. They have turned aside from what is considered true (BDAG, 309).

Conclusion (3:12-15)

the winter (3:12). Titus' plans are indefinite. They depend on (a) when Artemas or Tychicus reaches Crete; (b) when Titus' work is completed at Crete; and (c) the time of year and sailing conditions. Where is Paul now? Possibly he is in Macedonia[81] and he will hike (or sail around the Gulf of Corinth) to Nicopolis. Paul wants Titus to meet him at Nicopolis before or after the winter season, when the west winds begin to blow. Because sailing on the open sea was so dangerous, no one sailed from mid-November to mid-March.[82] Travelers were warned of weather hazards beginning in mid-September until mid-February. Thus, Paul would plan to visit key churches (1 Cor 16:6) or cities during these times. A good winter harbor was free from sudden, frequent, and violent winds.[83] Therefore, if Titus, Artemas, and/or Tychicus are to travel safely, they need to sail between the six months of April through September. The trip between Crete and Nicopolis might take 10 days up to a month.[84]

Several ancient cities at that time were called **Nicopolis**.[85] Most likely, this Nicopolis is in Achaia (Greece),[86] facing the Sea of Adria in Illyricum (Rom 15:19), not far from Dalmatia (2 Tim 4:10), because of its location and size. It is "by far the most important and famous city of this name."[87] It was founded by Octavian Augustus to celebrate his victory[88] over Mark Antony at the Bay of Actium in 31 BC. Herod the "Great" built many public buildings there for the inhabitants (Josephus, *Ant.* 16.5 [147]).

Paul continues his ministry strategy of sending his coworkers to different places depending on their spiritual gifts and the needs of different churches.[89] Titus' organizational and peacemaking gifts will, most likely, next be needed at Nicopolis.

---

81. 1 Tim 1:3; Phil 2:24.

82. See 2 Tim 4:21. Land travel was also closed Nov-March. See Titus 1:5. Acts 27:9; 28:11; Josephus, *J.W.* 2.10.5 (203); Bruce 1990: 534; Rapske 1994: 3, 22.

83. Smith 1880: 85.

84. Approximately 325 miles by sea. Lightfoot 1913: 38.

85. They were in Egypt, Pontus, Bithynia, and Cilicia. *IDB* 3:548; *OCD*, 734.

86. Later called the province of Epirus (Zahn 1953: 2:54).

87. Zahn 1953: 2:54.

88. *Nikē*, "victory"; and *polis*, "city."

89. See Titus 1:5.

Coworker **Artemas** is nowhere else mentioned in the Bible.[90] **Tychicus** (literally, "fortuitous")[91] was originally from Asia and has accompanied Paul as a coworker since the late 50s until just before Paul's death in the late 60s. He accompanied Paul and others with the donation for the poor Christians in Jerusalem.[92] They traveled together from Greece to Asia to Syria. He was with Paul in Rome during both the first and second imprisonments.[93] Paul sends him twice to Ephesus, once to Colosse, and now to Crete. He may have carried the letters to the Ephesians and the Colossians. Paul describes his role and mission in Ephesians and Colossians in almost the same words: "the beloved brother and faithful minister in the Lord."[94] Although "brother(s)" and "sister(s)" are common ways for the early Christians to indicate their close relationship, Tychicus and Onesimus are the only individuals called "*beloved* brother." Tychicus is a reliable minister[95] with a special gift. He was sent to the churches in Asia so that they would know "the things" concerning Paul and his coworkers in Rome and, thereby, have their "hearts" encouraged.[96] "The things concerning us" (*ta peri hēmōn*) is an important phrase for Paul. For example, in Philippians, followers of Christ should show their interest in Christ by showing interest in one another because all believers are members of Christ's body.[97] This is *agapē* love. By "encouraging their hearts," Tychicus would support the Christians in Crete.[98] Tychicus seems to have the gift of encouragement (Rom 12:8), a helpful role to follow Titus' previous organizational efforts.

Teach People to Keep Busy in Good Works (3:13–14)

Paul will send Artemas or Tychicus to Titus and Paul, in turn, wants Titus to **send** Zenas and Apollos: **Zenas the lawyer and Apollos—diligently send on their way, that nothing may lack to them** (3:13). Zenas and

---

90. *Artemas* is later called one of the Seventy and bishop of Lystra (Lock 1924: 158; Bernard 1922: 182).
91. The adjective form of *Tychē*, "fortune, providence, fate" (LSJ, 1839).
92. Acts 20:4; Rom 15:25–27; 2 Tim 4:12.
93. Eph 6:21–22; Col 4:7–8; 2 Tim 4:12.
94. Eph 6:21. Col 4:7 adds "co-slave."
95. See 1 Tim 3:8 (Spencer 2013).
96. Eph 6:22; Col 4:8.
97. Phil 1:12, 27, 29; 2:4–6, 19–21, 23, 30; 3:7–8; 4:10, 18.
98. See Titus 2:15.

Apollos, having similar interests, both being learned men, probably made like-minded companions. **Zenas** is only mentioned here in the Bible.[99] He was a **lawyer** ("learned in the law") either Jewish or Gentile. One lawyer (*nomikos*) is mentioned in the Septuagint (Eleazar, a priest in ancestry, but a lawyer by profession [4 Macc 5:4]), more in the New Testament. Some Jewish lawyers had tested and questioned Jesus' teachings and authority and, thus, Jesus had some strong criticism for them.[100] Zenas, though, is a lawyer who served God's kingdom as one of Paul's colleagues in ministry.

Apollos,[101] a native of Alexandria, Egypt, was called "learned" by Luke (an educated man himself) and was gifted in teaching and bold, charismatic rhetorical speaking. He was effective in speaking as a Jew to other Jews.[102] Even though the church at Corinth created a competition between the leadership of Paul and Apollos,[103] Paul never shows any resentment toward Apollos. He even is willing to send him back to Corinth (although Apollos himself is not willing to return at that time [1 Cor 16:12]). Paul sees that Apollos builds on Paul's own ministry: Paul "plants" and Apollos "waters" as together they work on God's "field" (1 Cor 3:6-9).

Why were **Zenas** and **Apollos** in Crete? Did they bring Paul's letter to Titus at Crete[104] or had they already been (or will they stay) at Crete for a while ministering alongside Titus? We cannot be sure. However, their presence at Crete would be very helpful since the heterodox teachers were raising many questions about the use of the law and especially questions about the place of the Old Testament law in the Christian life (1:10, 14; 3:9). They could help Titus, a Gentile, in addressing the legal and Jewish questions raised by the church in Crete.

But now it is time for Titus to exert his own effort and organizational gifts to help them go **on their way** (2 Cor 8:17; Titus 3:13). Paul wants Titus to place high importance and exert much effort (**diligently**)[105] in helping

---

99. His name is related to *Zeus* and is probably an abbreviation of *Zēnodōros*, "gift of Zeus" (Kohlenberger 1995: 394-95; Robertson 1934: 172). According to tradition, he became bishop of Diospolis or Lydda (Lock 1924: 158; Baring-Gould 1898: 10:397).

100. Matt 22:35; Luke 10:25; 11:45-52.

101. *Apollōs* may be short for *Apollōnios*, *Apollodōros*, or *Apollōnidēs* (BDAG, 116; Robertson 1934: 172, 189).

102. Acts 18:24-28. Some scholars think he wrote Hebrews (Farrar 1883: 186-88).

103. 1 Cor 1:11-12; 3:3-4, 21-23.

104. Zahn 2: 49; Towner 2006: 801; Fee 1988: 214-15.

105. *Spoudaiōs* and *spoudaizō* in Titus 3:12 and 13 are used similarly in Gal 2:10; Eph 4:3; Phil 2:28; 1 Thess 2:17; 2 Tim 2:15; 4:9; Heb 4:11; 2 Pet 1:10.

Zenas and Apollos as travelers. Titus has to equip them with everything they need for the journey (**way**), which will include finding the right ship, obtaining provisions, escorting them to the ship, possibly giving them money for the trip and letters of introduction, and praying for them.[106]

The next verse serves to reinforce Paul's exhortation to Titus to help **Zenas** and **Apollos** in their journey, and, as well, serves as an apt summary for the whole letter: **and let our people keep on learning also to stand forth with good deeds for necessary needs, lest they may be unfruitful** (3:14). By following 3:13 with this verse, Paul implies that the church should join Titus in preparing Zenas and Apollos for travel. Practice in doing loving actions is a way experientially to learn to do them. This verse hearkens back to the faithful saying in 3:8.[107] Doing **good deeds** helps other Christians, helps educate those who do the good deeds, should be limited to genuine needs, and is a result of one's faith (3:13–14). The good deeds they are to do are limited by the phrase **for necessary** (*anankaios*) or indispensable **needs**,[108] not luxuries.

Akarpos is a lovely metaphor (3:14). The faith of believers should have a "harvest" (*karpos*) of good deeds. As seeds result in produce or a harvest, God's word cast into our hearts[109] should result in a harvest of outward goodness. The outward deeds demonstrate the inner attitude.[110] As Jesus explained, "from their fruits you will recognize" whether a tree is good or bad (Matt 7:20; 12:33) and the kingdom of God is for those who "produce its fruit" (Matt 21:43). Bearing much fruit glorifies the Father (John 15:8). Therefore, Paul seeks **fruit** in his converts (Phil 4:17; Titus 3:14).

Final Greetings (3:15)

Paul concludes the letter: **All the ones with me greet you. Greet the ones loving us in faith. Grace be with all of you** (3:15). Artemas and Tychicus (3:12) and others are with Paul. Paul rarely is alone. He may be single, but he is not solitary. He writes the letter to Titus, but he lets other believers

---

106. Zahn 2: 54; LSJ, 1494; Acts 15:3; 20:38; 21:5; Rom 15:24; 3 John 6–8; 1 Macc. 12:4; Josephus, *Ant.* 20.2.5 (50); Towner 2006: 802. See also 2 Tim 4:21.
107. See Titus 3:8.
108. E.g., Heb 8:3; Acts 13:46; 2 Cor 9:5; Phil 1:24; 1 Cor 12:22–23.
109. Titus 3:5; Matt 13:3–23; Jas 1:18.
110. Matt 3:8. Deeds are active (1 Cor 14:14) and outward (e.g., Gal 5:22–23).

know. Everyone with Paul sends a written "kiss" toward Titus.[111] Then, Paul commands Titus to greet not everyone, but only those **loving us in the faith**. At first glance, Paul may appear unnecessarily restrictive. However, previously he had commanded Titus to reject divisive people (3:10), even as he commanded the churches not to associate with those who are disobedient.[112] The kiss of peace is not to be extended to those who are not at peace with God's message.

Ancient Greek letters would terminate with a final "farewell" ("be in good health")[113] and begin with a greeting (*chairō*).[114] Paul, in comparison, refers to **grace** (*chairō* or *charis*), both at the beginning and end of this letter (1:4; 3:15) and many of his letters. He does not clarify to whose grace he refers. Earlier in the letter, "grace" is a quality that flows from God and Jesus Christ.[115] Thus, again good deeds (3:14) are placed under the larger rubric of grace (3:5, 15).[116] As in 2 Corinthians 13:13 (14), Paul adds **all**. The churches at Crete and Corinth are besieged by heterodox persons. Nevertheless, God's grace is for them too. It is for everyone. Grace envelopes deeds in Paul's message to Titus.[117]

Fusing the Horizons: The Place of Grace

What is the foundation of all good behavior? It is grace, mercy, love, salvation, kindness. When I was a college student and not yet a confirmed believer in Jesus as Lord of the Universe and as my Lord, I was invited to attend a meeting of the InterVarsity Christian Fellowship. It was a Friday night. The night was a supreme example of what *not* to do as a bearer of good news. The Christian

---

111. See also Rom 16:16; 1 Cor 16:20; 2 Cor 13:12; 1 Thess 5:26. Among friends the greeting is accompanied by a kiss (BDAG, 144).

112. 1 Cor 5:11-13; 2 Thess 3:14-15.

113. *Hrōnnymi*, LSJ, 1578.

114. 2 Macc 11:21, 33; Josephus, *Life* 44, 65 (226-27, 365, 366); Hunt 1932: 268-309.

115. Titus 1:4; 2:11; 3:4-7. In many of Paul's letters, the closing blessing refers to the grace of the Lord Jesus (1 Cor 16:23; 2 Cor 13:13 [14]; Gal 6:18; Phil 4:23; 1 Thess 5:28; 2 Thess 3:18; Phlm 25). "The Lord be with you" is the way Boaz greeted his reapers, a model for the way Jews should greet each other (Ruth 2:4; *m. Ber.* 9:5).

116. The closing blessing is identical to Hebrews 13:25. It is almost identical to 1 Tim 6:21; 2 Tim 4:22; Col 4:18, but they omit "all."

117. See further Spencer 2000: 107-119.

who invited me to come at the last moment told me to go on my own because she was coming with her boyfriend. Did I feel abandoned? Yes. I was attending an all women's college and I had to go across town by bus to an all men's college at night. It was my first time. I was terrified! I had to find a specific classroom building in a strange school, but all the buildings were deserted and nameless and there was no one to ask. The Christian group met on the top floor of one empty building. No signs or people were at the bottom to welcome me. But, as I rode across town in the empty college bus and walked across the strange quad and slowly dragged my feet up the many stairs, I felt as if I were in a clear bubble, a cloud, that enveloped me and brought me along. My feet still moved, but this bubble stayed with me throughout the journey, enabling me to do the impossible—what even appeared to be ridiculous. But, when I finally arrived, I was wholeheartedly welcomed by the Christian believers with open arms.

God was with me. God is still with me. God was with me as I entered the kingdom and God is with me as I live each day in the kingdom. In the old covenant, God allays Moses' fears when God tells Moses: "I will be with you" (Exod 3:12). Jesus, Emmanuel ("God is with us"), also promises, "Behold, I myself am with you every day, until the end of the ages" (Matt 1:23; 28:20). Paul too tells the Athenians that God would always be with them too because in God "we are living and we are moving and we are being" (Acts 17:28).[118] Thus, as I experienced personally, Grace is the contextual bubble in which good deeds are done and Grace carries, guides, and instructs us all along the way.

---

118. See further Spencer 1998a: 26–27.

Introduction to 2 Timothy

INTRODUCTION

Occasion

Unlike Titus and 1 Timothy, in 2 Timothy,[1] Paul is now in prison. Paul is the Lord's "prisoner" who is "suffering for the gospel" (1:8, 12). Paul mentions his own suffering many times (he suffers hardship for the gospel, "even to the point of being chained like a criminal," while, in contrast, "the word of God is not chained" [2:9] and he quotes a "saying" that encourages Christians who suffer [2:11]). Paul summarizes his life (3:10–11; 4:7–8) and the inevitability of persecution for a Christian (3:12). He discusses "death," which has been "abolished" by Christ Jesus (1:10). Unlike the situation in the other prison epistles (Phil 1:14; Col 4:7–14), all in Asia "have turned away" from or left Paul, including Phygelus and Hermogenes (1:15), Demas (4:10), Crescens, Titus (4:10), and Alexander (4:14). At his first defense, all "deserted" him (4:16). In contrast, Onesiphorus' household was "not ashamed" of Paul's "chain." Instead, when Onesiphorus' household arrived in Rome from Ephesus, he eagerly searched for Paul and found him (1:16–18). In this context, Paul's main message to Timothy is not to be ashamed of his imprisonment, but rather to "share in suffering" (2:3; 4:5).

Similar problems continue to occur at Ephesus as had been occurring earlier in Ephesus and Crete: "wrangling over words" (2:14), "stupid and senseless controversies" (2:23), women who do not know the "knowledge of the truth" (3:7), false teachers (3:7; 4:3), and myths (4:4).

Instead of expecting release (Phlm 2:2; Phil 2:24; 1:25–26), Paul describes impending death (4:6; cf. Phil 2:17). At his first defense, he was rescued from "the lion's mouth" (4:17). Yet he still expects to write (4:13), and he expects to see Timothy before winter impedes transportation (4:21). According to tradition, to avoid arrest, Paul had rented a villa or room

---

1. See Spencer 2013, Introduction to Pastoral Letters. Authorship of Pastoral Letters.

outside the city near San Sebastiano. Arrested in AD 66, he spent about nine months imprisoned.[2] Although he no longer had the mild conditions of his first house arrest (Acts 28:16, 30; 2 Tim 1:17), yet his trial was delayed, probably because he appealed to the emperor, again pleading his Roman citizenship and previous acquittal.[3] Paul and Peter at the end were imprisoned in the Mamertine Prison, one of the principal prisons of Rome, below which was the dungeon of the Tullianum. Traditionally, Paul and Peter were both killed June 29, AD 67. Paul was executed on the Ostian Way outside Rome. Both Paul and Peter were interred in a marble tomb in San Sebastiano on the Appian Way for a year and seven months. Paul was then moved by Lucina in AD 69 near the Ostian Way on the Via Valentiniana, where his coffin remains to this day.[4]

No clear traditions recount exactly where in Rome Paul was being held during the writing of this last letter. Probably, not under house arrest, yet not at the Mamertine dungeon (where any writing would be impossible), he may have been incarcerated in a military camp or palace in the city, bound to a soldier, as had been Agrippa.[5] Paul was allowed to have friends visit him.

Titus and 1 Timothy clearly mention the locale of the readers of his letter—Crete (Titus 1:5) and Ephesus (1 Tim 1:3)—but 2 Timothy is not as explicit. Most likely, Timothy is still in or has returned to Ephesus (c. one to four years later than 1 Tim, AD 64–66), because Onesiphorus' household, who had visited Paul in Rome, had rendered service in Ephesus (1:18) and was present now with Timothy (4:19). Prisca and Aquila had been in Ephesus (Acts 18:19, 24–26) and were also now with Timothy (2 Tim 4:19). If Timothy was in Ephesus, being part of Asia, he would indeed "know" that all in Asia had deserted Paul (1:15). Paul sent Tychicus to Ephesus to replace Timothy so that Timothy could leave (4:12).[6] Second Timothy is the last letter written by Paul in the canon.

---

2. Barnes 1933: 60; Morton 1937: 472.

3. Barnes 1933: 42, 60; Finegan 1981: 23–24, 35.

4. Barnes 1933: 44, 58, 62, 65–68, 71–72, 78, 98–99, 101–4, 133–35, 149–51, 153, 156–57; Morton 1937: 473–76; Finegan 1981: 24, 29–30, 34, 36, 224; Barnes 1903: 93–94, 96, 99; Zahn 2, 1953: 62; Eusebius, *Hist. eccl.* 2.25; *Acts Peter* 40.

5. Josephus, *Ant.* 18.6.7 [195, 203–4] vs. 6.10 [235–37]; Witherington 2006: 324.

6. Neither Paul, nor Timothy, appear to be in Thessalonica, Galatia, Dalmatia, Troas, Corinth, or Miletus (Robertson 1931, 4: 9–13, 20). Zahn (1953, 2: 18–19) concludes Timothy is in Asia Minor, but not Ephesus.

Analytical Outline of 2 Timothy

Paul's overall purpose in 2 Timothy is to encourage Timothy to join in suffering with him for the gospel which he learned, unlike others who have abandoned Paul.

I. Letterhead: Paul reminds Timothy of "the promise that brings life in Christ Jesus" (1:1–2).

II. Timothy should not be ashamed to suffer for the gospel, nor of Paul suffering (1:3—2:13).

A. Timothy should not be ashamed because of his faith and heritage (1:3–7).

B. He should not be ashamed because of the gospel and Paul's own example and teaching (1:8–14).

C. Timothy should follow the example of those of Onesiphorus' household, who were not ashamed of Paul's chains, instead of others in Asia who turned away from him (1:15–18).

D. Timothy also should join in suffering (2:1–13).

III. Timothy needs to remind the people of these things, instead becoming a vessel for good works, while himself avoiding ungodly talking (2:14–26).

A. He should treat truth with integrity and avoid ungodly talking (2:14–19).

B. He should become a vessel prepared for good works, pursuing virtues, avoiding controversies, gently guiding the opposition because they may repent (2:20–26).

IV. Timothy needs to continue in his ministry of evangelism and sound teaching despite opposition (3:1—4:8).

A. Timothy needs to turn away from lack of genuine piety (3:1–5).

B. Some of the people who have an outward godliness will take women as prisoners, although eventually their folly will become evident (3:6–9).

C. Timothy needs to follow Paul's model, because the godly in Christ will be persecuted, while evil people will be deceived (3:10–13).

D. He needs to remain in the Scriptures, which prepare him for every good work (3:14–17).

E. Paul exhorts Timothy, in light of Jesus' judgment, to proclaim the word at all times, because a time is coming when people will turn from healthy teaching to myths (4:1–5).

F. Paul and all who love the Lord will receive a just crown (4:6–8).

V. Paul wants Timothy to come soon, because he has been left alone by all except Luke, he needs supplies, and he was opposed by Alexander and abandoned by all except the Lord (4:9–18).

VI. Paul sends final greetings (4:19–22).

A. Paul greets Prisca and Aquila and Onesiphorus' household (4:19).

B. He explains where Erastus and Trophimus are (4:20).

C. He reiterates: come soon (4:21a)!

D. Christians at Rome greet Timothy (4:21b).

E. Paul blesses Timothy and the church (4:22)

2 TIMOTHY 1

Address (1:1-2)

Paul reminds Timothy that he was appointed an **apostle**[1] **of Christ Jesus through God's will**.[2] This appointment is indispensable for Paul's conversion. Paul had been redirected from persecution of Christians to promotion of Christianity. Ananias had told him that God had chosen him to know "God's will" (Acts 22:4-5, 14). Paul had previously referred to this crucial change in his life and to eternal life (1 Tim 1:12-16). Paradoxically, in a situation where death is imminent, Paul emphasizes the **promise of** eternal **life**, only present **in Christ Jesus**.[3]

In the first letter, Paul addresses Timothy as "genuine child" (1:1), as he did also Titus (1:4), but now Paul writes **to Timothy, beloved child** (1:2). **Beloved** is a term that Paul has used to describe a father-son (or parent-child) relationship. A good father or parent "puts in (the) mind" (*noutheteō*)[4] of the child good content, teaches, warns, exhorts, admonishes, because the parent is genuinely concerned for the child, unlike a pedagogue, an enslaved instructor who has been ordered to teach the basics (1 Cor 4:14-17; Gal 3:24). To the Corinthians, Paul had described **Timothy** as a **beloved child** because he had begotten him spiritually (*gennaō*) and Timothy's way of life was identical to his spiritual father's (1 Cor 4:15-17). Beloved children imitate their parent(s), as believers should imitate God (Eph 5:1-2). Loving parents provide a good model.[5] Thus, using **beloved** for Timothy reminds Timothy of their loving familial relationship which they had had for about twenty years since Acts 14:8.[6] Although Paul uses

---

1. See 1 Tim 1:1 (Spencer 2013).
2. He refers to God's will also in 1 Cor 1:1; 2 Cor 1:1; Eph 1:1; Col 1:1.
3. Paul will return to the topic of life in 1:10. See Titus 1:2; 3:7; 1 Tim 1:16; 4:8; 6:12, 19.
4. Thayer, 429.
5. See also 1 Thess 2:7-12, where Paul uses the image of a father (and mother) with his own children who appeals and encourages and pleads to them to lead lives worthy of God. "Beloved" is also used by God the Father about God the Son: Matt 3:17; 12:18; 17:5; Mark 1:11; 9:7; Luke 3:22; 2 Pet 1:17.
6. See also Phil 2:22.

"beloved" for many specific Christian believers[7] and for many churches,[8] Timothy is the only **beloved child**. Also, "beloved child" presages the advice Paul will pass on to Timothy in this letter, as father passes advice to a son.[9] Moreover, in itself, "beloved" calls out to Timothy to respond because love evokes love since Paul will exhort Timothy to do some difficult actions (such as share in suffering).[10]

Timothy Should Not Be Ashamed to Suffer (1:3—2:13)

Paul's main point of the first section of his letter is to exhort Timothy not to be ashamed to suffer for the gospel, nor of Paul suffering (1:3—2:13). Paul gives three reasons: (a) Timothy should not be ashamed because of his faith and heritage (1:3–7); (b) Timothy should not be ashamed because of the gospel and Paul's own example and teaching (1:8–14); (c) Timothy should follow the example of those of Onesiphorus' household, who were ashamed not of Paul's chains, instead of others in Asia who turned away from him (1:15–18). Therefore, Timothy also should share in suffering (2:1–13).

Paul Thanks God (1:3–5)

While in 1 Timothy 1:3–4 Paul jumps right into his concern about the heresies at Ephesus and the following of his previous directions to Timothy, in 2 Timothy 1:3–5 Paul begins with an affirmation of Timothy: **I have gratitude to God, to whom I serve from my parents' time in a clean conscience, as I have unceasing remembrance concerning you in my prayers by night and by day, longing to see you, remembering your tears, that I might be filled with joy, having remembered the genuine faith in you, which dwelled first in your grandmother Lois and in your mother Eunice and I am persuaded also in you** (1:3–5).

---

7. Epenetus, Ampliatus, Stachys, Persis, Tychicus, Epaphras, Onesimus, Luke, Philemon (Rom 16:5, 8, 9, 12; Eph 6:21; Col 1:7; 4:7, 9, 14; Phlm 1, 16).

8. Rome, Corinth, Philippi (Rom 1:7; 12:19; 1 Cor 10:14; 15:58; 2 Cor 7:1; 12:19; Phil 2:12; 4:1).

9. E.g., 1:13–14; 2:22; 3:10–14.

10. **Beloved** is also a term used to describe all believers in God's new covenant as beloved brothers and sisters, not masters and slaves or servants (Rom 11:27–29; 1 Tim 6:2; Phlm 16; Jas 2:5). **Grace, mercy, peace from Father-God and Christ Jesus our Lord** (1:2) is the same greeting used in 1 Tim 1:2. See 1 Tim 1:2 (Spencer 2013).

Many ancient private letters began with a reference to prayer and reasons to be thankful for the reader (**I have gratitude**).[11] Paul begins by thanking God whom he serves. Implicitly, he will compare his own situation with that of Timothy's. His family too has worshiped God (**God, to whom I serve from my parents' time**).[12] Not only was Paul a Pharisee, but his father was a Pharisee (Acts 23:6). His parents were devout, having him circumcised on the eighth day, rearing him according to the strict legal requirements of the written and oral Torah (Phil 3:5–6). Thus, Paul became "zealous for God" (Acts 22:3), even if misdirected.

When defending himself before the Sanhedrin, Paul describes himself as having lived before God "with a good conscience" (Acts 23:1).[13] Paul's **conscience** is his interior faculty for personal discernment of good and evil. It affects his conduct and motives for action. Conscience arises from knowledge that the subject shares with himself or with someone else. When Paul's knowledge about Jesus was redirected (1 Tim 1:13–16), the basis for his convictions changed and his conscience was restructured since it had never been destroyed (vs. 1 Tim 4:2).

Paul now changes focus from his reasons for gratitude to God for his own upbringing to Timothy's upbringing. Paul has **unceasing remembrance concerning** Timothy in his **prayers** (1:3). In a similar unceasing manner ("without intermission"),[14] Paul had remembered the believers in Rome (1:9) and in Thessalonica (1 Thess 1:2–3). Paul practiced what he preached to others (1 Thess 5:17). What Timothy, the Romans, and Thessalonians had in common was they were people not currently present with Paul, and Paul eagerly desired to be in their presence (**longing to see you**), but he was not able to do so at that time.[15] He wanted to be with Timothy but was in prison. Paul took his concerns and feelings of disquiet and thanksgiving and shared them with God.[16] The loving expressed by

---

11. 2 Macc 1:1–9, 11–2:18; Aune 1987: 163, 177, 185–86.

12. "Parents" is a likely translation of *progonos* since in 1 Tim 5:4 the same term refers to parents, maybe grandparents (Spencer 2013).

13. See 1 Tim 1:5 (Spencer 2013); Titus 1:15.

14. *Adialeiptōs*, Thayer, 11.

15. Paul also "longed" to see the Philippians (Phil 1:8; 4:1). He had never met the Roman church, but planned to go there. He had been in Thessalonica but was forced to leave.

16. The Jewish Sabbath began at night and ended with the day. Thus, Paul's point is that he spent time in prayer, both **by night and by day**. See Acts 20:31; 1 Thess 2:9; 3:10. Devout Jews would pray three times a day, at dusk, 3 p.m., and dawn, to correspond with

the spiritual parent, Paul, was reciprocated by the child, Timothy (1:4). Paul in his prayers remembered Timothy's **tears.** *Dakryō/dakryon* refer "to shed tears, weep silently."[17] Tears may express outwardly inward concerns. Timothy is concerned for Paul. Did Timothy cry when Paul was arrested in Rome again?[18] Timothy was like his mentor Paul, who had told the elders from Ephesus how he had served the Lord "with all humility and tears," and, as a father, he exhorted them with tears (Acts 20:19, 31). Tears were an aspect of Paul's love for the Corinthians (2 Cor 2:4). Both Timothy and Paul modeled on Jesus himself, God incarnate, who prayed with both silent tears and loud shouts (Heb 5:7) and wept upon seeing the grief expressed by humans mourning the death of Lazarus, even though he knew he would resurrect him from the dead (John 11:25–26, 32–44). God's compassion may be demonstrated in tears, but these types of tears from this suffering world will all be wiped away by God when God dwells with humans in the new earth (Rev 7:17; 21:4). Somehow the end of the prayers and longing to see Timothy, remembering his tears, will result in Paul being **filled with joy**, if he indeed sees Timothy. And, indeed, he will ask Timothy to come soon (2 Tim 4:9, 21).

Paul remembers Timothy's tears and Timothy's **genuine faith** (1:5). To **remember** is an important act in the Bible (e.g., 1 Cor 11:2) and here particularly as Paul faces his own death. Later, he will ask Timothy to cause other believers to remember ("remind"; 2:14).[19] Peter, too, in his last letter, focuses on reminding his readers.[20] Paul's **joy** is not only to see Timothy, but to see Timothy in light of his **genuine faith.** His faith is without hypocrisy.[21]

Faith is described metaphorically as a friend who **dwells within** (*enoikeō*) someone, even as the Holy Spirit dwells within the church.[22] In

---

the three daily offerings in the temple in Jerusalem.

17. In contrast to *klaiō* ("to weep audibly") or *odyromai* ("to give verbal expression to grief"), *thrēneō* ("to give formal expression to grief"), *alalazō* ("to wail in oriental style") or *stenazō* ("to express grief by inarticulate or semi-articulate sounds, *to groan*") (Thayer, 347).

18. See also *TLNT* 2:496: "The captive cannot get this wrenching farewell scene out of his mind."

19. See also Titus 3:1.

20. 2 Pet 1:12–13; 3:1. Only Peter and Paul use the noun *hypomnēsis* in their last letters.

21. He is not an actor or pretender (*hypokritēs*; Thayer, 52, 643; BDAG, 1038). See 1 Tim 1:5 (Spencer 2013).

22. 2 Tim 1:14; Rom 8:9, 11 *oikeō en hymin;* Thayer, 217; The church body is also

the same way, as faith dwelled in Paul's **parents** and grandparents when they worshiped the God revealed in the Old Testament, so too faith dwelled in Timothy's grandmother Lois and mother Eunice when they worshiped the same God in the New Testament times. Moses commanded the Hebrews to read the law to all the men, women, children, and foreigners living in the cities every seventh year so they could listen and learn to fear the Lord and follow carefully the law (Deut 31:10-13). In many places in the Old Testament, parents are exhorted to teach their children about God's great deeds.[23] God's words are to be remembered: "Teach them to your children, talking about them when you sit at home and when you walk along the road, when you lie down and when you get up" (Deut 11:19; TNIV).[24] Godly instruction should come from the father and mother (Prov 1:8), but Timothy's father was a Gentile and thus did not undertake Timothy's biblical training (Acts 16:1). Even some Romans esteemed the education of "the good old days" when mothers (not servants) trained their children, as did Cornelia, the mother of Sempronius and Tiberius Gracchus, Aurelia mother of Caesar, Atia of Augustus, so that the child might "lay hold with heart and soul on virtuous accomplishments" (*Dial.* 28). While the Roman focus might be more on an occupation such as "the army, or the law, or the pursuit of eloquence,"[25] a devout Jew would instead focus on God's revelation. Timothy learned the holy Scriptures from infancy from his mother and grandmother (2 Tim 3:15). Timothy and at least also Eunice became believers in Jesus as the Messiah in Lystra (Acts 16:1).

God's Gift (1:6-7)

Paul then returns to his earlier point: **I am persuaded** (a genuine faith) **dwells also in you** (1:5). Yet, though **genuine faith** dwells within Timothy, as it did in his mother and grandmother, he needs to act more: **For this reason I remind you to keep stirring into flame God's gift, which is in you through the laying on of my hands** (1:6). Paul has remembered (*mneia*) Timothy in his prayers, remembered (*mimnēskomai*) Timothy's

---

the sanctuary of God wherein dwells God's Spirit (1 Cor 3:16; 2 Cor 6:16). *Oikeō* is used literally in 1 Cor 7:12-13 to describe a husband and wife living together in the same household. The aorist tense suggests dwelling had a beginning (Towner 2006: 454).

23. Passover—Exod 13:8-16; Mount Horeb—Deut 4:9-14; nature of God—Deut 6:4-9.

24. See also Ps 78:4-7; Prov 22:6; Joel 1:2-3.

25. Although goodness and self-control are also mentioned by Tacitus (*Dial.* 29).

tears, remembered (*hypomnēsis*) Timothy's faith, and now he calls to remembrance or **reminds** (*anamimnēskō*)[26] Timothy to act on this "genuine faith" that he has. If in 1 Timothy 4:14, Paul exhorts Timothy not to neglect his spiritual gift, now he tells him to keep lighting it up again, **stirring into flame** or causing to blaze again[27] **God's gift** (1:6) of evangelism (2 Tim 4:5). *Anazōpyreō* is a concrete image. *Zōpyron* is an ember of a fire or a hot coal[28] that is used to kindle a fire. Paul repeats the preposition *ana-* (*anamimnēsko . . . anazōpyreō*; 1:6). *Ana-* implies repetition or "motion upwards."[29] As long as a fire has hot coals, it can be easily stirred up into a blaze of fire. Spiritual gifts from God can become dormant.

Why would evangelism be such a difficult gift to heighten at this time? Timothy only has to see Paul's situation to become cautious before he reaches out aggressively with the good news into his society. Paul is in prison again and this time the circumstances are less hopeful for release (1:8; 4:7, 16). No wonder Paul explains: **for God did not give to you a spirit of fear but of power and of love and self-control** (1:7). In English, "Timothy" and "timid" form a quotable word-play, but not in Greek (*Timotheos* vs. *deilia*). Timothy might become fearful not because of his own personal nature, but more because of the dangerous situation in which the Christians find themselves, suffering persecution for their faith (1:8). For a good reason, Timothy might be fearful since he himself will eventually be imprisoned in Rome as well (Heb 13:23). If Timothy indeed was a former soldier,[30] he might very well appreciate the first two adjectives: **fear** and **power** (1:7). **Fear** describes the disciples when their boat was swamped by waves from a fierce storm (Matt 8:24–26). Spicq explains: Paul "stirs up 'the good soldier of Jesus Christ' (2 Tim 2:3) to undertake and pursue combat (1 Tim 1:18), according to the traditional military maxim, dating back to Deuteronomy: 'Conquer...fear not and be not disheartened.'"[31]

Power (*dynamis*) or "strength" is the antithesis of fear (1:7). Courage takes strength. The best strength comes from God (1:8). A soldier must

---

26. All these Greek words are cognates.

27. LSJ, 104; BDAG, 62. See 1 Tim 4:14 (Spencer 2013).

28. Thayer, 37; LSJ, 760.

29. LSJ, 98. The use of Timothy's gift in 2 Timothy 1:6 requires less work than in 1 Tim 4:14 ("neglect" vs. "rekindle").

30. See 1 Tim 1:18; 6:12 (Spencer 2013); 2 Tim 2:3.

31. *TLNT* 1:302. See Deut 1:21. In contrast, Judas Maccabees prayed that God make Lysias' enormous army "fearful" and not bold (1 Macc 4:28–32). See also Josh 1:9.

also have **self-control** (*sōphronismos*) (which Timothy will also need if he is to flee youthful passions; 2:22). This is the same quality required of the women at Ephesus (1 Tim 2:9, 15).[32] These three military qualities (fearlessness, strength, self-control) are still insufficient in themselves. They must be combined with **love** (*agapē*),[33] because Paul and Timothy do not fight a physical battle, but a spiritual one. The aim of the order is love,[34] a love which comes from Christ Jesus (1 Tim 1:14).

Join in Suffering (1:8-12)

Paul concludes with direct exhortations to Timothy: **Therefore, do not begin to become ashamed of the testimony of our Lord nor of me, his prisoner** (1:8a). The aorist subjunctive prohibition suggests that from Paul's perspective Timothy is not yet ashamed of Paul.[35] Paul had previously described Timothy as a model of someone who lives a costly life (1 Cor 4:9-17).[36] But, Paul is concerned that Timothy could desert him too. Jesus challenged the crowd and his disciples to deny themselves, take up their crosses, and follow him, assuring them that he will be ashamed of those who are ashamed of him and his words (Mark 8:38; Luke 9:26). Witnessing in behalf of Jesus is worth the difficulties because Jesus gives life and salvation. Paul had said in 1 Timothy 1:12 that he is not ashamed because of whom he trusts.[37] Onesiphorus' household also modeled believers not ashamed of being identified with a prisoner (1:16-17). In contrast, other believers appeared to have left Paul, possibly because they were ashamed of Paul or fearful of their own safety (4:10, 16).

The opposite of being ashamed of Jesus and Jesus' believers is to **join in suffering for the gospel according to God's power** (1:8b). If Jesus is a crucified Messiah (1 Cor 1:23) whose death on the cross was a shameful way to die in its time, how can the followers of this Messiah not suffer difficulties

32. See 1 Tim 2:15 (Spencer 2013).

33. The four qualities are described in a polysyndeton (using a conjunction between each one), thus, equal in importance.

34. See 1 Tim 1:5; 4:12; 6:11 (Spencer 2013).

35. The aorist subjunctive suggests the prohibition of a thing not yet done (Robertson 1934: 851–53). Twenty-seven percent of the uses of *epaischynomai* (**ashamed**) in the NT occur in 2 Tim (which is only .89 percent of the NT) showing how important this topic is in 2 Tim.

36. See Spencer 1989.

37. See also Rom 1:16; Phil 1:20.

(Heb 12:2)? Peter reiterates: suffering as a Christian is not shameful (1 Pet 4:16). Jesus taught that, if he had been persecuted, so would be his disciples (John 15:20; 2 Tim 3:12).[38]

Paul uses a unique word. **Join in suffering** is one word in Greek (*synkakopatheō*).[39] *Kakopatheō* ("suffer") without the preposition "with" is also repeated later in the letter to describe Paul's own suffering from his imprisonment and to challenge Timothy to endure suffering (2:9; 4:5; 1:12 *paschō*). The use of the preposition *sun* accentuates to "suffer together *with* someone."[40] Paul describes by the preposition ("with") how a communal aspect helps the sufferer in the midst of suffering.

However, Paul and Timothy and other believers are not to "join in suffering" simply for their own interpersonal enrichment, but **for the gospel**. Paul invites others to join him because he is inviting them to follow their crucified Messiah. But, how can Paul and Timothy have the strength to suffer for the gospel? They can only do so **according to God's power** (1:8). What is that power or strength? Paul describes it in an extended modifier: **the one having saved us and called us to a holy calling, not according to our works, but according to his own purpose and grace, the one having been given to us in Christ Jesus starting from eternal times, on the one hand, having been revealed now through the appearing of our Savior Christ Jesus, on the other hand, having abolished death but having brought to light life and immortality through the gospel** (1:9–10). God's power accomplished several things: it **saved us** and **called us to a holy calling** (1:9).[41] That calling is one not based on one's own **works**, accomplishments or actions (i.e., suffering for the gospel in itself does not save). Rather, it is a calling according to God's **own purpose**[42] and grace. God's **grace** contrasts with **our works**. Paul further describes the grace in four ways: the one (1) having been given to us in Christ Jesus before eternal times; (2) having been revealed now through the appearing of our Savior Christ Jesus; (3) having abolished death; and (4) having brought to light life and immortality through the gospel. Paul begins and ends this pericope referring to the **gospel** (1:8, 10). The calling has four actions in time. First,

---

38. See also Spencer 1994: 74–91.
39. See also 2 Tim 2:3.
40. BDAG, 951.
41. See 1 Tim 6:12 (Spencer 2013).
42. Or "goal," as in Acts 27:13.

starting from[43] **eternal times** refers to God's continuous, immeasurable time as opposed to human specific time.[44] In other words, before human time ever existed, God's power had a holy calling for humans in Christ Jesus, according to God's purpose and grace. That calling is a "godly life in Christ Jesus" (3:12), or a calling to be holy (1:9).[45] Ephesians also describes this calling as "for good actions, which God prepared beforehand, that in them we might walk" (2:10), or God chose humans "to be holy and blameless before him in love" (1:4), in contrast to such actions as "godless vain talking" and succumbing to "youthful passions" (2 Tim 2:16, 22). The second action refers to the incarnation (**the appearing of our Savior Christ Jesus**), which highlights Jesus, the Messiah, the Savior, the deliverer, who gave his life as a ransom for many.[46] Later, Paul will repeat: faith in Christ Jesus brings salvation (2 Tim 3:15). Elsewhere, Paul uses **the appearing** (*epiphaneia*) to refer to Jesus' return to earth for judgment,[47] however, in 2 Timothy 1:10 Paul refers to the incarnation by using the past tense (**having been revealed**), indicating this "appearing" has already occurred, similar to Titus 2:11 and 3:4,[48] where Jesus is the embodiment of God's grace and salvation.

The third action is **having abolished death** (1:10). The fourth, and final, action is **having brought to light life and immortality through the gospel** (1:10). **Abolish** might be more exactly rendered "making of no effect." Christ Jesus deprived **death** of its strength, power, force, and influence. Death is now unemployed and inactive and inoperative.[49] Christ's resurrection or **life** demonstrated God's victory over death (see also 2:8). Christ also nullified the power of death by having entered its domain. Rather than having been overwhelmed by it, he returned from death, not spreading darkness and death, but rather bringing to the light life and immortality.[50] Death has not yet been literally abolished. The state of having to be enslaved to sin has been abolished (Rom 6:6; 7:6). Death separating

---

43. *Pro*, Robertson 1934: 622.
44. See Titus 1:2; 1 Tim 6:12 (Spencer 2013).
45. Lock 1924: 87; Fee 1988: 229.
46. Mark 10:45. See 1 Tim 1:1; 2:3; 4:10 (Spencer 2013); Titus 1:3; 2:13; 3:4–7.
47. 2 Tim 4:1; 1 Tim 6:14; Titus 2:13; 2 Thess 2:8.
48. The verb *epihainō* is used, instead of the noun *epiphaneia*, as in 2 Tim 1:10.
49. Thayer, 336. Death is "idle," as soil that does not produce plants with fruit is idle or inoperative (Luke 13:7).
50. Rom 14:9; 2 Cor 4:7–12; Heb 2:14.

us from God's love has been abolished (Rom 8:38–39). But, death, the last enemy, will be completely made inoperative at the very end of time (1 Cor 15:24–26; Rev 20:14).

Paul has just presented a synopsis of **the gospel**, which has to do with life and immortality, rather than death (1:9–10). Paul now ends this extended main clause (1:8–11) with an adjectival clause, **for this gospel I myself was appointed a herald and an apostle and a teacher** (1:11). Previously mentioned in 1 Timothy 2:7,[51] these three roles also follow a synopsis of the good news (1 Tim 2:4–6). This gospel (2 Tim 1:9–10) is so marvelous, it is worthy of Paul's appointment (1:11) and it is worth suffering for (1:12). Consequently, Paul says he is **not ashamed**—he is a prisoner (1:12)—as he had exhorted Timothy not to be ashamed.[52] Paul reiterates why he is not ashamed, because he knows two things: **for I know in whom I trusted and I am persuaded that he is powerful to guard my deposit into that day** (1:12). In the past, Paul has trusted and continues to **trust** the Savior Christ Jesus who appeared, made death ineffective, and brought life and immortality (1:10). How appropriate to trust someone victorious over death as one faces one's own death! Jesus is trustworthy. Jesus is also **powerful** (1:12). He is powerful to guard until the second coming (**that day**) Paul's **deposit** (1:12). Elsewhere, Paul exhorts Timothy to **guard** "the deposit" (1 Tim 6:20), which appears to be the order of love from a clean heart and a good conscience and a genuine faith (1 Tim 1:5, 18).[53] In light of the historical context and the theme of suffering, Paul may be saying that his gospel message will not be imprisoned, even though he is.[54] The message that has been given to him (**my deposit**) is also guarded by Jesus himself.

---

51. See 1 Tim 2:7 (Spencer 2013).

52. See 1 Tim 1:8 (Spencer 2013).

53. See 1 Tim 6:20 (Spencer 2013). Is the **deposit** the gospel? Does Jesus guard the gospel, which God entrusted to Paul, who in turn entrusted it to Timothy, who will in turn entrust it to others (2:2)? E.g., Dibelius and Conzelmann 1972: 105. Or, is "deposit" a metaphor for Paul's own life or Paul's own commitment to Christ and his gospel? E.g., Fee 1988: 232; Mounce 2000: 488. Witherington III suggests "my deposit" might refer to people in Paul's charge (2006: 320). Any of these interpretations is possible.

54. See also Acts 28:31.

Guard Sound Words (1:13-14)

Paul now returns his attention to Timothy: **Keep holding onto a model of sound words which you heard from me in faith and love, the one in Christ Jesus. Guard the good deposit through the Holy Spirit, the one dwelling among us** (1:13-14). The **deposit** is the **sound** or healthy **words** that Timothy heard from Paul himself (1:13). Paul exhorts Timothy to **keep holding**[55] the **model** or pattern or standard of words that he received from Paul. Paul himself was a model or example of one aspect of the gospel message: Christ's mercy toward sinners.[56] These words or teachings promoted spiritual health (**sound**).[57] In contrast, some people only want teaching that promotes disease (1 Tim 1:10; 2 Tim 4:3). True words themselves are health-inducing, but the listener must also receive the words in a receptive manner, **in faith and love.** Faith and love, already mentioned in this letter as exemplary virtues, are two key ingredients in healthy teaching.[58] Those who are not receptive to health-inducing words may be attempting to alleviate their spiritual illnesses by superficial or harmful ways (2 Tim 4:3). Ultimately, however, the faith and love that enabled Timothy to hear Paul's message came from **Christ Jesus**, who is exemplary of faithfulness and love.

The words Paul passed on to Timothy are not only "healthy," they are also **good** and a **deposit**, entrusted for safekeeping (1:14).[59] Even as Jesus guards Paul's deposit, simultaneously Timothy needs to guard his deposit.[60] Timothy received Paul's sound teaching **in** (*en*) **Christ Jesus'** faith and love (1:13). *En* basically signifies "within."[61] It is as if Timothy lived within the surrounding presence of Jesus. Simultaneously, Timothy is to guard his deposit **through** (*dia*) **the Holy Spirit** (1:14). The Holy Spirit as "the agent is conceived as coming in between the non-attainment and the attainment of

---

55. Or "gripping onto."
56. See 1 Tim 1:16 (Spencer 2013).
57. See Titus 1:13. Healthy words and teaching are also mentioned in 1 Tim 1:10; Titus 1:9; 2:1; 2 Tim 4:3.
58. See 1 Tim 1:5, 14 (Spencer 2013); 2 Tim 1:5, 7.
59. See 1 Tim 6:20 (Spencer 2013).
60. **Guard** is aorist imperative, which may: (1) continue the broader overview of the present imperative "keep holding" (1:13); (2) treat the act of guarding as a single whole action; or, (3) be an "impressive" aorist which is more authoritative and solemn than the present (Robertson 1934: 832, 856).
61. "That the location is within the bounds marked by the word with which it occurs" (Robertson 1934: 586-87).

the object in view."[62] Timothy is ultimately responsible to guard his deposit, but he needs to do so by means of the Holy Spirit. The Holy Spirit can empower him to do the guarding.[63] But how near is the Holy Spirit? The Holy Spirit is very near, because the Holy Spirit is **the one dwelling among us** (1:14).[64]

Example of Believers in Asia (1:15)

Paul now illustrates by negative and then positive examples those who have not and have guarded their deposit (1:14), those who have and have not been ashamed of Paul, and those who have and have not joined in suffering with Paul (1:8). Timothy knows about the first negative example because he most likely is in Ephesus in Asia:[65] **You know this, that all turned away from me, the ones in Asia, including Phygelus and Hermogenes** (1:15). **Asia** had many Jews.[66] In Jerusalem, some Asians opposed Stephen; others opposed Paul (Acts 6:9; 21:27; 24:19). At first, Paul, Silas, and Timothy were not allowed by the Holy Spirit to preach the good news in the province of Asia (Acts 16:6), referring to the province that included Ephesus. Asia was bounded by the province on the north of Mysia, on the south of Caria, and on the east of Phrygia and by the Aegean Sea on the west.[67] But eventually Paul went to Ephesus in Asia with Priscilla and Aquila (Acts 18:19—20:1, 18), where many became believers, including Epaenetus, the first convert to Christ in Asia (Rom 16:5), and Tychicus, Trophimus (Acts 20:4), and Onesiphorus' household. The believers formed many churches who send greetings to the church in Corinth (1 Cor 16:19).[68] Thus, Paul experienced the great moving of the Holy Spirit in Asia, but also great difficulties. He remembers his earlier experience in Asia as having received the "sentence

---

62. The root idea of *dia* is "be-tween, in two," "passing between two objects or parts of objects" (Robertson 1934: 580–83). See 1 Tim 2:15 (Spencer 2013); 1 Cor 8:6.

63. See 1 Tim 4:1 (Spencer 2013); Titus 3:5.

64. See 2 Tim 1:5 and Rom 8:9, 11. Other qualities of the Spirit are described in 1 Tim 4:1 and Titus 3:5. In contrast, "spirit" most likely refers to the human spirit in Timothy and Jesus in 2 Tim 1:7; 4:22; 1 Tim 3:16.

65. See Introduction to 2 Timothy.

66. See Introduction to 1 and 2 Timothy (Spencer 2013). **Phygelus** is attested only by inscriptions from Ephesus and Miletus (Witherington III 2006: 323).

67. Bruce 1990: 354; *OCD* (1970: 131) set the boundaries of Asia as Bithynia on the north, Lycia on the south and Galatia on the east.

68. Seven churches in Asia are addressed in Rev 1:4, 11.

of death," because Paul and Timothy and other coworkers were "so utterly, unbearably crushed that we despaired of life itself" (2 Cor 1:8–9). Sadly, now again Asia is giving Paul difficulties. **All turned away from** Paul does not include Onesiphorus' household and Tychicus (2 Tim 4:12). Thus, Paul speaks of the majority. How devastated Paul must have felt when those whom he taught for many years rejected him at this difficult time in his life! But, likewise, Jesus when he was arrested and crucified was rejected by even his close disciples.[69] Paul highlights two particular individuals in Asia: **Phygelus and Hermogenes** (1:15).[70]

Example of Onesiphorus' Household (1:16–18)

In contrast to most believers in Asia was Onesiphorus' household: **Might the Lord give mercy to Onesiphorus' household, that often it refreshed me and was not ashamed of my chain, but having been in Rome diligently sought me and found me. Might the Lord give to them (it/him) to find mercy from the Lord in that day** (1:16–18a). **Onesiphorus** could be *Onēsiphoros* (a male) or *Onēsiphoron* (a female).[71] Paul was probably visited not by one person but by a group of people,[72] not necessarily the entire household. *Oikos* may refer to a set of apartments, all a person possesses, or to a homestead and all the people who live in the house. It would include the extended family and workers in the family business who lived in the housing complex, in other words, all the persons economically dependent on one master (children, adult sons, slaves, freedpersons, clients, and spouses of all these persons). A household was a partnership, a group

---

69. John 18:15–18, 25–27; 20:19.

70. The second-century (AD 185–195) forgery by an elder of Asia Minor, *Acts of Paul and Thecla*, recounts Demas and **Hermogenes**, the coppersmith, as Paul's travelers who pretended they loved him and were jealous of Paul's positive estimation of Onesiphorus. They believed the resurrection had already taken place. *Acts Paul* 3.1, 4, 14; 2 Tim 2:17–18. In contrast to this author, Paul was positive toward marriage: *Acts Paul* 3.5, 11–12, 16 vs. 1 Tim 4:3; 5:14.

71. Both endings have been found, but many ancient references refer to the neuter form, *Onēsiphoron*, which refers to females (*New Docs* 4:181–82). However, the second-century elder who wrote the *Acts of Paul and Thecla* named Onesiphorus was a "man" with a wife Lectra and children Simmias and Zeno from Iconium (3.2). Also in tenth-century codex 181.

72. *Autō* in 1:18 may refer either to the masculine or neuter singular dative ending, thereby, referring either to *oikos*, "household," or "him," or "it," but **household** is the closest antecedent.

of twenty to thirty people, not all related by blood ties, dwelling or working together.[73] The New Testament has both male and female "heads of households," such as Cornelius, Crispus, Stephana(s), and Lydia.[74]

Two times Paul asks the Lord to be merciful to this household (1:16, 18). **Mercy** is a significant attribute of God, to which Paul refers in the address of both 1 and 2 Timothy (1:2). Paul sees that the Lord was merciful in forgiving him his great sin as a persecutor of Christians.[75] "Mercy" is a frequent word in the Old Testament, being included in many of God's self-descriptions, such as "the Lord God, compassionate and *merciful*, persevering and very *merciful* and true and keeping justice and *mercy* for thousands."[76] Clearly, Paul is asking for Onesiphorus' household to be blessed, but does Paul have a more specific request in mind? For instance, Jesus reprimands the Pharisees who have not forgiven the repentant tax collectors and sinners (Matt 9:11–13). Has this household committed some great sin in the past or is Paul simply asking God that they be blessed in a general way[77]?

Paul gives two reasons why this household should be blessed: (1) often it refreshed Paul, and (2) it was not ashamed of Paul's chain.[78] *Onēsiphoros/on* literally is "bringing advantage, beneficial"[79] and, indeed, this household was greatly beneficial to the Apostle Paul. When its members **refreshed** Paul, literally they caused him "to cool again, to cool off, to recover from the effects of heat."[80] The focus in *anapsychō* appears more to be in bringing

---

73. Spencer 2005: 70–71.

74. Acts 10:2; 11:14; 16:15; 18:8; 1 Cor 1:16; 16:15–18. Inscriptions of female heads of households in Asia Minor have been found, both widows and married women (Spencer 2005: 71). The married younger widows would become rulers of their households (*oikodespoteō*). See 1 Tim 5:14 (Spencer 2013).

75. 1 Tim 1:13–16; verb, *eleeō*.

76. Exod 34:6–7; LXX. See also Exod 20:5–6; Deut 5:9–10; 7:9–10. God shows mercy by forgiving and saving and renewing people dead in their trespasses (e.g., Eph 2:4–5; 1 Pet 1:3), giving a child to Elizabeth, who had been barren (Luke 1:57–58, 72, 78), accepting Gentiles (e.g., Rom 15:9), providing a wife for Isaac (Gen 24:12, 14, 44), and helping Joseph to prosper (Gen 39:21).

77. As in Gen 27:28; 28:4; 40:14; Num 6:25; Ruth 1:9. Some commentators think Onesiphorus is dead (Robertson 1931: 615; Fee 1988: 236–37; Witherington III 2006: 324–25).

78. Paul's wrist was chained to the soldier. Normally a prisoner was chained with one chain of the left hand to a soldier (e.g., Acts 28:20). In severe cases two chains for two soldiers were used, as in Acts 12:6.

79. LSJ, 1231.

80. Thayer, 40, 43; Josephus, *Ant.* 15.3 (54). Rest on the seventh day for animals,

God's presence to an evil situation than simply helping Paul rest and become stronger. The household represented Christ to the prisoner, Paul, who represented Christ as well, because, just as this household visited Paul ("the least of these") in prison, they were, in effect, visiting Jesus (Matt 25:40), and they did so not just once but **often** (many times).

By visiting Paul, they demonstrated they were **not ashamed** of his imprisonment (1:16).[81] Moreover, Paul was not easy to find in Rome. They had to place importance on and be conscientious in their searching.[82] Paul now asks for the Lord's mercy in **that day**, most likely referring to the second coming of Jesus (1:12; 4:8).

Paul concludes by reminding Timothy: **And to everything in Ephesus it/they ministered, as very well you know** (1:18b). We, however, do not know how much this household did at Ephesus, but in Rome they served Paul by their presence and actions, comforting him in his afflictions.

---

servants, and strangers was intended to help people "cool off" or be "refreshed" (*anapausis*; Exod 23:12). This same verb is used to describe the effect of relief by David's music from an evil spirit on Saul (1 Sam 16:23; LXX). Peter describes the Lord's presence as "refreshing" (Acts 3:20). See also 2 Cor 7:13; Phlm 7, 20.

81. Agrippa was imprisoned simply because his freedman Eutychus heard him pray for Gaius to become emperor (Josephus, *Ant.* 18.6.5-6 [168-91]).

82. BDAG, 939. See Titus 3:13 and Introduction 2 Tim.

2 TIMOTHY 2

KEEP EMPOWERED AND ENTRUST PAUL'S TEACHINGS (2:1–2)

Paul, having mentioned his attitude to his imprisonment, the power of Jesus (1:12), the soundness and importance of Paul's own words (1:12–13), the receptiveness of Timothy (1:13), the presence of the Holy Spirit (1:14), the negative example of some believers (1:15), and the positive example of others (1:16–18), returns again to exhort Timothy: **Therefore, you, my child, keep on being empowered in the grace, the one in Christ Jesus, and what you heard from me through many witnesses, entrust these things to trustworthy humans, who are able also to teach others** (2:1–2). Paul has given many reasons how and why Timothy can continue to be empowered. By using the pronoun **you**, Paul exhorts Timothy in particular to be like Onesiphorus' household and not like Phygelus and Hermogenes. He calls Timothy again **my child** to remind him of their special spiritual parent-child relationship.[1] Timothy's **power**[2] comes from Jesus to guard the message entrusted to him (1:12). Somehow, Timothy himself should make an effort, but yet that effort is done in Christ Jesus' grace (2:1).[3] Christ's grace has already accomplished many marvelous actions.[4] Yet, Timothy himself needs to participate in an ongoing process to allow Christ Jesus' strength to come into his life.

Timothy has to guard his own walk with Jesus and develop an army with which to fight. As Paul realizes his own death is imminent, he wants to strengthen Timothy and strengthen the church, thus Paul begins 2:2 describing what it is that Timothy needs to entrust to others: **what you heard from me through many witnesses**. The content of the education is of paramount importance. This content is validated by two sources: (1) **me** (i.e., Paul) and (2) **many witnesses**. Timothy directly heard from Paul about Jesus being the Christ and the Savior, having abolished death and having brought

---

1. See 1 Tim 1:2 (Spencer 2013).

2. Even when Paul was deserted by humans, he still could be strengthened by the Lord (4:17). See also Rom 4:16–21; Phil 4:12–13.

3. See also 2 Tim 1:8, 12, 14.

4. See 2 Tim 2:9–10.

eternal life (1:9–10, 13). He also learned from Paul the ramifications of the gospel, that it will entail suffering (1:8). Timothy models Paul's "way of life in Christ" (1 Cor 4:17), that their difficulties as believers demonstrate that their "extraordinary power" must come from God (2 Cor 4:7).[5]

Other agents that corroborate or support[6] what Timothy heard from Paul are **many witnesses.**[7] Timothy witnessed Christ's empowering but difficult work in his travels and even while Paul had been in prison in Rome previously. A **witness** might be a legal witness, acceptable in court, someone who can verify what he or she has seen or heard or known by any other means.[8] Both the Old and New Testaments are founded on the principle established in Deuteronomy: "By the mouth of two witnesses (not one), or by the mouth of three witnesses, shall every word be established" (19:15). This same principle works for historical witnesses.[9] Paul had already exhorted Timothy in Ephesus to make sure women, not educated previously in Jewish law, should now be educated (1 Tim 2:11). All were encouraged to seek leadership positions in the church by becoming godly persons (1 Tim 3:1). Now Paul reiterates that message to Timothy to **entrust** the gospel educational process to **trustworthy humans**. Part of the function of an elder is the ability to **teach others** (1 Tim 3:2). That same function is repeated here (2 Tim 2:2). Nevertheless, Paul does not require that only elders teach. Many people may have the gift of teaching (Rom 12:7; 1 Cor 12:28), some of whom may become elders.

In 1 Timothy, Paul has entrusted the order of "love from a pure heart and a good conscience and genuine faith" to Timothy (1:5, 18). Now he wants him to **entrust** the order to others.[10] In 2:2, a message is "placed

---

5. See Spencer 2001: 86–87, 106–7, 196–97.

6. Robertson 1931: 616; Lock 1924: 93.

7. Barnabas, Silas, Luke, Aquila and Priscilla, James, the Twelve, and many others, including Lois and Eunice (Acts 14:12; 15:40—16:1, 10; 18:2–5; 20:4—21:18; 2 Tim 1:5; 3:14–15).

8. See 1 Tim 5:19 (Spencer 2013); Thayer, 392.

9. Jesus was conscious that he needed two or more witnesses to testify of his person and life (John 5:31–39; 8:13–18; 10:25, 37–38; 15:26–27; 21:24). The Gospel of Luke ends with Jesus' commission to his disciples to testify of his teachings, that the Messiah suffered and rose from the dead and that repentance and forgiveness of sins is to be proclaimed to all nations (24:44–48). The disciples testify to Jesus throughout the book of Acts. In Acts, Paul and his coworkers spend much time discipling the new converts and appointing elders for each church (e.g., Acts 14:23; 15:36).

10. To **entrust** (*paratithēmi*) literally means "to place beside, place near" someone, as when bread and fish are placed before someone to eat (Thayer, 486). It is the cognate of

before" people, entrusted to them as a deposit, a deposit not to hide but to reveal to others. The recipients of this message are described in three ways: (1) humans, who are (2) trustworthy, and (3) able to teach others.

Some commentators want to limit **humans**, *anthrōpos*, to men only in 2:2 because they presuppose that the teaching offices are restricted to men only.[11] However, 1 and 2 Timothy have plenty of references where *anthrōpos* is clearly generic: prayer for all humans, God desires all humans to be saved, one mediator between God and humans, God is Savior of all humans, sins of some people, people of corrupt mind, rich people, no human can see God, people will love themselves, evil people.[12] Definitive lexicons define *anthrōpos* as a generic term in the singular and plural.[13] The assumption is that God's revelation cannot rise above the androcentrism of its culture. However, if Jesus could rise above the androcentrism of his Jewish culture, why cannot his disciples rise above the androcentrism of their cultures?[14] In addition, the culture of antiquity was not one culture but many cultures, some of which allowed women to take leadership.[15]

Paul wanted both women and men to be taught sound words in order to teach these to others. But, for the important process of accurate transmission, students must have two qualifications. They must be faithful or **trustworthy** (2:2).[16] Moreover, since the goal is not simply self-edification, such people must also have the gift of teaching and the motivation to **teach others**. Then they will all be able to join Timothy, Paul, and other believers in suffering, and, if they should die or move away or be arrested for the faith, the message to **join in suffering as a good soldier of Christ Jesus** (2:3) will continue.

---

parathēkē, "deposit," in 1:12, 14. E.g., Mark 6:41; 8:6–7; Luke 9:16; 10:8; 11:6; Acts 16:34; 1 Cor 10:27.

11. For example, Johnson explains that, although *pistois anthrōpos* "*can* be translated as 'faithful people,'" he renders it "faithful men," because the "androcentrism of the Pastorals is so profound and pervasive that a gender-inclusive translation is almost impossible . . . it actually camouflages the true voice of the writing, which is unmistakably that of a male writing to another male within the Mediterranean culture of antiquity" (1996: 58).

12. 1 Tim 2:1, 4, 5; 4:10; 5:24; 6:5, 9; 2 Tim 3:2, 8, 13. See 1 Tim 2:5; 6:11.

13. LSJ, 138, 141; BDAG, 81, have the generic as the primary meaning. See Spencer 1998c.

14. See 1 Tim 2:11 (Spencer 2013); Spencer 2004; Spencer 1985.

15. E.g., Macedonian women, such as Lydia. See 1 Tim 1:7 (Spencer 2013).

16. See Titus 1:6; 1 Tim 5:16 (Spencer 2013).

GOOD SOLDIER OF CHRIST JESUS (2:3-7)

Paul now has the third command to Timothy in the concluding part (2:1–13) of the first section of the letter (1:3–2:13): "Keep on being empowered" (2:1) and "entrust" (2:2). Now, he adds, **join in suffering** (2:3), returning to his earlier command (1:8), but modifying in what manner Timothy should join in suffering: he should do it **as a good soldier of Christ Jesus**. Fighting as a soldier has been a predominate image that Paul has used for Timothy.[17] Timothy is exhorted to be a good soldier under his commander who is **Christ Jesus**. His commander determines the campaign and weapons he uses: Timothy serves in a "good" campaign with weapons of "faith and a good conscience."[18] How does the image of being a **soldier** relate to suffering? A soldier has to endure difficulties. For instance, the Roman soldier might have to carry eighty pounds on an all-day march and then construct defenses at the end of the day.[19] But, soldiers did not work as individuals, but in companies.[20] That is why Paul calls Timothy to **join in** suffering. He does not endure difficulties alone.

A **good** soldier is further described: **No one serving as a soldier entwines himself in affairs of life, so that he might meet the needs of the one having enlisted him** (2:4). Following the orders of one's commanding officer is crucial. The centurion in Capernaum described his way of life: "For I myself am a person under authority, having under me soldiers, and I say to this one, 'Go,' and he goes, and to another, 'Come,' and he comes, and to my slave, 'Do this,' and he does it" (Luke 7:8). Often soldiers volunteered because they were attracted to the general's personality and reputation and felt their allegiance to him rather than to the State.[21] Soldiers were recruited by a commander to participate in that commander's campaign. Therefore, the good soldier would aim to **meet the needs of**, or please, that commander. They were not even allowed to marry until their term of service was

---

17. See 1 Tim 6:12 (Spencer 2013).

18. See 1 Tim 1:18–19 (Spencer 2013). There Paul uses the verb and noun cognate forms for "fighting."

19. Stephens 1987: 35.

20. E.g., Acts 23:23.

21. Similarly, the centurion Cornelius had a devout soldier serving under him he could trust to go to Joppa to find Peter (Acts 10:5–8). The persons responsible for recruitment were the *strategoi*, the military commanders. The *strategoi* also served as magistrates who presided over trials of prosecution for desertion or evasion of military service (*OCD*, 120, 1018).

completed.²² Towner considers **affairs of life** could be distractions related to "living, buying, and selling," not sinful in themselves, but activities that might interfere with active military responsibilities.²³ Paul was encouraging Timothy to be completely devoted to his commander, Christ Jesus, and to his citizenship in and his campaign for God's kingdom.

Paul now uses a related image: athletic competition: **But if also someone may compete in a contest, (s)he is not crowned unless (s)he might compete according to the rules** (2:5). A soldier could be decorated with a necklace, armband, and embossed disc placed on the corselet and a centurion could be awarded a gold crown or a silver spearshaft.²⁴ Athletics was itself an aspect of preparation for war, which entailed suffering.²⁵ In athletics, one contends for a prize.²⁶ In Paul's first illustration, the key is whom one serves (2:4); here it is how one serves (2:5). Athletics (as opposed to serving as a soldier) intensifies the emphasis on a goal. However, the prize is not awarded if the contest is not done **according to the rules**. Athletes who won games might receive generous monetary rewards as well as many other honors. A victor in the Sacred Games had a right to free sustenance or to a pension and was exempt from taxation. A victor might be awarded a crown or wreath.²⁷ But, "when money enters into sport corruption is sure to follow."²⁸ Sometimes, victory was bought and sold. For example, in 388 BC, Eupolus of Thessaly bribed his opponents in boxing to allow him to win the prize. In addition, each sport would have its own regulations.²⁹ So too, Timothy needed to follow Christ's rules (his teachings) to win the goal of affirmation by Christ at the last judgment.

The third illustration highlights why one serves: **It is necessary the laboring farmer first to share in the fruits** (2:6). On active duty, a soldier would not himself farm, but, when pensioned off, he might. Lystra,

---

22. Stephens 1987: 34. Nevertheless, many soldiers had common-law wives they married upon retirement.

23. Towner 2006: 493; Witherington III 2006: 330. Paul is not literally restricting Timothy from these activities, even as he is not literally requiring Timothy to be a soldier. Cf. Demas in 4:10.

24. Stephens 1987: 34–35.

25. Heb 10:32; *alēsis*. See 1 Tim 6:12 (Spencer 2013).

26. LSJ, 32.

27. To be "crowned" as an honor or reward (*stephanoō*) could refer to a gift of money, honor, libations, office, or wreathe (LSJ, 1642).

28. Gardiner 1930: 103.

29. Gardiner 1930: 99, 103, 107, 113.

Timothy's home town, was set in a fertile plain. Second Timothy 2:6 appears to refer to a more general reward for labor.[30] The soldier, athlete, and farmer **labor** hard and have rewards for their work.[31] In 2 Timothy, the farmer appears to be a tenant farmer who leases the land, rather than the landowner, because he looks forward to a **share** of the crops.[32] The **fruits** or reward for labor here appear to be salvation in Christ Jesus with eternal glory and living and reigning together with Christ (2:10–12). Thus, those who join in suffering as good soldiers of Christ Jesus endure difficulties, please Christ, live according to Christ's rules, and are rewarded. Whom one serves, how one serves, and why one serves are important in these illustrations.

Paul concludes this section: **Keep pondering what I am saying; for the Lord will give to you understanding in all** (2:7). Paul uses two synonyms: **ponder** (*noeō*) and **understand** (*synesis/syniēmi*). In contrast, the teachers of the law do not "ponder" or "grasp." They have no perception of spiritual truths based on careful faith-based thought.[33] Timothy should continue thinking about what Paul has said (2:3–6) or will say (2:8–13), so that his mind will apprehend its significance. Timothy should ponder to understand spiritual truth based on careful faith-based thought that effects action. Most commentators conclude that Paul wants Timothy to contemplate the meaning and application of the three metaphors that Paul just introduced (2:4–6).[34] If Timothy is to ponder some spiritual truth over

---

30. Paul's point is similar to 1 Tim 5:18 and 1 Cor 9:7 and Deut 25:4. First Tim 5:18 has to do with literal wages for a worker. See 1 Tim 5:18 (Spencer 2013); Deut 20:6; Prov 27:18.

31. Mounce summarizes that the main point in all three illustrations is "share in suffering": "A soldier suffers by being forced to ignore civilian affairs. An athlete suffers by training properly. A farmer suffers by working hard" (2000: 507). The farmer especially needs patience, as James explains: "The farmer waits for the precious crop from the earth, being patient with it until it receives the early and the late rains" (Jas 5:7; NRSV).

32. E.g., Matt 21:33–41; BDAG, 196, 639.

33. Sometimes *noeō* is more intensive than *syniēmi*, as in "perceive (*noeō*) my understanding (*synesis*) of the mystery of Christ" (Eph 3:4), where understanding seems to summarize Paul's apprehension of the matter. *Synesis/syniēmi* often is simply a synonym for human wisdom (Matt 11:25; Luke 10:21; 1 Cor 1:19; 2 Cor 10:12), yet proconsul Sergius Paulus of Cyprus was a *wise* or intelligent man because he asked to hear the word of God from Barnabas and Saul (Acts 13:7). The twelve-year-old Jesus amazed the rabbinic teachers by his *understanding* (Luke 2:47). At other times *synesis/syniēmi* is a synonym of *noeō* indicating a level of comprehension that results in action as opposed to hearing that results in no comprehension (Isa 6:9–10, cited in Matt 13:13–15 and Acts 28:26–27; Rom 3:11; 15: 21; Matt 15:10; 17:13). See 1 Tim 1:7 (Spencer 2013). E.g., Matt 16:9, 12.

34. E.g., Fee 1988: 243; Mounce 2000: 510–11; Kelly 1963: 176. Marshall (1999: 731)

time, understanding the meaning of the three metaphors appears rather simple. However, if Paul wants Timothy to ponder the dangerous path of suffering that lies ahead for him, that would certainly take more time.[35] Timothy's path and Paul's path were reminiscent of Jesus' final path to Jerusalem (Luke 9:51–53).

God's Word Is Not Bound (2:8–9)

Paul now gives additional reasons why Timothy should endure suffering. It results in salvation for others and himself (2:8–13). Timothy needs to remember that, even though Paul is bound, God's word is not bound: **Keep remembering Jesus Christ, risen from the dead, from David's seed, according to my gospel, in which I suffer evil to the point of bonds as an evil doer, but God's word is not bound** (2:8–9). Paul still is developing the theme why Timothy should partner in suffering with him for the gospel. He has already mentioned how Jesus, full of grace, as Savior, destroyed death and brought life (1:9–10; 2:1). Now, he reminds Timothy to keep in his mind two things about Jesus Christ: (1) Christ was **risen from the dead** and (2) he is **from David's seed** (2:8). Throughout 2 Timothy, Paul employs "Christ Jesus,"[36] highlighting his status as Messiah (or **Christ**). This time Paul calls him **Jesus Christ,** possibly because he emphasizes Jesus as the descendant of King David and the prototype human who was raised from the dead. In Romans, Paul describes Jesus as "David's seed according to the *flesh*" (1:3).[37] Jesus, then, is an apt model of hope for Timothy because those

---

writes that Paul could be referring to 2:8–13 but that is less likely. Towner (2006: 496) concludes that 2:7 refers backward but also forward to the phrase that follows.

35. Towner (2006: 497) explains: "Timothy's path was leading to Rome and suffering. It was a hard path in every way. It involved first selecting new team members to fill the gaps caused by those who had left the mission team and who would expand the ministry in Asia. Then the challenge of suffering at Paul's side and in his place had to be faced." In addition, 2:7 would then bring together all the topics in 2:4–6 to allude back to 2:3, "join in suffering," and in 2:8 to allude forward to 2:9, Paul's own suffering, and to the trustworthy word in 2:11–13. The three illustrations in 2:4–6 are then a part of the picture.

36. 2 Tim has twelve references to "Christ Jesus." In 1 Tim, he uses "Christ Jesus" twelve times, "Jesus Christ" two times, "Christ" one time, while in Titus "Jesus Christ" predominates (three references) with one reference to "Christ Jesus" (UBS).

37. 1 Tim 2:11–12; 1 Cor 1:23–24. Nathan prophesized to David: "Your house and your kingdom will endure forever before (the Lord); your throne will be established forever" (2 Sam 7:16; TNIV); Isa 9:6–7; 11:1–5; Jer 23:5–6; 33:15–16; Matt 1:1, 6; John 7:42; Rev 5:5; 22:16; Ignatius, *Eph* 18.2.

who suffer now will have hope for the future since the crucified Messiah is also the risen Messiah.

Paul has used the phrase **my gospel** two times previously.[38] Here, the phrase reminds Timothy of what he has "heard" from Paul (2:2). Paul is highlighting that the gospel he preaches includes suffering. Paul suffers to the point of being imprisoned unjustly, even as Jesus was crucified between two criminals, although he was righteous, Paul is in **bonds** (*desmos*), but God's word is not **bound** (*deō*; 2:9). Ironically, Paul had bound male or female followers of the Way in Damascus,[39] but now he was bound himself for the same reason he bound others. He writes that he is treated as **an evil doer**.[40] Ultimately, Paul realizes he had been persecuting Jesus (Acts 9:4–5), who himself had been bound,[41] unjustly, and was now sharing his fate. But, no matter the situation, those who suffer unjustly for Christ's sake can still promote their message of good news (4:17).

On account of this[42] **I endure all things on account of the elect, in order that also they themselves might attain salvation in Christ Jesus with eternal glory** (2:10). By implication, Timothy, too, should endure suffering, thereby helping others. The principle idea in **endure**[43] in a context of suffering is perseverance in one's faith in Christ despite persecution for that faith. "The person persevering to the end, this one will be saved," Jesus taught his disciples.[44] Paul considers Jesus' teaching from another perspective. The person who perseveres even through imprisonment (not only saves him/herself, but also) can help other believers.

Elect is frequently used in the New Testament for believers in a context of suffering. To be "elect" is to be special or precious to God.[45] One of the things the church is elected or picked out or chosen for is for suffering

---

38. Rom 2:16; 16:25. The message entrusted to Paul: 1 Tim 1:11; 1 Cor 15:1–2; Gal 1:11; 2:2.

39. Acts 9:2, 14, 21; 22:5. See 1 Tim 1:13 (Spencer 2013).

40. Ramsay (1893: 249) explains that *kakourgos* "refers expressly to the *flagitia*, for which the Christians were condemned under Nero, and for which they were no longer condemned in AD 112." Mounce 2000: 514.

41. Matt 27:2; Mark 15:1; John 18:12, 24.

42. "This" is neuter to allude back to "gospel."

43. See 1 Tim 6:11 (Spencer 2013). Thayer, 644. Literally it is used for "remain behind" in, e.g., Luke 2:43; Acts 17:14.

44. Matt 10:22; 24:13; Mark 13:13; also Rom 12:12; Jas 1:12; 5:11; 1 Pet 2:20.

45. See 1 Tim 5:21 (Spencer 2013); also Titus 1:1; Ps 105:6; Isa 43:20–21; Col 3:12; 1 Pet 1:1; 2:9.

on behalf of its testimony to Jesus Christ.[46] People are called by God, but to become "elect," they must persevere until the end.[47] Of course, Jesus, the Messiah, *the Chosen One*, is the ultimate model of someone who perseveres.[48] By persevering as a Christian, Paul serves as a model for other believers who are (and will) suffer for their faith, with the ultimate goal that they **attain salvation in Christ Jesus** (2:10). That salvation comes not with a temporary glory, but an **eternal glory**[49] (a glory that is continuous and immeasurable).[50]

Paul concludes this first section of his letter (1:3—2:13) with a pithy summary statement that is an authoritative, accurate, and fully reliable teaching from God: **The word is trustworthy:**[51] **for if we died together, also we will live together; if we persevere, also we will reign together; if we will deny, also that one will deny us; if we are unfaithful, that one remains faithful, for he is not able to deny himself** (2:11-13). This summary statement expresses the value of sharing and persevering in suffering. Paul has four conditional clauses, where each condition (protasis) results in a conclusion (apodosis).[52] These four sets of clauses (a condition followed by a conclusion) concern themselves with four concerns in times of persecution: death, perseverance, denial, and unfaithfulness.

In the same way as Paul earlier put priority on Jesus as "risen from the dead" (2:8), Paul puts priority on living and reigning with Jesus (2:11-12). He begins with **for if we died together** (2:11), using the past tense (aorist). The aorist treats the act of dying as a single whole.[53] "Death" is a synecdoche of the afflictions a Christian endures. Paul himself had been near death many times and now he looks forward to it again.[54] Paul looks at death

---

46. See Spencer 1990a: 56–57; Matt 24:22, 24, 31; Mark 13:20, 22, 27.

47. Matt 22:14; Rev 17:14.

48. Heb 12:2–3; Luke 23:35; 1 Pet 2:4, 6. The title **elect** for an individual may signify a believer who has had to suffer in behalf of Jesus, e.g., 2 John 1, 13; maybe Rom 16:13; 1 Pet 5:13. Later "elect" came to signify a clerically ordained person (Spencer 1985: 111).

49. See also 2 Tim 4:18; 2 Cor 4:17; 1 Pet 5:10.

50. See 2 Tim 1:9.

51. See Titus 3:8; 1 Tim 1:15 (Spencer 2013).

52. A first class condition assumes the reality of the condition (Robertson 1931: 618).

53. Robertson 1934: 831–32, 846.

54. 2 Tim 2:9; 1 Cor 15:31; 2 Cor 4:10; 11:23 "in death many times"; also Hendricksen 1957: 257; In contrast, others interpret "death" as metaphorical, "dying as incorporation into Christ's death through baptism (Rom 6:3)" (Bassler 1996: 145; Lock 1924: 96; Towner 2006: 509; Mounce 2000: 516); "death to sin and self which every Christian

from the standpoint of the future: **also we will live together**. He correlates death with life (*zaō*), alluding to his previous references to "eternal life."[55] A number of verbs begin with the preposition *sun* ("together with"):[56] *synapothnēskō* ("die together"), *syzaō* ("live together"), and *symbasileuō* ("reign together") (2:11-12). They complement Paul's central imperative to Timothy: to "suffer together with" (*synkakopatheō*; 1:8; 2:3). All of these verbs describe the action of being "together with" or accompanying someone. The object of each of these verbs is omitted: die with *whom*? Live with *whom*? Reign with *whom*? Primarily, Paul refers back to Christ Jesus (2:10),[57] but he probably also includes other believers. In the same way, "join in suffering" has a double allusion: Timothy suffering for the gospel and for Christ Jesus and Timothy suffering with Paul.[58]

The second set of clauses begins with the ongoing present tense and ends with the future tense: **if we keep persevering,**[59] **also we will reign together** (2:12a). Believers become joint heirs with Christ, "if we suffer together that also we may be glorified together."[60] Heirs reign over their kingdoms.[61] When Jesus by his blood ransomed his people, he made them a kingdom, rulers on earth, and priests to serve God.[62] But, Paul presents the difficulties in living as a Christian in an antagonistic world (death and the need to persevere), before he presents the rewards (life and reigning). Otherwise, believers might want to reign in order to avoid any costs to discipleship (1 Cor 4:8-13). The first two sets of clauses end with a positive conclusion. Death results in life, perseverance in victory.

---

undergoes in baptism" (Kelly 1963: 179-80).

55. 1 Tim 1:16; 6:12; Titus 1:2; 3:7.

56. Robertson 1934: 626-28.

57. Paul's message to Timothy is similar to his message to the Philippians. He desires to know Christ and "the power of his resurrection and the fellowship of his sufferings, becoming like him in his death" (3:10).

58. Paul has expressed both ideas in other letters. He told the Romans that if they died with Christ, they would also live with him (Rom 6:8). He also told the Corinthians that Paul and Timothy loved them so much they would die together and live together with them (2 Cor 7:3).

59. See 1 Tim 2:10 (Spencer 2013).

60. Rom 8:17; also, 1 Pet 4:13. Martyrs and those who persevere through trials in particular will reign (Luke 22:28-30; Rev 3:21; 20:4).

61. Spencer 1985: 68-69.

62. Rev 5:9-10; 22:5; Dan 7:27.

In a time when one's testimony for Jesus Christ, "risen from the dead, from David's seed" (2:8), might cause difficulties, the temptation is to deny one's faith or become unfaithful: **if we will deny, also that one will deny us** (2:12b). **Denying** one's faith may be by words or by action.[63] Several believers in Rome had already denied Jesus, by deserting Paul.[64] Jesus had warned his disciples that whoever denies our Lord before others, he also would deny him/her before his Father in heaven (Matt 10:33). Human action results in divine action. Instead, Jesus' followers were to deny *themselves* and take up their cross daily and follow him (Luke 9:23).

To deny someone is to say "no" to someone.[65] God allows human action and decision. However, human unfaithfulness does not nullify God's faithfulness: **if we are unfaithful, that one remains faithful, for he is not able to deny himself** (2:13).[66] Paul described himself as **unfaithful**, a blasphemer, persecutor, and violent person who received mercy.[67] But even though humans may not remain consistent, God the Trinity always will keep God's promises. God's very nature is truth and faithfulness and cannot act outside itself.

Avoid Ungodly Talking, Become a Vessel for Good Works (2:14–26)

With this summary statement (2:11–13), Paul concludes the first section of his letter, explaining why Timothy should not be ashamed to suffer for the gospel, nor of Paul's suffering (1:3–2:13). What Paul has just told Timothy is not simply for Timothy's own edification, but it is to be passed on to others: **these things keep reminding** (2:14a). **These things** refer to what Paul has just said in 1:3—2:13.[68] Timothy is also to remind the church about matters brought up in more length in 1 Timothy and Titus: **while charging in the presence of God not to dispute about words, useful for nothing, for destruction of the ones hearing** (2:14b). In this second section of his letter,

---

63. 1 Tim 5:8; Titus 1:16.

64. 2 Tim 1:15; 4:10, 14–16. Despite promising to die together with Jesus, should it be necessary, and never to desert him, Peter did desert him and would not even acknowledge he had been with him (Mark 14:29–31, 68–72).

65. See Titus 2:12.

66. Also Rom 3:3–4.

67. See 1 Tim 1:13 (Spencer 2013).

68. See 2 Tim 1:5.

Avoid Ungodly Talking, Become a Vessel for Good Works (2:14-26)

Paul exhorts Timothy to remind the people while himself avoiding ungodly talking and instead become a vessel for good works (2:14-26). Timothy should treat truth with integrity and avoid ungodly talking (2:14-18). Despite ungodly talking, God's firm foundation stands (2:19). Timothy should become a vessel prepared for good works, pursuing virtues, avoiding controversies, gently guiding those of the opposition because they may repent (2:20-26). Before Timothy can leave Ephesus for Rome, he needs to help the church mature spiritually. Part of joining in suffering has to do with ensuring integrity in one's own actions and exhorting others to do the same.

Treat Truth with Integrity and Avoid Ungodly Talking (2:14-19)

Paul commands Timothy solemnly to charge the church **in the presence of God** (2:14). Paul uses **charge** (*diamartyromai*)[69] twice in this letter to avoid negative behavior and in 4:1, for Timothy himself to act in a positive manner. Paul charges him **not to dispute about words** (*logomacheō*, 2:14).[70] At Ephesus, there continued to be battles about **words**, arguments about topics that led to spiritual error.[71] These words are described in two ways: (1) **useful for nothing** and (2) **for destruction of the ones hearing** (2:14). Paul also describes these words as "godless" and "empty," leading to more "ungodliness," as "a spreading cancer" and deviating from "the truth" (2:16-18). These words are not beneficial or of any use; they are destructive to those listening.[72]

In contrast, Timothy must: **Make every effort to present yourself approved to God, a worker who does not need to be ashamed, rightly**

---

69. "To exhort with authority in matters of extraordinary importance" (BDAG, 233). Also "call gods and men to witness, protest solemnly" (LSJ, 403). *Diamartyromai* is *martyromai* ("call to witness") intensified by the preposition *dia-*, thus to testify about a serious content in a serious manner (Luke 16:28; Acts 2:40; 8:25; 10:42; 18:5; 23:11; 28:23). Paul used the verb several times in his farewell speech in Miletus to the Ephesian elders to describe his own ministry (Acts 20:21, 24).

70. Paul uses the verb cognate (*logomacheō*) in 1 Tim 6:4 (*logomachia*).

71. See 1 Tim 6:4 (Spencer 2013).

72. **Destruction** (*katastrophē*; 2:14) is a strong word in the OT. While literally referring to turning around and down (as to overturn a table; e.g., Matt 21:12; Mark 11:15; LSJ, 915), metaphorically, it refers to a total destruction of an area, such as God's destruction of Sodom and Gomorrah by brimstone and fire, resulting in death (Gen 13:10; 19:21, 25, 29). Often it refers to God's judgment of the ungodly (2 Chr 22:7; Job 8:19; 15:21; 21:17; 27:7; Prov 1:18, 27). Thus, the result of these word-battles for the hearer is not simply to waste time, but to have oneself condemned.

handling the word of truth (2:15). Timothy must not concern himself with being **approved** by those who are on a road to destruction. Rather, his judge is God. And, although he has been saved by grace (1:9), he still needs to **make every effort** (*spoudazō*) to please God. As Onesiphorus' household made extensive effort to find Paul (1:17), Timothy is to make that same extensive effort to present himself approved. These are times of urgency, when Paul exhorts his coworkers to hasten and exert themselves in coming to see him.[73] With that same urgency, he wants Timothy to work on his spiritual maturity. **Approved** (*dokimos*) may be used to describe pure metals that sustain their structure even if cast into a furnace.[74] They are genuine. Humans too demonstrate the genuineness of their character by persevering through trials (Jas 1:12). Timothy also should extend effort to persist as a genuine believer and thus become approved or commended by God.[75]

Paul further defines what it means to be **approved** by God with three modifiers: (1) a **worker**, (2) **who does not need to be ashamed**, and (3) **rightly handling the word of truth** (2:15). A **worker** is someone who "makes every effort." Therefore, they are **not ashamed.** Paul alludes to Jesus' exhortation to his disciples: of those who are ashamed of Jesus and of his words, Jesus "will also be ashamed when he comes in the glory of his Father with the holy angels."[76] Of what not to be ashamed has been an important topic in this letter: the testimony of the Lord and of Paul, the Lord's prisoner.[77] Now, Timothy himself is to be unashamed, probably because he is making every effort to present himself approved to God and he is **rightly handling the word of truth** (2:15). By the context, it appears that others, by their word-battles, are not interpreting the word of truth **rightly** (e.g., but rather, deceptively; 3:13).

How should Timothy handle the word of truth? He should do so **rightly**, that is, cutting it in a straight line (*orthotomeō*).[78] Wisdom can "*rightly* direct" one's paths (Prov 3:6) and righteousness blamelessly *cuts*

---

73. 2 Tim 4:9, 21; Titus 3:12, 13. 40 percent of the uses of the verb (*spoudazō*) and the adverb (*spoudaōs*; six of fifteen times) are found in the Pastorals.

74. Gen 23:16; 1 Kings 10:18; 1 Chr 28:18; 2 Chr 9:17; Zech 11:13.

75. 2 Cor 10:18.

76. See also 2:12b. Mark 8:38, NRSV; Luke 9:26.

77. 2 Tim 1:8, 12, 16.

78. LSJ, 1250; Thayer, 453; Robertson 1931: 619; Fee 1988: 255; Bassler 1996: 151.

straight paths, as opposed to ungodliness (Prov 11:5). The **word of truth** is used for the gospel orally communicated[79] in the New Testament. It may also be in written form, but when it is correctly interpreted, it directs their paths in the right direction, so that *orthotomeō* ("straight-cutting") then affects *orthopodeō* ("straight-walking").[80] The opposite of falsifying God's word by shameful and deceptive means (2 Cor 4:2) is handling it correctly.

Such handling of the word of truth was not occurring in Ephesus. So, Timothy needs to **keep avoiding the godless empty talk; for they will increase to more ungodliness and their word as a spreading gangrene will increase, among whom are both Hymenaeus and Philetus, who, concerning the truth, have deviated, saying, the resurrection already is past, and they are upsetting the faith of some** (2:16–18).[81] All three Pastoral Letters have similar descriptions of the heresies (see table on the following page).

The difference is that 2 Timothy does not specifically refer to genealogies, a negative use of the law,[82] defiling of the conscience,[83] asceticism, and the circumcision party. Thus, either Paul did not repeat in his second letter to Timothy every aspect of the problems in Ephesus or there have been improvements in some areas since his previous letter around three to four years earlier. What does remain consistent are word-battles, empty talk, heresy, deception, women's involvement, unhealthy self-serving teaching, myths, harm, demonic aspects, godless behavior, and false piety.

---

79. Eph 1:13; Col 1:5; Jas 1:18. LSJ, 1250; Thayer, 453.

80. Gal 2:14; Acts 14:10; Heb 12:13.

81. See 1 Tim 1:9; 6:20 (Spencer 2013); Titus 3:9. **Godless** (*bebēlos*) acts are unholy ones that lead to lack of piety and **empty talk** (*kenophōnia*) are sounds that are empty or without a truthful goal and therefore deceive. Titus 3:9 also refers to arguments, contentions, and battles as does 2 Tim 2:14, 16–18. 1 Tim 6:20 also refers to "godless" (*bebēlos*) and "empty talk" (*kenophōnia*).

82. 2 Tim 2:5 vs. 1 Tim 1:8–10; Titus 3:9.

83. Although Paul does refer to his "clean conscience" in 2 Tim 1:3.

Similarities in Heresies in the Pastorals[84]

2 Timothy (AD 64–66)	1 Timothy (AD 62–64)	Titus (AD 62–64)
I. Word-battles[85]		
Fights about words, controversy (2:14, 23)	Controversy (2:8; 6:4–5)	Controversy, battles (3:9–11)
Empty talk, useful for nothing, foolish, stupid (2:14, 16, 23 vs. 2:21)	Empty talk, unuseful use of law (1:6, 8–10; 5:13; 6:20)	Empty talk, useless (1:10; 3:9)
II. Problems with True Teaching		
Heresy: resurrection already past (2:18)	Heterodoxy, problems with Christology: Jesus, human, was unique moderator for all (1:3; 2:4–6; 6:3, 5, 20–21)	Jewish Christian heresy (1:10, 14)
Deceptive, not true, false (2:18, 25; 3:8, 13; 4:4; vs. "straight" 2:15)	Deceptive, not true (2:14; 4:1–2; 6:3, 5)	Deceptive, against truth (1:10, 12, 14, 3:3)
Education necessary, women never learn (2:2; 3:6–7)	Education necessary, especially for women (1:7; 2:11–12)	Education necessary: elders, male and female, teach (1:9; 2:3)
Not healthy (1:13; 2:17; 4:3)	Not healthy (1:10; 6:3–4)	Not healthy (1:9, 13; 2:1–2, 8)
Self-serving; loving money (3:2; 4:3)	Self-gain (6:4–5)	Self-gain (1:11)
Myths vs. legal (2:5; 4:4)	Myths, genealogies, legal (1:4, 8; 4:7)	Myths, genealogies, legal (1:14; 3:9)
III. Result		
Destruction, judgment, demonic, slanderous vs. approved (2:14, 19, 26; 3:3)	Satanic, slanderous (3:6–7, 11; 4:1; 5:15)	Harmful, slanderous (1:12; 2:3; 3:11)
Godless behavior, idle, spreading cancer (2:16–17)	Godless (1:5, 9; 2:10; 4:1, 7; 6:6, 20)	Godless (1:6–8, 15–16; 2:3, 5, 12)
Outward piety (3:5)	False piety: asceticism (4:3)	False piety (1:16)

---

84. See Titus 1:10.

85. See 1 Tim 6:4 (Spencer 2013).

Godless empty talk has two basic results: (1) **they will increase to more ungodliness and** (2) **their word as a spreading gangrene will increase** (2:16–17). **Ungodliness** is the negation of worship (*sebeia*). **Godless empty talk** is not static, it increases. Its ramifications increase, while genuine worship decreases.[86] Paul then repeats the same concept using a simile: **as a spreading gangrene** (2:17). *Gaggraina* is "a disease involving severe inflammation, which if left unchecked can become a destructive ulcerous condition, *gangrene, cancer*."[87] This illness is **spreading** and is destructive (*nomē*).[88] Not all growth is healthy.

Gangrene is gradual and painful. It is massive death of tissue, an infection that may be caused by overly tight bandaging or the growth of bacteria that live without oxygen but enter the body through a wound. The bacteria produce a toxin that spreads into the surrounding tissues and kills them. The cure is removal of the dead tissues.[89] What does gangrene have in common with **godless empty talk** (2:16)? An outside source causes spiritual death and unhealthy growth, spreads, and eventually results in people losing, not gaining, their salvation (2:19). Paul then gives an example of two people: **among whom are both**[90] **Hymenaeus and Philetus, who, concerning the truth, have deviated, saying, the resurrection already is past, and they are upsetting the faith of some** (2:17–18). **Hymenaeus** (mentioned in 1 Tim 1:20) apparently has won over a coworker, **Philetus**. Along with Alexander, Hymenaeus had abandoned the conscience, the interior faculty for the personal discernment of good and evil, as guided by faith or trust in God for an external law structure.[91] Both Hymenaeus and Alexander had been acting in a diabolical manner: deceiving and speaking falsely instead of furthering truth, peace, righteousness, and love.

Wrong teaching about the **resurrection** (*anastasis*) has been mentioned elsewhere in the New Testament. Some Greeks might not want to believe in a bodily resurrection because the body or matter was considered

---

86. See Titus 2:12; 1 Tim 4:15 (Spencer 2013). *Asebeia* ("ungodliness") is a synonym of *bebēlos* (**godless**; 2:16). Paul had previously exhorted Timothy to progress in his spiritual life, but in 2 Tim he describes a negative progression, of ungodliness and deception (2:16; 3:13).

87. BDAG, 186.

88. BDAG, 675.

89. *CE* 10: 567; Hippocrates, *Artic.* 69; *Mochl.* 35.

90. A singular verb is used for two people, thereby the totality is emphasized (Robertson 1934: 405).

91. See 1 Tim 1:5, 19–20 (Spencer 2013).

evil (Acts 17:18, 32). The Sadducees, unlike the Pharisees, believed there was no resurrection at all.[92] Some, at the church in Corinth, like the Sadducees, believed there was no resurrection from the dead (1 Cor 15:12). But, Paul explains, if the dead are not raised, then Christ has not been raised, and people's sins are unforgiven (1 Cor 15:16–17). Paul presents a correct sequence: Christ is the first to resurrect, then Christ returns, at which time those who belong to Christ resurrect (1 Cor 15:23). Jesus and Paul confirmed the belief of most ancient Jews that there would be at the judgment two resurrections: one to life, one to condemnation.[93] This is a foundational doctrine (Heb 6:2), previously mentioned in this letter (2 Tim 2:8, 11). Now, at Ephesus, Hymenaeus and Philetus had been promoting a different slant on the resurrection claiming at some point in the **past** the resurrection occurred and this event has changed the state of affairs. In the fictional second-century *Acts of Paul and Thecla*, the author has the villains Demas and Hermogenes hold to a similar view, believing that the resurrection has already taken place in the children (14). Both cases seem to propose a type of Gnosticism where "knowledge of the true God" results in resurrection or reincarnation. We cannot fully understand this heresy of Hymenaeus and Philetus, but it must have had ramifications for human behavior. Possibly by believing the **resurrection is past**, they then thought judgment was past.[94] In that case, they might live immoral lives[95] or legalistic, ascetic ones (1 Tim 1:9; 4:3). Sometimes those who propose excessive legalism are the very people who live unrighteous or ungodly lives. Their rules are so excessive, no one could ever obey them, including themselves.[96]

Thus, Paul exhorts all who claim to be Christian, including Timothy: **Nevertheless, the firm foundation of God stands, having this seal: the Lord has known the ones who are his, and all naming the Lord's name**

---

92. Matt 22:23; Mark 12:18; Luke 20:27; Acts 4:1–2; 23:6–8.
93. Luke 14:14; John 5:29; 11:24; Acts 24:15; 2 Macc 7:14.
94. 2 Clem 9.1 joins judgment and resurrection.
95. 1 Cor 15:32; 2 Tim 2:19, 22.
96. Also, Col 2:21–23. Commentators suggest that **the resurrection already is past** could refer to these believers now living (1) in the resurrection age to come, which required celibacy and food restrictions, since in the resurrection there was no marriage and no physical body (1 Tim 4:3; Matt 22:30; Mark 12:25; Luke 20:35–36); or (2) in the spiritual resurrection stage that began with baptism. The later Menander claimed his disciples received the resurrection by being baptized into him and thereby no longer dying but being immortal (Irenaeus, *Haer.* 1.23.5) (Towner 2006: 527–29; Marshall 1999: 753; Lock 1924: 99; Fee 1988: 256; Bassler 1996: 152; Kelly 1963: 185).

must stand away from unrighteousness (2:19). Paul appears to allude to the Old Testament incident wherein Korah and 250 chiefs insist they could offer sacrifices in the tabernacle as did Aaron and his sons. At that time, Moses told Korah and his followers that **God has known the ones who are his**, who are the "holy ones," set apart, chosen as priests (Num 16:5). Then Moses exhorted the rest of the Hebrews to separate themselves from the people who had questioned whether the Lord had sent Moses and Aaron, so as to avoid falling into the earth when it opened up in judgment: literally, they had to "stand off away from" (*aphistēmi*) the tent of Korah and the others if they wanted to stay alive (Num 15:27). Paul's allusion to this incident shows that the heresy of Hymenaeus and Philetus was a dangerous one that would result in condemnation for any attracted to it.

Unrighteousness implies immoral behavior because Paul now proposes in a positive manner its opposite, righteousness[97]: **But in a great household there are not only golden and silver vessels but also wooden and clay, and, on the one hand, some are into honor, but, on the other hand, some are into dishonor; therefore, if some might purify themselves from these things, (s)he will be a vessel into honor, consecrated, useful to the master, prepared for every good work** (2:20–21). In contrast to battling about words, which is "*useful* for nothing" (*chrēsimos*; 2:14), Timothy and the church are to make themselves **useful**[98] (of good service) **to the master** (2:21). Paul uses an extended illustration, comparing people (household servants) with different types of **vessels** (*skeuos*). This is a large household with many different vessels. A **vessel** is moveable property, any item that can be carried.[99] It includes the moveable items in the temple (Num 1:50; Heb 9:21). Thus, if Christians as a group are God's sanctuary (e.g., 1 Cor 6:19–20), individually they are vessels in the sanctuary. Whereas in Romans 9:21–23 the focus is on the potter and the malleability of the clay, in 2 Timothy 2:20–21 the focus is on the pot and human responsibility.[100] In 1 Thessalonians 4:4, the vessel symbolizes the human body, and one's

---

97. See Titus 3:6.

98. The use of *euchrēstos* in 2:21 adds *eu-* (good) to *chrēstos* which heightens its positive value. *Chrēstos* is a characteristic of God, God as forgiving, bringing health and wholesomeness. See Titus 3:4; *TLNT* 3:511–16.

99. E.g., Gen 31:37; 45:20; Exod 30:27; Matt 12:29; Luke 17:31; Rev 18:12.

100. **Vessel** is a term the Lord used for Paul himself: "a chosen vessel to carry my name" (Acts 9:15). In 2 Cor 4:7, the focus is on an unimpressive jar that hides a treasure inside. The vessel is a life of difficulties of a genuine Christian worker (4:8–10). In 1 Pet 3:7, the vessel symbolizes the human body, its physical strength.

own use of it for an honorable or dishonorable purpose, sexual holiness or impurity (vv. 4–7). Thus, the reference to fleeing youthful passions (2:22) follows naturally from the earlier reference to vessels.

Timothy, and others in the church, can make themselves into vessels for honorable uses. This result is dependent on the condition: **if some might purify themselves from these things** (2:21). **These things** appears to refer to all the negative behavior previously mentioned: disputing about words that are useless and destructive, engaging in godless empty talk, and unrighteousness (2:14–19). But, he will also apply unrighteousness to youthful passions and foolish and non-instructive arguments (2:22–23). The subjunctive tense (**might purify**) indicates that purification is a possible but not an accomplished goal. A vessel of **honor** is further defined in three ways: (1) **consecrated**, (2) **useful to the master**, and (3) **prepared for every good work** (2:21). The vessel is **consecrated** or made holy. In 1 Timothy, Paul described everything created by God, including marriage and all foods, as "rendered holy" or "sanctified" (*hagiazō*) by God's word and prayer.[101] As Jesus prayed, believers are sent into the world but they are not from the world (John 17:14–19). They too are to work on being holy *de facto* in an unholy world.

An honorable vessel, like a household servant, is available for service by the master of the household, by implication, the Lord (2:19). This vessel has been **prepared** ready for use for **every good work** (2:21). **Every good work** has a double meaning, literally, for its intended use in the household, and, metaphorically, for holy or good behavior.[102]

---

101. See 1 Tim 4:5 (Spencer 2013). In the OT, *hagiazō* refers to something or someone set apart for God. For example, the first born son is set apart for God (Exod 13:2). Priests must undergo a lengthy process of offerings, washing, putting on special garments, being anointed with oil, and sprinkled with blood in order to be able to minister in the sanctuary (Exod 19:22–23; 28:37; 29:1–46). That lengthy process has been superseded by Jesus' perfect offering (Heb 9:13–14; 10:10, 14, 29: 13:12) so that now faith in Christ Jesus sanctifies (Acts 26:18; 1 Cor 1:2; 6:11.) Nevertheless, each believer now works to make actual in their own lives and in other lives what Christ has accomplished in God's sight (e.g., Eph 5:26–27).

102. Also 3:17. If a vessel for **honor** has clearly positive connotations, then a vessel for **dishonor** would have negative connotations. Dishonor appears to refer to the negative behavior Timothy is to avoid. But, could the difference in 2:20–21 between a vessel of honor and a vessel of dishonor simply refer to "special/valued" vs. "ordinary/everyday/cheap" use (NRSV, NLT, REB), instead of "noble/honour" vs. "ignoble/dishonour" (NIV, KJV, NTME) (2:20–21)? Probably not, in this case, because "noble" vs. "ignoble" fits better in the context. In Rom 9:21–22, similar terminology of "dishonor" refers to objects made for destruction, while in 1 Cor 12:23 the opposite of "honor" is not "dishonor," but what "we think" has less honor.

Avoid Ungodly Talking, Become a Vessel for Good Works (2:14-26) 113

Paul now warns Timothy to continue to beware of specific temptations: **But keep on fleeing the youthful passions and keep on pursuing righteousness, faith, love, peace, accompanied by the act of calling upon the Lord from a clean heart** (2:22). **Passions** (*epithymia*) or "desires" are strong feelings turned upon something.[103] They can be good or harmful. They can refer to coveting what belongs to another,[104] such as wealth, but since in this verse they are modified by **youthful,** and Timothy himself was probably in his late twenties or early thirties,[105] what belongs to another is probably sexual.[106] Similar language is used in 1 Thessalonians 4 to exhort Christians to control their "vessel."[107] The same verb **flee** (*pheugō*) is used in 1 Corinthians 6:18 ("flee sexual immorality").[108] In the same way as sheep will flee from strangers (John 10:5), Timothy should flee from youthful passions. But, he should not leave a vacuum in his being. The same active intensity should be directed to **keep on pursuing righteousness, faith, love, peace** (2:22). The first three of these attributes were mentioned in Paul's personal exhortation to Timothy in 1 Timothy, attributes Timothy was to **keep pursuing.**[109] **Faith** and **love** are two key concerns at Ephesus.[110] Later, Paul will explain that Scripture helps in training in **righteousness** and faith (3:15–16).[111] **Peace** was included in the opening greetings,[112] but here is reiterated because, if Timothy pursues peace, he will be able to be gentle with his opponents (2:24–25).

Timothy is to keep pursuing these four virtues while **calling upon the Lord from a clean heart** (2:22b). In this letter consistently, human action and God's action occur concurrently. While Timothy flees from harmful

---

103. See 1 Tim 6:9 (Spencer 2013).

104. Exod 20:17; Deut 5:21.

105. See 1 Tim 4:12 (Spencer 2013).

106. **Passions** can also be interpreted in a more general way to refer to any general desires characteristic of youth contrary to **righteousness, faith, love, peace**, especially those which would lessen patience toward opponents, such as impulses to impatience, love of disputation, self-assertion, self-indulgence, headstrong passions (Lock 1924: 101; Towner 2006: 544; Fee 1988: 262 vs. 274). See also 3:6.

107. *Epithymia, hagiasmos, timē, skeuos* (1 Thess 4:4–7).

108. Sexual immorality, like disunity and heresy, affects the whole body of believers as God's sanctuary (1 Cor 3:16–17; 6:18–19; 2 Cor 6:14–17; Spencer 2001: 114–15).

109. See 1 Tim 6:11 (Spencer 2013).

110. 1 Tim 1:5, 14; 2 Tim 1:13.

111. See 1 Tim 1:5, 14, 19 (Spencer 2013).

112. 1 Tim 1:2; 2 Tim 1:2; Titus 1:4.

passions and pursues helpful virtues, he regularly appeals to the Lord for help in growth in these four virtues. For, ultimately, "everyone who calls on the name of the Lord will be saved" (Rom 10:13; Joel 2:32). In 1 Timothy 2:1, Paul describes several different types of prayer. All of them may be found in 2 Timothy. Second Timothy 2:22 and 1:3–4 contain requests: Paul longs to see Timothy and exhorts Timothy to call on the Lord. Paul intercedes for Onesiphorus' household in 1:16, 18. He continually thanks God (1:3), and he asks the Lord to bless Timothy (4:22). In prayer, Paul too serves as a model for Timothy. But, the basis of the prayer must be a **clean heart**. Paul had previously summarized Timothy's commission as "love from a clean heart and a good conscience and genuine faith."[113] If within one's inward self, one prays with evil intentions, one's prayers will not be answered. Paul describes his own prayers as done with a "clean conscience" (1:3).

Temptation can come from one's strong passions (2:22), but they can also come from external sources: **and keep on averting the foolish and non-instructive arguments, knowing that they give birth to battles** (2:23). In 2:16, Paul had warned Timothy to keep on avoiding (*periistēmi*) "godless empty talk" because ungodliness would spread. Now, he adds to that warning, to **keep on averting**, declining, or refusing (*paraiteomai*) **arguments** or disputes that lead to spiritual error.[114] Disputes can be caused by a search for the truth. But, these disputes are **foolish** and **non-instructive**. **Non-instructive arguments** is the opposite of what Timothy is to do in 2:25. These arguments do not seek to guide, like the daily instruction and supervision of conduct of a minor, as God's grace instructs.[115] These arguments, like the "old women's myths" are neither instructive nor edifying.[116] Arguments that do not search for the truth and for guidance eventually **give birth to battles** (*machē*; 2:23).

Paul continues the imagery (2:21) of the household slave with a master: **But it is necessary the Lord's slave not to battle, but to be kind before all, apt in teaching, patient, giving guidance in gentleness to the ones opposing oneself, whether perhaps God may grant to them repentance into knowledge of truth** (2:24–25). Timothy is to become involved in conversations with those with whom he disagrees, but in a different manner. He is **not to battle**,[117] as in armed combat aiming to destroy his enemies

---

113. See 1 Tim 1:5 (Spencer 2013).
114. See Titus 3:9.
115. See Titus 2:12.
116. See 1 Tim 4:7 (Spencer 2013).
117. *Machomai*, "to battle" (2:24), is the verb form of *machē*, "battle" (2:23).

at all costs. Rather, he is to converse using four means, the first of which is **to be kind** (*ēpios*; 2:24). *Ēpios*, when referring to heat and cold, is "mild, less intense" and in actions, "soothing, assuaging," as opposed to strong or angry.[118] Eusebius defends the traditional view that 2 Timothy was written during Paul's second imprisonment because during the first Roman imprisonment that Luke describes in Acts: "Nero's disposition was *gentler* and it was easier for Paul's defence on behalf of his views to be received, but as he advanced towards reckless crime the Apostles were attacked along with the rest" (Eusebius, *Hist. eccl.* 2.22). A kind conversation, not one in anger, is less likely to result in a battle. Moreover, Timothy is to display this kind attitude to all, not just those with whom he agrees.

Paul uses two synonyms for instruction: *didaktikos* (2:24) and *paideuō* (2:25). *Didaktikos*, **apt in teaching**,[119] a quality needed for overseers, was especially needed in a context of heterodoxy. In a gentle manner, Timothy was to teach the truth. Timothy, instructed by Paul, was qualified to cause to learn.[120] In teaching, the focus is more on content. Anyone of any age can choose to learn a skill or new content. (Prisca and Aquila may have returned to Ephesus to help Timothy in this educational process; 2 Tim 4:19.) In contrast, to guide (*paideuō*) focuses more on conduct and the relationship of an adult and a minor. Paul describes the law as a pedagogue (*paidagōgos*; teacher) that instructs a minor until he or she becomes the heir who has now received faith.[121] But, before, in the middle, and after these two concrete words (teach and guide), Paul intersperses three synonyms: *ēpios* (**kind**), *anexikakos* (**patient**), and *prautēs* (**gentleness**) (2:24–25). If **kind** refers to a soothing, conciliatory manner, **patient** (*anexikakos*) is even stronger, referring to holding one's self firm (*anechō*) to endure evil or difficulties or wrongs (*kakos*).[122] This is a type of endurance that perseveres in the faith despite persecution[123] or that perseveres in love with other believers.[124] Of course, Timothy is not to accept or promote falsehood because the goal is **knowledge of truth** (2:25), not knowledge of falsehood. Love,

---

118. LSJ, 776; TLNT 2:176.

119. See 1 Tim 2:12.

120. LSJ, 371, 421.

121. Gal 3:25; 4:1–7. Cf. Rabbi Gamaliel did more than teach Paul content, he guided him (Acts 22:3).

122. Thayer, 44–45.

123. 1 Cor 4:12; 2 Thess 1:4.

124. Eph 4:2, 15; Col 3:13.

after all, "rejoices in the truth" (1 Cor 13:6), not in falsehood. Such guidance is given not in anger, impatience, or haughtiness, but **in gentleness** (*prautēs*; 2:25). *Prautēs* is a significant attribute of Jesus (Matt 11:29), which signifies gentleness, humility, non-contentiousness, goodness, and reliance on the Lord's care.[125] This is the way to correct sinners,[126] with a soft voice.[127]

A soothing, firm, and soft manner might educate and guide those who persist in placing themselves in opposition[128] to Timothy (2:25). Timothy educates and guides, but God grants **repentance**. Divine sovereignty and human responsibility work cooperatively together. Paul's opponents: **might become sober again (and escape) from the trap of the devil, captured alive by him into that will (2:26)**. Being **sober** is an important qualification for an overseer, elder, and minister.[129] Those who are not continually sober cannot understand the Lord's will and be filled with the Holy Spirit (Eph 5:17–18). They may not even notice that they have been captured alive by a trap of the devil to do his will (2:26). Paul has used the imagery of a **trap** twice in 1 Timothy (3:7; 6:9) to describe a snare that suddenly catches animals unawares.[130] Possibly, the gentleness and patience, the soothing soft voice, the persistence in teaching and guidance is needed with the opponents because, like trapped animals, their will is limited, their lack of freedom blinds them from seeing the truth. Even animals trapped in "Have-a-Heart" cages can become so terrified that they do not leave when the door of the cage is opened.

---

125. See Titus 3:2.

126. 1 Cor 4:21; Gal 6:1.

127. LSJ, 1459.

128. Thayer, 50.

129. 1 Tim 3:2, 11; Titus 2:2–3. False teaching may act as a narcotic (Towner 2006: 549).

130. See 1 Tim 3:7 (Spencer 2013).

2 TIMOTHY 3

Timothy Needs to Continue in Ministry despite Opposition (3:1—4:8)

In this third major section (3:1—4:8) of the letter, Paul exhorts Timothy to continue in his ministry of evangelism and sound teaching despite opposition, turning away (3:1–5) from those who lack genuine piety, opposing the truth and taking women as prisoners. Eventually their folly will become evident (3:6–9). Instead, Timothy needs to follow Paul's model, expecting the godly in Christ to be persecuted and evil people to be deceived (3:10–13), while Timothy remains in the Scriptures, which prepare him for every good work (3:14–17). Paul exhorts Timothy, in light of Jesus' judgment, to proclaim the word at all times because a time is coming when people will turn from healthy teaching to myths and Paul will be gone (4:1–6), to receive with all who love the Lord a just crown (4:7–8).

Lack of Genuine Piety (3:1–5)

As in 1 Timothy 4:1, Paul mentions the last days: **And know this, that in the last days difficult times will be present** (3:1). These **last days** are now here, having already begun with Jesus' incarnation and life, after Pentecost.[1] And, in these last days, life for an evangelist will be more **difficult**.[2] If being captured alive by the devil's trap sounds terrifying (2:26), Paul depicts days so violent as to be compared to possession by demoniacs who prohibit any human from passing through them (Matt 8:28). Paul describes people characterized by nineteen negative qualities: **for people will be loving themselves, loving money, boastful, haughty, blasphemous, disobedient to parents, unthankful, unholy, unloving, irreconcilable, slanderous, without self-control, savage, not loving the good, traitors, reckless, deluded, loving pleasure more than loving God, having an outward form**

---

1. See 1 Tim 4:1 (Spencer 2013).

2. *Enistēmi* (**be present**) normally refers to the present age (Rom 8:38; 1 Cor 3:22; Gal 1:4; 2 Thess 2:2; Heb 9:8–9).

of godliness but denying its power (3:2–5).³ The first two and the last word of the series (*philautos, philarguros, philēdonos*) all begin with *philos*, a friendship type of love. But, having such objects of love does not develop friendship with God, faith and love in Christ Jesus (1:13), salvation, living, reigning, and enduring with Christ Jesus (2:10–12), enduring with the truth (2:18, 25), and escaping the devil's trap (2:26). The first love is **love of self**. The second love is **love of money** (silver), a visible deity.⁴ The final love summarizes one aspect of all these negative qualities: pleasure is loved more than God (*philotheos*; **loving pleasure,** 3:4).⁵ Timothy and the church could never join Paul in suffering for the gospel, if love of self, money, or pleasure superseded their love for Christ Jesus.

The concrete negative qualities that follow relate to one or more of these three bad friendships. Those who do not acknowledge or thank God may end being **boastful** or having false pretensions.⁶ In reality, they may love self or money more than God. **Haughty** (*hyperēphanos*) is a more intensive synonym of "boastful" (*alazōn*; 3:2). To be haughty is to cause oneself to be resplendent, brought forth into the light, to shine more than others, having an undue sense of one's importance bordering on insolence.⁷ Many of the qualities in the 2 Timothy 3:2–5 list may also be found in Romans 1:30–31 because, like haughtiness, they are a result of not acknowledging God or being humble before God, but, being a friend of the world instead of a friend of God.⁸ God opposes such haughty people.⁹ Such boastful and haughty attitudes may easily turn to **blasphemy** or slander, being demonic qualities (3:2). Disrespectful language about God or about other human beings was a continual problem at Ephesus and Crete. A result of the heresy at Ephesus, it had been a problem for Paul himself.¹⁰

---

3. These attributes are listed in asyndeton, without any conjunctions between the qualities, the first eighteen in staccato fashion. They are each one Greek word, except for "disobedient to parents" (3:2). Each word is three to five syllables long. The rhythm ends at 3:4b, thereby emphasizing the remaining 3:4b–5.

4. See 1 Tim 6:10 (Spencer 2013).

5. See Titus 3:3.

6. Rom 1:21, 30; LSJ, 59–60. Some in business who do not plan humbly, sensitive to the Lord's will, may also end up boastful (Jas 4:16).

7. BDAG, 1033; Thayer, 641, 647–48. Wealthy people can become haughty (1 Tim 6:17).

8. Rom 1:21, 30; Jas 2:23; 4:4, 6–7.

9. Jas 4:6; 1 Pet 5:5; Prov 3:34.

10. See 1 Tim 1:13; also 1 Tim 1:20; 6:1, 4 (Spencer 2013); Titus 3:2.

Paul now lists five words that all begin in Greek with *not* (the *a* privative): **disobedient, unthankful, unholy, unloving, irreconcilable** (3:2–3). **Disobedience to parents** (3:2) may appear of a different character than the other qualities in this list. However, children's attitudes to parents is important, being also mentioned in 1 Timothy (3:4–5; 5:4, 8) and Titus (1:6) and in the Ten Commandments (Exod 20:12). Disobedience is a quality of the heretical circumcision party (Titus 1:16) and of non-Christians (Rom 1:30). Disobedience contrasts with righteous wisdom (Luke 1:17). These are children who refuse to be persuaded by Christ's truth.[11]

Unthankful (*acharistos*) is a characteristic of non-Christians (Luke 6:35) because non-Christians do not thank God or honor God despite creation manifesting God's power and divine nature (Rom 1:20–21). Thankfulness (*charistos*) is an aspect of God's grace (*charis*), which overflows from God's character toward humans (2 Tim 1:9; 2:1). Unthankfulness to God may result in acts lacking holiness that are profane (*anosios*; **unholy**). Obedience to parents (3:2) should be based on a relationship of affection between parents and children,[12] but in these last days this is lacking. Some people refuse to make a truce with God; they are implacable or **irreconcilable**.[13] **Slanderous** (*diabolos*; 3:3) is a synonym of "blasphemous" (*blasphēmos*; 3:2), employing the same word as the Slanderer *par excellence*, the devil, for the act of lying, deceiving, speaking falsely against others.[14]

Paul then has a second set of words that begin in Greek with the *a* privative: **without self-control** (3:3), without strength, dissolute (*akratēs*),[15] not tame, **savage** (*anēmeros*), and **not loving the good** (*aphilagathos*). **Lack of self-control** is a servant of love of self-pleasure, possibly leading to **savage**, bestial, behavior, as opposed to gentle behavior (2:24–25)[16] that ends with no longer **loving the good**. Loving goodness is an essential quality for an elder, the opposite of demonic behavior.[17]

---

11. See Titus 3:3.

12. "Affection," *storgē*; LSJ, 262, 1650 vs. *astorgos*, **unloving** (2 Tim 3:3; Rom 1:31).

13. *Aspondos*; LSJ, 260.

14. See Titus 2:3.

15. Husband and wife are not to deprive one another sexually too long for the sake of prayer because then they could be tempted by lack of self-control (1 Cor 7:5). See also 1 Tim 2:15 (Spencer 2013); 2 Tim 1:7.

16. BDAG, 79, 438; LSJ, 137, 771; Thayer, 45.

17. See Titus 1:8.

Paul continues with two attributes that begin with the same preposition (*pro*; "before").[18] To give or hand over in a treacherous manner is to be a **traitor**,[19] such as Judas Iscariot, who betrayed even Jesus, God incarnate (Luke 6:16), and those who betrayed the prophets who foretold the coming of Jesus, the Righteous One (Acts 7:52). Alexander, the metal worker, appears to have been such a person betraying Paul (2 Tim 4:14–15). *Propetēs*, literally, is "falling forwards" or "down" and thus a precipitous or **reckless** act.[20] Not loving goodness, people will fall down and act recklessly (without thought). The end result is their brain is clouded with smoke, making their mind unclear. They are **deluded**,[21] **loving pleasure** (*philēdonos*) more than **loving God** (*philotheos*; 3:4).

Unlike Romans 1:18–32, where Paul depicts those who do not claim to be believers, these similar qualities in 2 Timothy 3:2–4 describe actions of those who claim to live in a **godly** manner (*eusebeia*; 3:5). In genuine godliness one dedicates oneself to please God in one's words and actions. One's life is offered as worship of God.[22] *Morphōsis* and its cognates *morphē* and *morphoō* refer to **an outward form of godliness** seen by the eye that reflects an inward nature or essential attribute.[23] For example, when Jesus was transfigured (*metamorphoō*), his outer glory represented his true inward nature as God.[24] In contrast, the external or outward visible form of godliness of the behavior Paul describes (3:5) is not authentic. Probably, this description is similar to the ascetic behavior described in 1 Timothy 4:3 and the Jewish heresy described in Titus 1:16. Paul had written about not denying one's faith,[25] but denying ungodliness (Titus 2:12), but here, he writes of **denying** the power of godliness. What could be the **power** of **godliness**? Most likely, it refers to having the authentic "form" (*morphōsis*), where the outward piety reflects an inward piety.[26] Genuine godliness has power or strength, which is the antithesis of fear (1:7). That power comes from God who saves and calls according to the purpose and grace mani-

---

18. Robertson 1934: 620.
19. *Prodotēs*; BDAG, 867.
20. Acts 19:36; Thayer, 541; BDAG, 873.
21. See 1 Tim 3:6 (Spencer 2013).
22. See Titus 1:1; 1 Tim 4:8 (Spencer 2013).
23. E.g., Lightfoot 1913: 110, 127; *TLNT* 2:524; Job 4:16.
24. Matt 17:2; Mark 9:2; Phil 2:6.
25. See 2 Tim 2:12.
26. See Titus 1:16.

fested by Christ Jesus who abolished death and gave life and immortality (1:9–10).

Timothy, in contrast, must: **keep turning yourself away from these**[27] (3:5b). *Apostrephō* can be used as an exemplary or non-exemplary action. In a non-exemplary manner, some people turned away from Paul (1:15) and others turn away from truth (Titus 1:14), but, in an exemplary manner, believers need to turn away from evil.[28] Timothy must reject all the behavior listed in 3:2–5. However, since the pronoun **these** (*toutous*) in 3:5 is masculine plural, does this suggest Timothy must turn away from the people (3:2) who exhibit such behavior? If so, how can he then dialogue with his opponents with the intention to help them repent (2:24–25)? Or, must Timothy turn away only from the behavior itself, as in 2:16, 23, not the people *per se*?[29] Timothy certainly must reject these behaviors, and, keeping away from people who do these behaviors is an aspect of turning away from their behavior. As Paul tells the Corinthians: "bad company destroys good morals" (1 Cor 15:33). Yet, he must also be open to teach those who are teachable (2:24–26).[30]

Women as Prisoners (3:6–9)

People (rather than behavior) is suggested by the next sentence, because from the type of people listed in 3:2–5 comes this group: **For out of these (people) are the ones going into the households and taking prisoner attractive women, overwhelmed with sins, being led by manifold passions, always learning and never being able to come into knowledge of truth** (3:6–7). Paul uses the present participle to suggest this action is present and ongoing. These people do two things: **go into**[31] households and **take prisoner** women (3:6). They themselves already have been taken prisoner by the devil to do the devil's will (captured alive in a trap; 2:26),

---

27 Thayer, 68; Matt 5:42.

28. Acts 3:26; Rom 11:26; 2 Tim 2:16, 23.

29. Then the pronoun *toutous* would be translated as **these things**, being resumptive, referring to all that precedes in a general way (Robertson 1934: 698).

30. Towner (2006: 561) thinks the 3:5 command refers to people who are completely hardened in opposition, the core of the movement, that can no longer be reached, as in 1 Tim 1:20.

31. *Endynō* signifies "to enter into an area through devious means or pretense, *slip in*" (BDAG, 333).

and now they take others prisoners as subservient captives of war.[32] They are not motivated by love of God (3:4), but by love of themselves, money, or pleasure (3:2, 4). Who does the imprisoning? They are described by the generic *anthrōpos* (**people**; 3:2) or the generic masculine plural (**these**, *toutous*; **the ones**, *hoi*; 3:5–6). Thus, the false teachers probably include women as well as men.[33] Some younger widows would be likely dispersers of these falsehoods (1 Tim 5:13, 15). In conservative wealthy homes, the women might live in *gynaikeia*, the part of the house belonging to women, and only women could enter that section.[34]

Some women in particular are the victims.[35] Paul uses the diminutive for women (*gynaikarion*; 3:6).[36] Most commentators think "little women" is a derogatory term,[37] but it is not necessarily.[38] The first-century (AD 50–120) Stoic philosopher Epictetus used *gynaikarion* as a positive term for an attractive woman. Wars arise to win her, he writes (*Diatr.* 2.22 [23]). Men wish to please her (3:1[32]). Attractive women capture the "citadel (acropolis)" of fever within men (4.1[86]).[39] It is also a term of endearment for "a little wife and child" (*Ench.* 7). These women are described in three ways: (1) **overwhelmed with sins**, (2) **being led by manifold passions**, and (3) **always learning and never being able to come into knowledge of truth** (3:6–7). **Overwhelmed** (*sōreuō*) is a metaphor, literally signifying "to heap together" or "to heap up."[40] In Romans 12:20, Paul refers to Proverb 25:22, *heaping up* burning coals on an enemy's head. Hospitality for one's enemies results in a judgment against them, but a reward from God, whereas, in 2

32. Luke 21:24; 2 Cor 10:5.

33. See 1 Tim 1:3 (Spencer 2013).

34. E.g., Philo, *Spec. Laws* 3.31 (169–70); *Flaccus* 11 (89); Spencer 1985: 50.

35. Obviously not Prisca (4:19). Irenaeus cites the example of the magician Marcus who emphasized deceiving and seducing wealthy women by flattery (*Haer.* 1.13.3).

36. LSJ, 363; BDAG, 208; Robertson 1931: 624. The diminutive is used by *Marcus Aurelius Antoninus* 5.11.

37. BDAG, 208; Robertson 1934: 155; Fee 1988: 272; "silly women" (NTME, REB, KJV, NRSV, NIRV, YLT); "weak women" (TEV, NASB, ESV); "weak-willed women" (NIV 1984); "weak-minded women" (GW); "gullible women" (TNIV, NIV 2011); "immature women" (CEB); "foolish women" (NLT).

38. MM (133): "society ladies borne by caprices in various directions and full of idle curiosity"; "little women" (WYC); Bassler (1996: 160): "the term is not as pejorative as the NRSV translation"; "vulnerable women" (NLT); in Spanish, "mujercillas" (RV, BA).

39. See also Epictetus, *Diatr.* 2.18 (18); 3.22 (36–37). Witherington III (2006: 353) refers to predators of handsome boys and pretty women.

40. Thayer, 612; cf. 2 Tim 4:3.

Timothy 3:6, sin has been heaped upon these women. These women have never comprehended the nature of the gospel that Christ Jesus came into the world to save sinners and, therefore, is merciful to every sinner.[41] They have not been freed. They continue to sin. They are **led**, not by God, but, by **manifold passions.** Paul had previously warned Timothy to flee "youthful passions" (2:22), strong feelings and desires turned upon something or someone inappropriate. Paul does not specify what kind of passions the women have. It could be sexual or financial[42] or different since they are **manifold**, but they are not good desires.[43] As a result, despite Paul's goal for everyone, but especially women who have not been educated properly[44] (i.e., although they **learn** by study [*manthanō*]), they have not reached the goal: **knowledge of truth** (3:7).

Paul then compares these false teachers to Jannes and Jambres: **But just as Jannes and Jambres opposed Moses, in the same way also they themselves oppose the truth, humans who corrupted the mind, discredited concerning the faith. But they will not advance any more, for their folly will be quite plain to all, as also happened to those persons** (3:8–9). **Jannes and Jambres** were names given to two of the magicians called in by Pharaoh in Egypt to oppose Moses. After Aaron had turned his staff into a snake, the court magicians were able to do the same, but then Aaron's serpent swallowed up theirs. Later, with the Lord's help, when Aaron is able to turn dust into gnats, the magicians could not copy that act. Therefore, they told Pharaoh: "This is the finger of God" (Exod 7:11–13; 8:18–19).[45] The teachers at Ephesus, like Jannes and Jambres, may have appeared impressive to these women, but in reality they were opposing the person(s) chosen

---

41. 1 Tim 1:13–16; also Titus 3:4–7.

42. See 1 Tim 3:11; 6:9 (Spencer 2013).

43. Also Titus 3:3.

44. See 1 Tim 2:4, 11 (Spencer 2013).

45. A number of later Jewish and Christian documents referred to Jannes and Jambres (or Mambres). The *Damascus Document* (which may be earlier or contemporary with 2 Tim) notes: "For in ancient times there arose Moses and Aaron, by the hand of the prince of lights and Belial, with his cunning, raised up Jannes and his brother during the first deliverance of Israel" (CD V.17b–19). In the first century BC/AD *Pseudo-Philo* wrote that Jambres sinned in the days of Moses (47.1). In the first through third centuries AD, a book was written about *Jannes and Jambres*. Around the third or fourth century, the *T. Sol.* said that Jannes and Jambres called to their aid the demon Abezethibtou when they opposed Moses in Egypt. It said: "I am the adversary of Moses in (performing) wonders and signs" (25.4). The Pythagorean philosopher, Numenius, refers to Jannes and Jambres as "sacred scribes" who practiced "magic" (Eusebius, *Praep. ev.* 9.7–8).

by God to promote God's message. As Jannes and Jambres were shown not to be empowered by the only true and most powerful God, so too these false teachers will be shown to oppose the truth and be less powerful. Does this mean that the Ephesians were still impressed by magic since Paul mentions two magicians? Lock suggests that since this church is fond of Jewish myths and genealogies and magic (Acts 19:19), Paul gives them an example of magicians whose folly was exposed.[46]

In addition to opposing the truth, they are characterized by two phrases: **corrupted the mind** and **discredited concerning the faith** (3:8). God destroys in punishment those who destroy God's temple.[47] However, humans may destroy or **corrupt** their own minds.[48] Whose minds are destroyed here?[49] Do the false teachers only destroy their own minds ("humans of corrupted mind") or also the minds of the female students ("humans having corrupted the mind")? Both will happen. (They are deceived and deceiving; 3:13.) What is the end result? They are **discredited** or not approved when it comes to the **faith**.[50] Ground that produces thorns and thistles eventually will be burned (Heb 6:8). An ominous future looms before these false teachers.

Everyone needs to **advance** or progress (3:9) in a positive manner.[51] Paul promises that false teachers, like Jannes and Jambres, will not progress in their influence, because their corrupted **mind** (*nous*; 3:8) will be revealed as a lack of mind or no mind (*anous*, **folly**; 3:9) to all people.

Follow Paul's Model (3:10–13)

Timothy, instead, needs to follow Paul's model because the godly in Christ will be persecuted while evil people are being deceived (3:10–13): **But, you, follow after my teaching, way of life, way of thinking, faith, compassion, love, perseverance, persecutions, sufferings: what happened to me in Antioch, in Iconium, in Lystra, what persecutions I endured and from all the Lord rescued me** (3:10–11). Throughout this letter, Paul has

---

46. Lock 1924: 107. See *goēs* 3:13.
47. 1 Cor 3:17; 2 Pet 2:12.
48. 2 Cor 11:3; Eph 4:22.
49. The verb **corrupt** is plural nominative to match **humans**, but **mind** is singular accusative.
50. See Titus 1:16; cf. 2 Tim 2:15.
51. See 1 Tim 4:15 (Spencer 2013).

interspersed negative (what not to do) and positive (what to do) comments. With the explicit pronoun **you** (3:10), Paul personally addresses Timothy. He had warned him to keep turning away from the people who love themselves, money, and pleasure more than they love God (3:2–5). Instead, Timothy is to **follow** after nine aspects of Paul's life.[52] The first three attributes are close in meaning: his **teachings** and leading or conduct (**way of life**, and **way of thinking** or goals).[53] The next attribute, of course, is the central one: **faith**. In Titus 2:2, the male elder was to be "faithful, loving, persevering," the same exact words and sequence Paul has used in 2 Timothy 3:10 (but in 2 Tim **compassion** is inserted after **faith**). Paul uses these same three attributes to refer to Timothy.[54] The battle at Ephesus is over faith and love.[55]

Paul highlights three specific reflections of faith, which are fruits of the Spirit (Gal 5:22–23) and also attributes of God: **compassion, love, perseverance** (3:10). God had been **compassionate** with Paul by being merciful toward him, forgiving him.[56] Paul will later exhort Timothy to be compassionate (4:2). To **persevere**[57] until the end is the trait Timothy most needs if he is to join in suffering with Paul despite **persecutions** and **sufferings**. Jesus had warned his disciples that the believer without roots falls away when trouble or persecution arises, unlike the believer in "good soil" who hears the word, understands it, and bears fruit (Matt 13:21–23). However, no trouble or hardship or persecution could ever separate a believer from Christ's love (Rom 8:35).[58] While *diōgmos* (**persecutions**) is concrete and specific,[59] *pathēma* (**sufferings**) is more abstract and general.[60] Paul uses *pathēma* to refer to the sufferings of Christ,[61] the sufferings from living as a Christian,[62] and the sufferings from one's own mortality living in a fallen

---

52. As Esther had followed Mordecai (Esth 2:20), so Timothy was to follow Paul.
53. See 2 Tim 1:9.
54. See 1 Tim 6:11 (Spencer 2013).
55. 1 Tim 1:14; 2:15; 2 Tim 1:13.
56. See 1 Tim 1:16 (Spencer 2013).
57. See 2 Tim 2:10, 12.
58. The church of Thessalonica had been renowned for its perseverance and faith despite persecutions and pressures (2 Thess 1:4).
59. The noun *diōgmos* comes from the verb *diōkō*, "to make to run or flee, put to flight, drive away" (Thayer, 153).
60. *Pathēma* comes from the verb *paschō* to feel, in a bad sense, to feel misfortunes, to suffer, to undergo evils, to be afflicted (Thayer, 472, 494).
61. 2 Cor 1:5; Phil 3:10.
62. 2 Tim 1:12; 2 Cor 1:6–7; Gal 3:4; Col 1:24; Phil 1:29; 1 Thess 2:14; 2 Thess 1:5.

world.⁶³ Now, he presents some specific illustrations of difficulties Timothy had learned about early in their acquaintance from Paul's ministry at Antioch, Iconium, and Lystra. He picks three cities in the province of Galatia, the governing center of Phrygia, Antioch in Pisidia, nearby Iconium, and Timothy's own home town, Lystra, in the region of Lycaonia.⁶⁴

At first at the synagogue in Antioch of Pisidia, the message of Paul and Barnabas was enthusiastically received. But some Jews, filled with jealousy at the large crowds, slandered them and contradicted their words, eventually stirring up so much persecution against them they had to leave the region.⁶⁵ At Iconium, also at first in the synagogue, many believed. But again the unbelieving Jews stirred up persecution against them and tried to stone them (Acts 14:1–5). Thus, Paul and Barnabas arrived in Lystra just having been persecuted extensively for their faith. At Lystra, Paul and Barnabas were again well received after they healed a crippled man. However, Jews from the earlier cities followed Paul and Barnabas to Lystra (Acts 14:8–19). They persuaded the crowds to stone Paul and dragged him out of the city, thinking he was dead. When Paul returned to Lystra, what did he emphasize in his teaching? "It is through many persecutions that we must enter the kingdom of God" (Acts 14:22). Paul reminds Timothy of this very message: **what persecutions I endured** (3:11). And yet the **Lord rescued** him from them all. Even in Lystra, he got up and traveled by foot the next day (Acts 14:20).⁶⁶

From these illustrations, Paul concludes: **Likewise**⁶⁷ **all the ones wishing in a godly manner to live in Christ Jesus will be persecuted** (3:12). Being an apostle, Paul is not in a unique position when it comes to suffering: **All . . . will be persecuted.**⁶⁸ Why? They will be persecuted because they desire **to live in Christ Jesus in a godly manner** (*eusebōs*). In a world that is not genuinely godly, not dedicating itself to please God in its words and actions,⁶⁹ godly living can become an indirect judgment, and those

---

63. Rom 8:18; 1 Cor 12:26. Further, see Spencer 1994: chaps. 2, 4.

64. Ramsay 2001: 95–96, 99–101; Hansen 1994: 378–79.

65. Acts 13:14–50. It is probable that the persecution in Antioch and hinted at in Lystra included beating by lictors according to Ramsay (2001: 97–98).

66. See 1 Tim 4:12 (Spencer 2013). David also describes the Lord as rescuing the righteous from all their afflictions (Ps 33:19; LXX) (Fee 1988: 277).

67. *De kai* together signify heightened emphasis: "but also" (BDAG, 213).

68. The verb form *diōkō* of the noun *diōgmos*; 3:11.

69. See 2 Tim 3:5; 1 Tim 4:7; cf. 1 Tim 2:2 (Spencer 2013).

being judged, because of jealousy or misunderstanding or falsehood, may occasion reprisal. **To live in Christ Jesus** reminds the reader of the sufferings Christ endured and Jesus' warning: "if they persecuted me, also they will persecute you" (John 15:20).

Lest Timothy be enticed, Paul reminds him again that evil people do not **advance** or progress to the better:[70] **But evil people and imposters will advance to the worse, leading astray and being led astray** (3:13). Paul describes the **evil people** as **imposters** (*goēs*). But, *goēs* also signifies "sorcerer, conjuror."[71] The use of *goēs* appears to allude back to the magicians or sorcerers Jannes and Jambres (3:8). These evil people both **lead** others **astray** and are themselves **led astray** (3:13), possibly by deceitful spirits (1 Tim 4:1).[72] Some of Paul's own coworkers had been led astray.[73]

Remain in the Scriptures (3:14–17)

Paul repeats again the personal pronoun **you** (3:14), directly exhorting Timothy, that in contrast to these evil people and imposters who have been led astray and now lead others astray, Timothy needs to remain in the Scriptures, which prepare him for every good work (3:14–17): **But, you, remain in what you learned and are firmly persuaded, knowing from whom you learned and that from infancy you know the holy writings, the ones being able to make you wise into salvation through faith, the one in Christ Jesus** (3:14–15). While **you** occurs once in 1 Timothy, near the end (6:11), and once in Titus (2:1), it occurs six times in 2 Timothy, showing how much Paul has focused this letter toward Timothy. Of these six references, four of them call Timothy to contrast himself with those who lead astray (3:9–10), evil people (3:13–14), those who follow myths (4:4–5), and Alexander, a harmful person (4:14–15).[74] Thus, the repetition of **you** intensifies the difficult context of people who could harm Timothy's faith.

---

70. 2 Tim 3:13; 2:16 vs. 3:9.

71. BDAG, 204; LSJ, 356. Incantations used to be uttered in a kind of howl (*goaō*; Thayer, 120). *Goēs* was a derogatory term used against Moses (Josephus, *Ag. Ap.* 2.16 [161]).

72. See Titus 3:3.

73. E.g., Demas: Col 4:14 vs. 2 Tim 4:10.

74. In contrast, 2 Tim 1:18; 2:1 are affirmative of Timothy.

Timothy had a two part process: he **learned** and then he was **firmly persuaded** (3:14). Over an extended period of time Timothy learned.⁷⁵ *Manthanō* may refer to the acquisition of knowledge or skill gained by instruction and, as well, to the thoughtful pondering for further understanding of the significance of something or someone.⁷⁶ Both aspects are pertinent here. The content of the learning is the holy writings. Timothy's learning contrasts with the learning of some women in the church, who never arrive at the "knowledge of truth" (3:7 vs. 1 Tim 2:4). Timothy has come to the knowledge of truth because he is now **firmly persuaded**. *Pistoō*⁷⁷ is a significant concept in the Old Testament. It can refer to God establishing or confirming a truth or a promise⁷⁸ or to humans confirming a truth.⁷⁹ Faithfulness is included.⁸⁰ Thus, Paul has observed that Timothy has moved from learning to commitment, confirming the truth of what he was taught by word and action.

Timothy's acquaintance with and regard for his teachers, which include Paul and many others, helps him persist.⁸¹ His teachers included Lois and Eunice, who taught Timothy **from infancy** (3:15).⁸² Lois and Eunice taught this man (Timothy) and were affirmed in it, and, now, Timothy is commanded to remember them. **Infancy** (*brephos*) can refer to a fetus still in the womb⁸³ or to a newborn child or nursing baby.⁸⁴ Timothy's mother Eunice and grandmother Lois began to teach Timothy at the earliest age possible!⁸⁵ Apparently, they did not even wait for five years of age (*m. Abot'* 5:21). The content of their education was the **holy writings** or Scriptures (3:15). A pious Jew of that time would consider the holy writings to refer to

---

75. **Remain** is in the present imperative showing an ongoing process. **Learning** and being **firmly persuaded** are in the aorist tense. Paul treats each of the two actions as a single whole, with emphasis on the completion of the actions (Robertson 1934: 832, 835).

76. See 1 Tim 2:11 (Spencer 2013).

77. *Pistoō* is related to *pistos* ("faithful") and *pisteuō* ("to trust or believe"). E.g., 1 Tim 1:16; Titus 3:8.

78. E.g., 2 Sam 7:16; 1 Kings 1:36; 8:26, LXX.

79. E.g., 1 Chr 17:24; 2 Chr 1:9; Ps 77:8, 37, LXX.

80. Sir 27:17; 29:3.

81. See 2 Tim 2:2.

82. *Manthanō* in 2 Tim 3:14 is the same verb used in 1 Tim 2:11.

83. Luke 1:41, 44; Sir 19:11.

84. Luke 2:12, 16; 1 Pet 2:2; 3 Macc 5:49.

85. See 2 Tim 1:5.

the twenty-two books of the Old Testament.[86] In accordance with Deuteronomy 4:2, Josephus mentions that no one has added, removed, or altered a syllable "and it is an instinct with every Jew, from the day of his birth, to regard them as the decrees of God, to abide by them, and, if need be, cheerfully to die for them" (*Ag. Ap.* 8 [42]).[87] **Writings** (*gramma*), by itself, refers to anything written, including the Bible.[88] The adjective **holy** clarifies to which writings Paul refers.[89] Paul himself treats the Old Testament as authoritative and reliable. He also treats the Gospel of Luke as Scripture.[90]

In addition, Paul explains that these holy writings are **the ones being able to make you wise** (3:15). A wise person could be someone learned, an expert, skilled in letters.[91] James defines genuinely wise teachers as people who prove their actions by their good conduct characterized by gentle wisdom (Jas 3:13). Therefore, in a practical sense, a wise person is one who in action is governed by piety and integrity.[92] The wise person understands the Lord's will (Eph 5:15–17) and will not be led astray (3:13). The law of the Lord makes even infants wise (Ps 18:7; LXX). By study of the law, righteous people become wiser than even their teachers or enemies (Ps 119:97–99). Since God is wise (Rom 16:27), God's writings make people wise.[93]

But not all wisdom leads to knowledge of truth.[94] Therefore, Paul clarifies to what kind of wisdom he refers with two prepositional phrases: **into salvation through faith** (3:15). The phrases explain the goal and means through which wisdom is obtained. To be saved is to be forgiven one's sins and, thus, be purified, made acceptable to a holy God. God, the Savior, does the purifying, but humans must cooperate in this process.[95] Study of the

---

86. E.g., Josephus, *Ag. Ap.* 8 (38). The Hebrew Bible groups its books at twenty-two or twenty-four (Harris 1969: 142–43).

87. Nevertheless, in practice, eventually the oral teachings or interpretation of the Scriptures, came to have equal or greater authority (e.g., *m. Qidd.* 1:10), which Jesus combatted (e.g., Mark 7:8–13).

88. Luke 16:6–7; John 5:47; Acts 28:21; Gal 6:11; 1 Macc 5:10. Josephus uses *gramma* to refer to the Old Testament (*Ag. Ap.* 1. 8 [42]).

89. Also Rom 1:2. These writings contrast with the Ephesians' writings of magicians (Acts 19:19; Lock 1924: 109).

90. See 1 Tim 5:18 (Spencer 2013). Peter cites Paul as Scripture (2 Pet 3:16).

91. Thayer, 582.

92. Ibid.

93. See also synonym Titus 2:2. All should learn from Scriptures (1 Tim 4:13).

94. E.g., Matt 11:25; Luke 10:21; 1 Cor 1:19–20; Isa 44:25; Jer 8:8–9.

95. See 1 Tim 2:3–4 (Spencer 2013); Titus 3:5.

Scriptures gives guidance toward the end goal of salvation. Moreover, the Scriptures must be studied through the lens of faith in Christ Jesus, which helps the Scriptures be handled rightly (2:15).[96]

Paul then further defines Scripture: **All Scripture is God-breathed and advantageous for teaching, for reproof, for restoration, for guidance, the one in righteousness, in order that God's person may be complete, being completed fully for every good work** (3:16–17). Paul highlights two key characteristics of Scripture: from whom does it originate and for what purposes is it helpful. The foundational truth is that it is **God-breathed**. In 3:15, he uses the plural "writings," while in 3:16 the singular "writing."[97] Every single one of the "holy writings" is God-breathed (3:16). God-breathed is a composite of two words: "God" and to "breathe forth" (*pneō*).[98] *Pneō* is often used literally of winds that blow, such as winds that blow down a house or a ship.[99] The Holy Spirit is analogous to the wind that "blows wherever it pleases" (John 3:8). The Spirit creates and keeps humans and animals alive.[100] Similar to breathing the breath of life into a mass of dirt and making Adam alive (Gen 2:7), God has blown life into the Scriptures. They are created by God and, therefore, are inspired by God. Human beings who received God's revelation mainly through prophets,[101] now have heard God-incarnate's message[102] recorded in God-breathed writings, true to his original message, and, as God-breathed, standing forever (Isa 40:8).

Therefore, they are useful for four goals: **teaching, reproof, restoration, guidance** (3:16). **Teaching** (*didaskalia*) and learning are crucial concerns in Ephesus.[103] Scriptures cause the reader to learn.[104] They also **reprove**, bringing deeds and thoughts out in the open for clarity and truth.[105] Read-

---

96. The Scriptures also prophesy about Jesus (Luke 24:27, 44; Acts 17:2–3; 18:28; Rom 1:2; 16:25–26; 1 Cor 15:3–4).

97. *Gramma* (3:15) and *graphē* (3:16) both come from the verb *graphō*, "to write" (Thayer, 120–21).

98. LSJ, 1425.

99. Matt 7:25, 27; John 6:18.

100. Ps 103:29–30; LXX. Poirier (2010: 92) agrees: *theopneustos* is "life-giving," but Scripture not only "contains" the life-giving gospel, **all** of it is life-giving.

101. 2 Sam 23:2; Jer 1:9; Ezek 3:4; 13:1; 2 Chr 18:13. God's Spirit gives prophetic authority in Scripture (Yarchin 2012: 363–81).

102. John 3:33–34; 1 Cor 2:10; Gal 1:11–17; 1 Thess 2:13; Rev 21:5; 22:6.

103. See 1 Tim 2:12 (Spencer 2013); Titus 2:15.

104. LSJ, 371, 421. Also Rom 15:4.

105. See Titus 1:13; 1 Tim 5:20 (Spencer 2013).

ers may learn that some actions done are sinful, and, thereby, reproved. But the process does not end with reproof, it continues on to **restoration**. "Health" is a frequent metaphor Paul uses in the Pastorals. "Straight" is a synonym. The word of truth should be handled "rightly," cut in a straight line (*orthotomeō*).[106] The Scriptures also help people to become "straight," restoring people to an "upright or a right state."[107] Epictetus exhorts his students: "What sort of a teacher, then, do you still wait for, that you should put off *reforming* yourself until he arrives?" (*Ench.* 51.1). In comparison, the Scriptures teach and restore or reform and are always available. Finally, Paul ends with **guidance** (*paideia*; 3:16), the day-by-day instruction activity Timothy was to do with his opponents (2:24–25). This guidance is not a worldly one; rather, it is **the one in righteousness** (3:16).

Scripture's final goal is: **that God's person may be complete, being completed fully for every good work** (3:17). In 1 Timothy 6:11, Paul had exhorted Timothy as **God's person** to flee the love of money and instead pursue "righteousness, godliness, faith, love, perseverance, gentleness." Now, he wants Timothy to be **complete** (*artios*; 3:17), "complete, perfect of its kind, suitable, exactly fitted" to the purpose; "full-grown," "sound, of body and mind"; "prepared, ready."[108] Thus, as a result of studying Scripture, Timothy is completely prepared **for every good work** (3:17), since all study of Scripture must be practical. Otherwise, its intended purpose has been distorted. Learning without knowing and applying the truth (3:7) is inconceivable to Paul. Learning Scripture while engaging in foolish arguments is contradictory (2:23). Studying Scripture is intended to prepare Timothy to be a vessel of the Master for holy behavior (2:21).

Fusing the Horizons: Why Study the Bible?

In summary, based on 2 Timothy, why should someone rely on the Bible?

---

106. See 2 Tim 2:15. *Epanorthōsis* has as its stem *orthos*, "straight, erect," the same root as in *orthotomeō*.

107. Thayer, 228.

108. LSJ, 249. BDAG (136) defines *artios* as "being well fitted for some function, complete, capable, proficient." Paul uses the same root twice: *artios* and *exartizō*. *Artizō*, the verb, signifies "get ready, prepare" (LSJ, 249). The *ex-* ("out of, from within"), which here functions as a perfective (Robertson 1934: 596; 1931: 628), intensifies the verb *artizō*, thereby signifying "to complete, finish" (LSJ, 587).

1. The Bible provides a standard of wholesome, true principles to guide us and help us teach others.[109]
2. The writers claim the messages are from God (3:16).[110]
3. The Bible is relevant no matter our situation (2:9; 4:17).
4. The Bible enables us not to be deceived nor to deceive others (3:13).
5. We follow wise teachers (faithful parents, guardians, grandparents, Sunday School teachers, pastors, professors, mentors, etc.) who know the Bible (3:14).
6. We experience the Bible's effects in our lives, by obtaining a wisdom that leads to salvation (3:15).
7. We are challenged to mature and change because the Bible exposes evil and restores (3:16–17).
8. The Bible prepares us for the judgment (4:1, 8, 18).
9. The Bible prepares us to minister to others (4:2).

---

109. 2 Tim 1:13; 2:2, 18–19, 22; 3:7, 16–17. Also John 10:35; 14:26; 16:13–15; 17:17; Acts 4:25; 1 Cor 13:6, Pss 12:6; 119:160; Prov 30:5–6.

110. Also 1 Thess 2:13; 2 Pet 1:20–21.

2 TIMOTHY 4

Proclaim the Word (4:1–6)

Paul then concludes by exhorting Timothy, in light of Jesus' judgment, to proclaim the word at all times because a time is coming when people will turn from healthy teaching to myths (4:1–5). He gives a solemn warning: **I am charging, in the presence of God and Christ Jesus, the one coming to judge the living and dead, and in his appearing and his kingdom: proclaim the word, take a stand in season, out of season, reprove, rebuke, encourage, in all compassion and teaching** (4:1–2). Believers need to mature spiritually (3:17) because they will face the judgment. Paul had used the exact first seven words in 1 Timothy 5:21 (**I am charging in the presence of God and Christ Jesus**) in similar locations in each letter (about one chapter before the close of the letter). He exhorts Timothy about a serious content in a serious manner[1] on three bases: (1) God as his witness, (2) Christ's appearing, and (3) Christ's kingdom. Christ Jesus is described as **the one coming to judge the living and dead** (4:1). A **judge** (*krinō/kritēs*) would decide what is just in court trials.[2] The last judgment is done by the Father with the Son.[3] But, the Father has entrusted all judgment to the Son "so that all may honor the Son just as they honor the Father."[4] Jesus promises that all who hear his word and believe him who sent him already have eternal life and do not come under judgment.[5]

Appearing (*epiphaneia*) is a synonym for the time when Jesus will judge the world (4:1). **Judgment** focuses on the serious preparation needed, while **appearing** focuses on the glorious event. "Appearing" is reminiscent of the Aaronic benediction: May the Lord "make his face *appear* (or shine) upon you" (Num 6:25). It is a metaphor for deliverance and blessing.[6] At

---

1. See 2 Tim 2:14.
2. E.g., Gallio, the high priest, governor, emperor (Acts 18:14–15; 23:2–3; 24:10; 25:10, 25). See also 1 Thess 4:16–17; 1 Pet 4:5; Rev 11:18; 19:2; 20:11–13.
3. John 8:16; Rom 2:16; 1 Cor 4:5.
4. John 5:22–23; Acts 10:42; Rev 19:11–16.
5. John 3:18; 5:24.
6. Pss 30:15–16; 66:1; 79:3; 117:26–27; 118:135, LXX.

the appearing all will know Jesus is God (Ezek 39:28). An "appearing" was a "glorious manifestation."[7]

Why now add **kingdom** (*basileia*) as the third basis for his charge (4:1)? After the judgment and the appearing, Christ will set up his kingdom. Paul looks forward to Christ's kingdom (4:18). Jesus did much teaching on God's kingdom,[8] as did Paul.[9] The kingdom is not food and drink but "righteousness and peace and joy in the Holy Spirit" (Rom 14:17). The wicked will not inherit it.[10] The perishable will become imperishable (1 Cor 15:50–55). People who are forgiven and lead a life worthy of God may enter Christ's kingdom.[11] As eternal life (2 Tim 1:1), Christ's kingdom begins now and extends forever.

Paul now gives his five-part charge: to **proclaim, take a stand, reprove, rebuke, encourage** (4:2).[12] Timothy is not merely supposed to do these actions because of his personal opinions or habits,[13] but he should do them based on remaining in what he learned from his knowledge of the Holy Scriptures and from his teachers (3:14–16). First, Timothy is exhorted to **proclaim the word**. Why does Paul *not* write "teach the word," "prophesy," "heal the sick," "do wonders and miracles" as one of these five main commands, especially since the first function of the Scripture is to teach (3:16)? Preaching or proclaiming is an action all believers are to do, but especially evangelists, such as Timothy and Philip.[14] A preacher is a herald, a messenger from the Scripture (**the word**) to the people.[15] A preacher or evangelist brings good news (Rom 10:14–15). Jesus at the end of his earthly ministry exhorted his disciples "to proclaim in his name repentance for

---

7. Thayer, 245. Antiochus called himself "Epiphanes" (*Epiphanē*) but he was superseded by the real God's *epiphaneia*, "manifest signs that came from heaven" that manifested God's power and glory and delivered the people (2 Macc 2:20–21; 3:24; 14:15; 15:27; 3 Macc 2:9; 2 Thess 2:8. See also 1 Tim 6:14 (Spencer 2013); Titus 2:13; 2 Tim 1:10; 4:8). Of the eleven references of the noun and its cognates in the NT, seven occur in the Pastorals (64 percent).

8. E.g., Luke 4:43.

9. Acts 19:8; 20:25; 28:23, 31.

10. 1 Cor 6:9–10; Gal 5:19–21; Eph 5:5; Rev 22:15.

11. Col 1:13–14; 1 Thess 2:12.

12. Paul uses five aorist imperatives that treat each action as a single whole irrespective of the time involved (Robertson 1934: 832).

13. Also 2 Cor 4:5.

14. 2 Tim 4:5; Acts 8:5; 21:8.

15. See 1 Tim 2:7; 3:16 (Spencer 2013).

forgiveness of sins to all nations."[16] Jesus himself proclaimed, "Repent, for the kingdom of heaven is near."[17] Timothy too will be proclaiming Jesus' kingdom (4:1).

In this difficult time, the next key action is to **take a stand in season, out of season** (4:2). Literally, **take a stand** means "to stand" (*histēmi*) "over" (*epi*) or make a stand. Sometimes simply standing and waiting is enough, as Cornelius' emissaries were waiting at the gate[18] or someone may be standing, affirming an action, as Paul affirmed the condemnation of Stephen (Acts 22:20). But, Timothy is charged to remain firm **in season** (at good times) and **out of season** (at bad times).[19] Timothy is to proclaim the gospel, that is, take his stand, whether it is convenient or inconvenient, opportune or inopportune.[20] And, he has no leisure to wait; he must be urgent.

In the same way as the Scripture **reproves** (3:16), Timothy too is to bring deeds and thoughts out into the open for the sake of truth (Eph 5:11) since proclamation of the word clarifies for hearers what is sin. A synonym of reprove (*elenchō*) is **rebuke** (*epitimaō*). *Epitamaō* in the New Testament often means to order something or someone *not* to do something, to speak or to act in a certain way.[21] For example, Jesus told his disciples, if believers sin, order them not to do so (rebuke, censure severely) but, if they repent, forgive them (Luke 17:3). Thus, if sinful deeds are brought out in the open (reprove or reveal), then the next step is to order the listener not to do them (rebuke).

---

16. Luke 24:47. See 1 Tim 1:15 (Spencer 2013).
17. Matt 4:17, 23; 9:35; Luke 8:1.
18. Acts 10:17; 11:11.
19. Good versus bad times is a subjective decision. For instance, Judas Iscariot sought a "good time" to betray Jesus (Matt 26:16; Mark 14:11; Luke 22:6). For Apollos to come to Corinth during the midst of the arguments there was not a "good time" (1 Cor 16:12). The disciples were so busy they could not find an opportunity to eat (Mark 6:31). In contrast, the Philippians took a while before they could arrange to send Paul money; there had been no good time (Phil 4:10).
20. BDAG, 407; Thayer, 259.
21. E.g., the disciples ordered adults not to bring their children to be blessed by Jesus (Matt 19:13; Mark 10:13; Luke 18:15. Peter ordered Jesus not to say he would suffer (Matt 16:21–22; Mark 8:31–32). Jesus ordered demons not to stay within people but to leave (Matt 17:18; Mark 1:25–26; 9:25; Luke 4:35, 41; 9:42). He also ordered the winds and waves not to be rough but to be calm and a fever to leave (Matt 8:26; Mark 4:39; Luke 4:39; 8:24).

The final step is *parakaleō*, which can include appealing to people, supporting or helping, and **encouraging** them.[22] Paul explains that he and Timothy "are ambassadors for Christ since God is *appealing*" through them. Therefore, the Corinthians should "become reconciled to God" (2 Cor 5:20). Appeal is one stage in the reconciliation process between humans and God. That appeal is done **in all compassion and teaching** (4:2). **Compassion** is a synonym for gentle mercy. It is the way Paul tells the Galatians a transgressor is to be restored (Gal 6:1). Paul himself was treated with compassion by Jesus.[23] So, Timothy should be loving toward sinners. And, now is when he should **teach** them. Education is a means of restoration,[24] returning Timothy to the first benefit of Scripture: teaching and guiding (3:16).

The urgency with which Paul exhorts is necessary: **For there will be a time when they will not endure the healthy teaching but according to their own passions they will accumulate teachers who scratch their hearing and, on the one hand, they will turn their hearing from the truth, while, on the other hand, they will turn away to the myths** (4:3–4). Paul writes in the future about events that have already begun,[25] but will get worse. Already some women are not coming to knowledge of the truth (3:6–7). Unhealthy doctrine is being taught at Ephesus (1 Tim 1:3, 10). Paul described some of the causes of susceptibility to deceptive teaching earlier: being overwhelmed with sins and being led by manifold passions (3:6). These same passions result in people not **enduring healthy teaching**, but, rather, **accumulating teachers** that do not bring health. To **endure** (*anexomai*)[26] can be used in a positive sense, if the objective is necessary, as to endure persecution for the faith,[27] an action Paul wants from Timothy, to join in suffering, because all who wish to live in Christ Jesus in a godly manner will be persecuted (1:8; 3:12). However, here "endure" is used in a negative sense, since the object should be repelled: **teachers who scratch their hearing** (4:3). As in Corinth, where the church had been accepting a "different gospel" than they had received, transmitted to them by "super apostles" who enslaved, consumed, trapped them, put on airs,

---

22. See Titus 2:15.
23. See 1 Tim 1:16 (Spencer 2013).
24. As in 1 Tim 2:11; 2 Tim 2:24–25.
25. See 1 Tim 4:1 (Spencer 2013).
26. Literally, "to hold one's self erect and firm" (Thayer, 45).
27. 1 Cor 4:12; 2 Thess 1:4.

and even slapped them (2 Cor 11:4, 20), at Ephesus, **healthy teaching**, the truth, would no longer be endured.[28] Instead, some would listen to teachers who **scratch their hearing** (4:3). Hearing is an important step in the communication and reception of the gospel. Faith comes from hearing.[29] The people Paul describes are impaired in their hearing.[30] They apparently want their ears scratched because they itch.[31] If someone had sores, they would itch and want the sores scratched to relieve the unpleasant sensation,[32] although that scratching would be the worst action they could do. Scratching would only make the itching worse. Since the sensation of being overwhelmed with sins and passions could be cured by the truth that brings greater health, a superficial cure, scratching, just makes the problem worse. In this case, the scratching is listening to **myths** (4:4). Mentioned in all the Pastoral Letters,[33] myths were speculative doctrines based on fictional stories, not historic truths. They promoted asceticism and legalism and concern with genealogies. These stories could be entertaining.[34] However, they did not prepare the listeners for persevering in persecution and suffering for their faith.

In contrast to these people, Paul gives Timothy four commands: **But, you, continue sober in all, endure hardship, do work of an evangelist, fulfill your ministry** (4:5). This is the final time Paul addresses Timothy directly as **you**.[35] In some ways these four commands contrast with the negative characteristics in 4:3–4. Instead of being unhealthy and lacking perception, Timothy is sober. Instead of merely following his personal passions, Timothy endures suffering. Instead of pursuing falsehood, Timothy promotes truth as an evangelist. Instead of destroying his health, he maintains it by using his spiritual gift to carry out his ministry fully. These

---

28. See 2 Tim 1:13; Titus 1:13.

29. Rom 10:17; Gal 3:2, 5; 1 Thess 2:13.

30. Literally, Mark 7:32–35; metaphorically, Matt 13:14–15 and Acts 28:26–27, citing Isa 6:9–10.

31. E.g., ears with impacted wax will itch.

32. *Knēthō* is a participle, passive or middle voice. The passive signifies "to itch," but the middle "to scratch" (LSJ, 964). Lock (1924: 113): "having itching ears, and desiring to get the itching checked," I think fits better in context than "being pleased, having their ears tickled by each new teacher."

33. See Titus 1:10; 2 Tim 2:16–18.

34. See Titus 1:14; 1 Tim 1:4; 4:3, 7 (Spencer 2013).

35. See 2 Tim 3:14.

four commands also recall previous charges to Timothy.[36] **Sober** has both a literal and a metaphorical sense. Being sober (*nēphō*) is an important attribute for elders and ministers.[37] Paul tells the Thessalonians to be sober for "those who are drunk get drunk at night," but, since they belong to the day, they should be sober (1 Thess 5:6–8). Synonyms are staying awake, having self-control, and keeping alert.[38] Thus, "sober" in 2 Timothy 4:5 hearkens back to "self-control" (*sōphronismos*) in 1:7. Timothy must be alert if he is to save himself and his hearers (1 Tim 4:16).

Earlier Paul had explained how he suffered evil (*kakopoieō*) to the point of imprisonment (2:9). Now he exhorts Timothy to "suffer evil" (**endure hardship**; *kakopatheō*). This verb is a synonym for the main theme of the letter, Paul's exhortation for Timothy to join in suffering with him for the gospel (1:8; 2:3). Paul explains next how he expects his own death. Timothy himself will experience difficulties from the Roman government (Heb 13:23).

The next command hearkens back to 1:6 ("to keep stirring into flame God's gift") and 1 Timothy: "Do not neglect the spiritual gift in you."[39] Here Timothy's spiritual gift is explicitly mentioned. An **evangelist**, as a minister of the word, is a messenger of God's good news of salvation who preaches, baptizes, and instructs people in the basics of faith. Having this gift would help Timothy pastor this church that needs to learn the basics of truth. But, in a time of persecution, being an evangelist would be dangerous. Nevertheless, Paul reiterates **fulfill your ministry** (4:5), carry it through to the end.[40] Paul himself reminds Timothy how Paul's own ministry was fulfilled at his first defense when all the Gentiles heard the good news (4:17).

Receive a Just Crown (4:6–8)

Paul concludes this section of the letter exhorting Timothy to continue in his ministry of evangelism and sound teaching despite opposition (3:1— 4:8) by describing his own future: **For I myself already am offered up and**

---

36. Paul begins with the present imperative (**continue sober**) that presents an overview and then moves to aorist imperatives (**endure hardship, do work of an evangelist, fulfill your ministry**), subsidiary concrete commands (4:5).

37. *Nēphalios*: Titus 2:2; 1 Tim 3:2, 11.

38. 1 Thess 5:6; 1 Pet 1:13; 4:7; 5:8.

39. See 2 Tim 1:6; 1 Tim 4:14 (Spencer 2013).

40. Thayer, 517. The Lord fulfilled his purpose for Paul (Ps 138:8).

the time of my departure stands near (4:6). This verse introduces one of Paul's most poignant descriptions of his present suffering and imminent death. While Paul exhorts Timothy to continue in ministry, Paul himself is in the final stage of his ministry. He compares himself to an Old Testament **offering**, though not a sin or guilt offering since Christ has already forgiven his sins. Neither is he a fellowship or peace offering because he knows God is present with him. He describes himself as a drink offering. Drink offerings of wine were combined with meal offerings every day, every Sabbath, and every festival at the temple, as together they were presented to the Lord (Hos 9:4).[41] Paul describes himself as presently (**already**) being such an offering.[42] He is not the one making the offering happen, but, nevertheless, by calling himself a drink offering, he sees his life as a gift being presented to God. The eventual giving of his life-blood is similar to the pouring out of red wine. He is indeed offering his body as a living sacrifice to God (Rom 12:1).

After he describes his forthcoming death in metaphorical terms, as an **offering**, then, in more literal terms, he states the **time** of his **departure stands near** (4:6). The Lord had rescued Paul from all his previous difficulties (3:11) but now the right time (*kairos*)[43] has come. Time is personified as a person (a soldier) **standing** nearby,[44] ready to escort him to **depart** life in the flesh (Phil 1:22–23).[45]

Paul then describes further why this is the right time in three almost parallel clauses: **I fought the good fight, I finished the race course, I kept the faith** (4:7). Life is first described as a **fight** (*agōn*), an image from athletics, which he had already used for Timothy (1 Tim 6:12).[46] The idea of effort

---

41. M. *Yoma* 3:5; Lev 23:37–38; Num 15:5; 28:24—29:39. Sometimes a drink was offered to the Lord in other contexts. Jacob offered a drink offering as thanksgiving for God's blessing to him and to consecrate the place where God had spoken to him, Bethel (Gen 35:9–15). David offered the water his three warriors (Joshebbasshebeth, Eleazar, and Shammah) drew from the well of Bethlehem in the camp of the Philistines as a drink offering because he wanted to honor their great sacrifice for him (2 Sam 23:8–17).

42. In contrast, in Phil 2:17 he considers the possibility, "if even."

43. BDAG, 497.

44. See 1 Tim 4:2 (Spencer 2013).

45. Thayer (39) describes **departure** (*analysis*) as a metaphor drawn from "loosing" from moorings preparatory to setting sail.

46. The perfect tense and middle voice (**I fought for myself**) accentuate that the fight began in the past and the active agent was Paul himself. In each clause the object precedes the verb giving emphasis to each object: fight, race course, faith.

is the very essence of athletics and the real prize is the honor of victory.⁴⁷ Paul has exerted effort as a believer and he looked forward to his prize, the "righteous crown" (4:8). A fight (or athletics) is a general term, a **race course** now indicates a specific type of sport. Paul had previously described his life to the elders from Ephesus as running in a race course. His goal was to "complete his race course and the ministry" that he received from the Lord Jesus (Acts 20:24). Ancient foot races were not run in curved tracks but in straight ones where runners fixed their eyes on a post at the end of the track, the goal.⁴⁸ Paul's goal was "to testify to the good news of God's grace" (Acts 20:24). He was seeking an imperishable prize. His running was purposeful.⁴⁹ Now, Paul was stating that he had finished the race course. The last clause describes the completion of his goal: Paul has **kept the faith** (4:7). *Tēreō* literally signifies "to guard."⁵⁰ It was often used as a synonym for "to obey," as in 1 Timothy 6:14, "to **keep** (obey) the commandment(s)."⁵¹ Paul had lived consistently in obedience to the mandates of the faith. He had exhorted Timothy to "keep" himself pure (1 Tim 5:22), as Paul kept the faith pure. Following Jesus who asked the Father to "guard" or protect from the evil one the people that he had given him (John 17:15), Paul had protected the faith, the gospel he preached, from the falsehoods promoted by the evil one.

To what does Paul look forward? **Henceforth, the righteous crown is laid up for me, which the Lord will grant to me in that day, the righteous judge, and, not only to me, but also to all the ones having loved his appearing** (4:8). Paul continues the athletic imagery, referring again to the **crown**.⁵² In 2:5, the focus was how one competes. In 4:7–8, Paul's focus is the completion of the race. Every city-state had its athletic festival, including Ephesus, which had its annual athletic games (the Ephesia).⁵³ Crown winners had many privileges, but "the most coveted prize in the Greek world was the wreath of wild olive which was the only prize at the Olympic Games. The real prize is the honour of victory . . . The branches for the

---

47. Gardiner 1930: 1–2.
48. Gardiner 1930: 128, 135.
49. 1 Cor 9:24–26; Gal 2:2; Phil 2:16.
50. See 1 Tim 6:13–14 (Spencer 2013). **Guard** is used literally in Matt 27:36, 54; 28:4; Acts 12:5–6; 16:23; 24:23; 25:4, 21.
51. Also Matt 19:17; 28:20; John 14:15, 21, 23; 15:10.
52. 4:7; See 2 Tim 2:5.
53. Gardiner 1930: 39, 111; Yamauchi 1980: 90–91.

crown were cut with a golden sickle by a boy both of whose parents were living, from the sacred olive tree that grew at the west end of the Temple of Zeus, where even to-day the wild olive may be seen."[54] The metaphor of an imperishable crown, or crown of life and glory that never fades, was used by several New Testament authors.[55] In times of persecution, a reward is important to motivate people to persevere.[56] In this last letter, Paul describes the crown as **laid up**, held in reserve for him[57] and mentions three things about it: (1) what kind of crown it is, (2) who will give it, and (3) who will get it (4:8).

Instead of olive branches, which are imperishable and become brittle, God's crown partakes of the same nature as the judge who bestows it. *Dikaiosynē* and *dikaios* may be rendered just or **righteous** (4:8), which describes God's character (Deut 32:4). It may refer to the judge in a court, but here it is the judge of an athletic contest. The highest honors were bestowed by emperors. Sometimes ancient matches were arranged beforehand,[58] however, Jesus as judge cannot be bribed, but is always just and holy. In the Pastorals, *dikaios* and *dikaiosynē* always are synonyms of "holy." Timothy has been exhorted to pursue this characteristic,[59] to be a person who observes God's rules. No one can be perfectly righteous, except Jesus, the Righteous One.[60] Nevertheless, at the final judgment, the pursuing of righteousness will be completed because it will be awarded.[61]

Apodidōmi (**will grant**) in 4:8 is clearly positive, while in 4:14 it is negative. It can be a reward or a punishment.[62] The verb is often used in legal situations, such as paying back debts,[63] paying taxes or shares,[64] paying wages (Matt 20:8), and giving conjugal obligations (1 Cor 7:3). The **crown**

---

54. Gardiner 1930: 2, 35–36.
55. 1 Cor 9:25; 1 Thess 2:19–20; Jas 1:12; 1 Pet 5:4.
56. Rev 2:10; 4:4, 10; 14:14; Heb 2:9.
57. E.g., Luke 19:20.
58. Gardiner 1930: 111–12.
59. 1 Tim 6:11; 2 Tim 2:22.
60. 1 Tim 3:16; 1 John 2:1.
61. See Titus 1:8; 3:5; 1 Tim 3:16 (Spencer 2013). "The crown that consists in righteousness and is also the reward for righteousness" (Robertson 1931: 631; Lock 1924: 115; Towner 2006: 616).
62. See 1 Tim 5:4 (Spencer 2013); Thayer, 60. Literally, it signifies to give back or to give over (Matt 6:4, 6, 18; Rom 2:6; 1 Pet 4:5; Rev 22:2).
63. Matt 5:26; 18:23–34; Luke 7:42; 10:35; 12:59; 16:2; 19:8.
64. Matt 21:41; 22:21; Mark 12:17; Luke 20:25; Acts 5:8; Rom 13:7.

of righteousness is the reward that Paul expects, the righteousness that comes from God based on faith (Phil 3:9). But this reward is not just Paul's, rather it is **to all the ones having loved his appearing** (2 Tim 4:8).

Does **appearing** refer to Jesus' incarnation or second return to judgment? Sometimes Paul clearly uses **appearing** to refer to Jesus' second return to judgment[65] but at other times to Jesus' incarnation.[66] These people have long **loved** Jesus' appearing (4:8). Thus, it could refer to the prospect of Jesus' second return or to the action of Jesus' first coming to earth or both. **The Lord will grant** clearly refers to the future, but the love of believers has been present for a while.[67]

COME SOON (4:9–18)

After this expectant look to the future (4:8), Paul has completed exhorting Timothy to continue in his ministry of evangelism and sound teaching despite opposition (3:1—4:8). Now Paul exhorts Timothy: **Make every effort to come to me soon** (4:9). This act of coming is Timothy's first step in joining Paul in suffering (1:8; 2:3). Paul then cites several reasons why he would like Timothy to come **soon**, before winter (4:21): (1) Paul is left almost all alone (4:10–11a); (2) he needs human and material resources (4:11b-13); and (3) he was abandoned at his first defense—and opposed (4:14–18). How was Paul abandoned while a group of Christians in Rome greet Timothy (4:21)? Probably Paul was incarcerated in a military camp or palace, where it was not as easy to have company as when he was under house arrest during the first Roman imprisonment.[68] Sometimes Bible students envision Paul as a self-sufficient independent minister, but these verses indicate how relational and communal and interdependent Paul was. He was building on the precedence of Jesus' action to send out the Twelve and the Seventy-two, "two by two."[69]

Paul mentions four coworkers: **Demas has abandoned me, having loved the present age, and he went into Thessalonica, Crescens into Galatia, Titus into Dalmatia; Luke is only with me** (4:10–11a). The most

---

65. 1 Tim 6:14; Titus 2:13. Towner 2006: 616.

66. 2 Tim 1:10; Titus 2:11; 3:4. Robertson concludes that "appearing" in 4:8 could refer to either (1931: 631).

67. See 2 Tim 4:1. **Appearing** in 4:1 could refer to the incarnation.

68. See 2 Tim, Occasion.

69. Mark 6:7; Luke 10:1.

disturbing coworker is **Demas**.⁷⁰ Demas, like Luke, was probably a Gentile.⁷¹ He, along with Luke, had kept Paul company during the first Roman imprisonment, when Paul was under house arrest.⁷² Paul describes Demas as: he **has abandoned me** (4:10). *Enkataleipō* (**abandon**) is an intensive word, signifying "to leave behind in the lurch or in straits" or "leave in the lurch one who is in straits," thus, "abandon."⁷³ Jesus cried out in Aramaic when on the cross: "My God, my God, why have you abandoned me?"⁷⁴ Paul had described his and Timothy's ministry as "being persecuted but not abandoned" (2 Cor 4:9). But, now, Paul felt abandoned in Rome by Demas. In contrast to those who love Jesus' appearing (4:8), Demas loved the **present age**.⁷⁵ He would not join Paul in suffering. He would not carry his cross with Jesus. He did not want to take the chance that he be imprisoned along with Paul. He probably returned home to Thessalonica in Macedonia.⁷⁶

When times became difficult, Demas no longer heeded the message Paul had given the Thessalonians, that they imitate Paul, Silvanus (Silas),

---

70. *Dēmas* is probably a nickname for *Dēmētrios*, *Dēmarchos*, *Dēmaratos*, or *Dēmodokos* (Robertson 1934: 172; Thayer, 132; BDAG, 222).

71. They are contrasted with Jews (Col 4:11–14).

72. Col 4:14; Phlm 24. Demas appears to be known by the Colossians although he was not one of them (Col 4:12–14). Demas, like Luke and Mark, was a "coworker" (*synergos*), a colleague in ministry with Paul, to whom the churches were to be subject, who prepares believers for ministry (1 Cor 16:15–16; Eph 4:11–12; Spencer 1985: 118; Ellis 1971: 437–52). Demas, along with Hermogenes, were included in the fictional second-century *Acts of Paul and Thecla* as fellow travelers with Paul to Iconium who were jealous of Onesiphorus and full of hypocrisy and flattery. The presbyter of Asia Minor has them espouse the doctrine that the resurrection has already taken place (*Acts of Paul* 1, 4, 12, 14; 2 Tim 2:18).

73. Thayer, 166; LSJ, 470; MM, 179. Also, 2 Tim 1:15.

74. Matt 27:46; Mark 15:34, citing Ps 22:1.

75. E.g., 1 John 2:15; Titus 2:12.

76. "Demetrius" was a common name in **Thessalonica** (Zahn 1953: 1:213, 441). Thessalonica, the capital of the province of Macedonia, was (and still is) a flourishing commercial and political center situated right on the Thermaic Gulf. The *Via Egnatia* crossed it. It was the most populous city in Macedonia, a "free city" that did not have to pay taxes to Rome but could levy taxes and conduct its own internal affairs (Strabo, *Geogr.* 7.7.4 [C323]; Donaldson 1985: 259–60). Paul visited Thessalonica in his second and third missionary journeys (Acts 17:1–9; 20:1–2). Many devout Greek men and women and some Jews were persuaded. However, a mob tried to harm Paul and Silas, but they escaped to Beroea. Some unbelieving Thessalonians even pursued them there (Acts 17:3–5, 10, 13). Other believing Thessalonians later accompanied Paul to Jerusalem when he brought the offering (Acts 20:4). Aristarchus, a Thessalonian, stayed with Paul during the first house arrest (Acts 27:2; Phlm 24).

and Timothy, a word they had received with joy in spite of persecution (1 Thess 1:6). Paul had warned them that they would suffer persecution, as did Christ Jesus, the prophets, and Paul and Silas (and Jason).[77] Even though Paul wrote extensively about the future of Jesus' return,[78] Demas preferred the present world. Unfortunately, he did not hold fast to what he was taught (2 Thess 2:15).

Crescens[79] and **Titus** (4:10) are not described as having abandoned Paul and loving the present age, but they leave to different regions, one to Gaul or Galatia, one to **Dalmatia**, the southern part of Illyricum. **Titus**, like **Demas** and Luke, was a Gentile.[80] He had been in Crete two to five years earlier and was to have met Paul at Nicopolis (Titus 3:12). **Dalmatia** is not far from Nicopolis. Possibly, Titus felt some urgency in returning to the area of Illyricum (Rom 15:19). Titus was a coworker of Paul but he was not in a hierarchical relationship with him. Paul had "left" Titus in Crete but did not "send" him to Corinth.[81] As Titus was a responsible, committed, mature Christian with the gift of organization and peacemaking, it is difficult to believe he would abandon Paul, but possibly his strength in organization might not gift him for the intensive personal support that Paul needed at this time.

Then comes the brief sentence filled with so much pathos: **Luke is only with me** (4:11a). Even in suffering for Christ's sake, the follower of Christ needs support, as Jesus needed support when he asked in Gethsemane before the crucifixion: "Simon, are you asleep? Could you not keep awake one hour?" (Mark 14:37; NRSV). In addition, the imprisoned person needs material support. When Agrippa was imprisoned by Tiberius, Antonia arranged certain concessions for him: the centurion handcuffed to him would be humane, Agrippa would be allowed to bathe every day, receive

---

77. 1 Thess 2:14–15; 3:3–4, 7; 2 Thess 1:4–5; Acts 17:3.

78. 1 Thess 4:14–17; 5:2–4, 23; 2 Thess 1:7–10.

79. The Greek name is rare (BDAG, 566). No additional information is given in the NT on **Crescens**. Later traditions associate Crescens with Chalcedon (as bishop) in northern Asia Minor, and with the founding of the churches in Vienne and Mayence (Brownrigg 1971: 92; Baring-Gould 1898: 15:323; Zahn 1953: 2:26; Lock 1924: 117; Kelly 1963: 213; Mounce 2000: 590). Vienne is in Gaul. Gauls also migrated to Galatia. If Crescens did go to Gaul and Titus to Dalmatia, they would be reaching out northwest and northeast from Rome (Hendricksen 1957: 319; Zahn 1953: 2:11–12, 25).

80. See Titus 1:4.

81. Titus 1:5; 2 Cor 8:6, 17, 23; 12:18.

visits from friends, have a bed, and other bodily comforts.[82] Paul was in prison and Luke visited and supported him (Matt 25:36).

Luke had felt called by God, along with Paul, Timothy, and Silas at Troas in Asia Minor, by the Macedonian appealing in a vision. Luke, taking leadership in maintaining the newly established church, remained in Philippi and returned with the large group that accompanied Paul with the offering for the Jerusalem Christians.[83] The Macedonian church had many strong Christian women and Luke's Gospel also emphasizes Jesus' ministry to women. Thus, Luke too must have been sympathetic to the leadership of women in the church. Along with Aristarchus, Luke accompanied Paul from Caesarea when he was sent to Rome and stayed with him during the house arrest.[84]

Paul describes *Loukas*, probably a nickname for *Loukanos*, as "the beloved physician" (Col 4:14), one of his coworkers.[85] "Beloved" indicates Paul and Luke had a close and affectionate relationship. Possibly Luke assisted Paul with his eye difficulties.[86] Luke may have been a freed slave, because slaves were often physicians. Sometimes physicians were generously paid.[87] Luke shows his education by his use of good literary Koine style[88] and his interest in detailed, comprehensive, orderly, truthful history in his two writings sent to Theophilus.[89]

---

82. Josephus, *Ant.* 18.6.7 (203–4).

83. Acts 16:9–17; 20:5—21:18.

84. Acts 27:1—28:16. Barclay (1966: 251) suggests that, when traveling to Rome under arrest, a prisoner was allowed to take two slaves with him as personal attendants. Luke and Aristarchus were willing to accompany Paul in those circumstances. Most likely, Luke completed the book of Acts during Paul's earlier imprisonment. I think likely that Luke researched his Gospel during Paul's two-year imprisonment in Caesarea (Acts 23:31—26:32). See also Zahn 1953: 3:128. Paul quotes Luke's Gospel in 1 Tim 5:18. Eusebius relates that Luke was Antiochene by birth (*Hist. eccl.* 3.4). Some Latin texts have "we" in Acts 11:27 (Zahn 1953: 3:2, 4–5, 51).

85. Phlm 24. Some early church fathers thought Paul referred to Luke's Gospel in 2 Cor 8:18 (e.g., Eusebius, *Hist. eccl.* 3.4; 5.8; 6.25; Zahn 1953: 3:6–7, 56).

86. Gal 4:13–15; 6:11; 2 Cor 12:7. Paul may have had ophthalmia (Reiter's condition or intermittent glaucoma).

87. E.g., a physician is paid twenty drachmas, the equivalent of twenty days work for a laborer (BDAG, 465).

88. E.g., Robertson 1934: 50, 57–58, 86, 106–7, 121–23, 1064–65, 1084, 1106.

89. See prefaces. Luke was buried in Constantinople in AD 357 (Zahn 1953: 3:7; Brownrigg 1971: 262). About Luke, Brownrigg summarizes: his character "emerges . . . as that of a highly sensitive and sympathetic person of wide interests and perception" (260).

Paul then asks Timothy: **Having picked him up, bring Mark with yourself, for he is useful to me for ministry** (4:11b). **Mark** must be somewhere near Ephesus, on the way to where Timothy will board a ship at Troas (4:13).[90] In this sentence, we are reminded that Paul and John Mark are now reconciled to each other. John Mark as a youth was reared in the Christian church. His mother, Mary, hosted the Jerusalem church in their home. Mark joined Paul and Barnabas on their first traveling outreach (Acts 12:25), but he deserted them in Perga in Pamphylia, thereby causing Paul not to want to take him on the second trip. Mark's cousin Barnabas advocated for him (Acts 13:13; 15:37–40). By the time Paul is first imprisoned in Rome (c. AD 59–62), Mark remains steadfastly with Paul as his coworker (Col 4:10; Phlm 24).[91] Mark became a consecrated "vessel," "useful" to the "master" (2 Tim 2:21) and **useful** for ministry (4:11), like Onesimus (though once not "useful" was now "useful"[92]), though we cannot be sure exactly how Mark would be **useful** to Paul for ministry. Zahn suggests that Mark possessed "a treasure of narratives from the lips of Peter and of other disciples of Jesus, who were accustomed to come and go to his mother's house."[93] Possibly, Mark might help in Paul's writing projects (4:13). Mark is also well acquainted with Rome and with the condition of the church

---

90. Possibly he was still in or near Colosse (Col 4:10).

91. **Mark** was also friends with the Apostle Peter. Mark's and Peter's friendship goes back to at least the early 30s, when Peter arrives to celebrate his release from prison (Acts 12:12). Among experiences Mark and Peter had in common were that even as believers they denied their faith not just once but at least twice. Mark may have been present (the "certain young man") when Jesus was arrested, and, when they tried to arrest him too, ran away naked (Mark 14:51–52. See also Barclay 1966: 157; Zahn 1953: 2:428, 447). Strong and consistent early traditions support a connection between Peter and Mark in the writing of Mark's Gospel (e.g., Eusebius, *Hist. eccl.* 2.15; 3.39; 5.8; 6.14, 25). Both Peter and Mark, in times of testing, failed in discipleship, but they were able to turn their lives around and become victorious Christians. Mark is remembered for traveling to Egypt and establishing churches in Alexandria (Eusebius, *Hist. eccl.* 2.16, 24; Zahn 1953: 2:431, 448; Baring-Gould 1898: 4:334).

92. Phlm 11; 1 Pet 5:13; Spencer 2007: 270–71; Lock 1924: 117.

93. Zahn 1953: 2:430; 377–79, 445–47, 451.

in that city.⁹⁴ Paul adds: **And Tychicus I sent into Ephesus** (4:12).⁹⁵ As in Crete, **Tychicus**' presence allows another of Paul's coworkers to leave.

Paul continues with a further reason he wants Timothy to hasten to Rome: **When you come, bring the cloak which I left in Troas with Carpus, and the books, especially the parchments** (4:13). Paul here assumes Timothy will come to Rome. These details have impressed many commentators as the type of simple details no forger would ever have.⁹⁶ Paul wants two items, something to warm the body and something to activate the mind. Even though Paul expects the final outcome not to go well, he still wants to keep active. The **cloak** (*phailonēs*) is a thick upper garment,⁹⁷ and is a solid reason why Paul wants Timothy to come before winter (4:21). Paul left this heavy cloak in **Troas**, the important seaport between Asia and Europe in Mysia in northwest Asia Minor on the Aegean Sea where Paul received his vision to go to Macedonia.⁹⁸ After being released from the first Roman imprisonment, Paul must have returned to Troas, where he left his cloak with **Carpus**.⁹⁹ Possibly, Paul had to leave Troas in haste.

94. Hendricksen 1957: 321. Lock (1924:117) suggests Mark was useful for "personal service in prison, or for missions to the city, or for help in worship," "as a comforter in trouble." Fee (1988: 294) suggests Mark provided "at least ministry to his personal needs" (also Kelly 1963: 214) but Marshall (1999: 817) responds that "one does not summon an experienced missionary simply to be a valet." Towner (2006: 626) summarizes Mark's role as "ongoing ministry in the Roman church" or "to assist in taking the mission into new parts."

95. See Titus 3:12.

96. Kelly 1963: 215; Fee 1988: 295; Mounce 2000: 592; Witherington III 2006: 378.

97. LSJ, 1912. Kelly describes the **cloak** as a "large, sleeveless outer garment, made of a single piece of heavy material, with a hole in the middle through which the head was passed," "used for protection against cold and rain" (1963: 215). Towner adds that it was expensive, made from goat hair, hide, or coarse wool (2006: 628). The *phailonēs* is not the threadbare cloak (*tribōn*) worn by the Stoic or Cynic philosopher or a fancy cloak (Arrian, *Epict. diss.* 3.23 [35]; 4.8 [15, 34]; LSJ, 1817).

98. *Trōas* is a contraction of *Trōias* ("Trojan"; LSJ, 1831–32). Alexandria Troas was near ancient Troy. It was founded by Antigonus, one of the successors of Alexander the Great, and it became a Roman colony. Strabo describes it as "one of the notable cities of the world" (*Geogr.* 13.1.26 [C593]). In two days Paul and his coworkers (Timothy, Luke, and Silas) sailed from Troas to Neapolis (Acts 16:8–11). Paul traveled to and from Macedonia through Troas also during the third missionary journey (Acts 20:5–13; 2 Cor 2:12–13). By this time, a Christian community was already established that met the first of the week. At Troas, Paul talked through the night (when Eutychus fell asleep from a window).

99. *Karpos*, literally, refers to "fruit," usually "fruits of the earth," such as corn (LSJ, 879). Traditionally, Carpus became bishop of Beroea in Thrace (Brownrigg 1971: 55;

He writes he left behind **the books** (4:13). A *biblion* could be as small as a document[100] or as large as a complete book.[101] In the New Testament, the emphasis is a literal document one touches.[102] A *biblion*, a strip of *byblos* made of Egyptian papyrus, could be a tablet, petition, book, and in the plural even a library.[103] Literary works made into scrolls did not usually exceed thirty-five feet. *Membrana* (a **parchment** scroll or codex notebook) were made from the skins of cattle, sheep, and goats. Quality parchment was developed in Pergamum in Mysia. It was more durable than papyrus and could be written on both sides of a sheet, washed off, and reused.[104] Many commentators have theorized that the *biblia* made of papyrus were copies of the Old Testament and the *membrana* were copies of Paul's own letters. Thus, the first collection of Paul's letters might be Paul's own private collection.[105] The phrase can be translated, **the books, especially the parchments**, which implies two different types of books, those of papyrus and parchment, or **the books, namely, the parchment ones**, which implies one type of books. At a minimum, Timothy had to transport Paul's library to the prison in Rome, especially the most durable ones, the ones made of parchment.

Paul warns Timothy: **Alexander, the metalworker, did much evil to me; the Lord will repay him according to his works; from whom also keep yourself away, for exceedingly he stood against our words** (4:14–15). The New Testament cites several **Alexanders**: son of Simon (Mark 15:21), high priest family member (Acts 4:6), a Jew in Ephesus who tried to make a defense before the mob (Acts 19:33–34), and a person in the church at Ephesus who by rejecting conscience made a shipwreck of his faith.[106]

Baring-Gould 1898: 11:319).

100. E.g., a certificate of divorce (Matt 19:7; Mark 10:4).

101. E.g., the Gospel of John (John 20:30; 21:25); the book of Isaiah (Luke 4:17, 20); the book of Revelation (Rev 1:11; 22:7, 9–10, 18–19).

102. A *biblos* emphasizes a literary work one reads (MM, 111). A *biblos* or *byblos* may also serve as a synonym for *biblion*, e.g., the book of Isaiah (Luke 3:4); the book of Psalms (Luke 20:42; Acts 1:20).

103. LSJ, 315, 333; MM, 110.

104. Metzger 2005: 8, 12, 14.

105. MM, 396; Kelly 1963: 216; Comfort 1992: 46, 49–50; Richards 1998: 160–66; Towner 2006: 629. According to Kelly, *membrana* was a technical term for a codex or leaf-book made of parchment, widely used for notebooks, account books, and first drafts of literary works (1963: 216).

106. See 1 Tim 1:20 (Spencer 2013).

Some scholars have suggested that the Alexanders in Acts 19 and 2 Timothy 4 were all the same person: "The character of this Alexander appears to have been all too consistent with that of the other two references."[107] Other scholars have suggested that only the Alexanders in the Pastorals are the same. Paul describes "the same person in a different setting, and his expulsion from the church may have been the cause of his relocation to another place where he continued to oppose the apostle."[108] However, Paul may have used the modifier **the metalworker** to distinguish this Alexander from the other two, especially the Alexander Paul had previously mentioned in 1 Timothy 1:19–20.[109] A *chalkeus* was a smith who worked in metal, such as copper, iron, bronze, and brass.[110] The smith's trade was widespread in the countryside. Smiths worked in tool rooms, temples, stables, on boats, and irrigating machines.[111] The name **Alexandros** means "defender of men,"[112] but he was no defender of Paul. Probably at Troas,[113] he harmed Paul. Paul does not specify what **evil** Alexander manifested, but possibly he accused Paul, thereby getting him arrested. This Alexander is so antagonistic to the Christian teaching (**our words**), Paul warns Timothy to be on guard against him (**keep yourself away**; 4:15). Thus, if Demas had been a passive opponent (4:9), Alexander was an active opponent (4:14–15).

Paul then concludes this section of his letter (4:9–18) by explaining his legal situation: **In my first defense no one came to my aid, rather all abandoned me; may it not be counted against them; but the Lord stood by me and he strengthened me, in order that through me the proclamation might be fulfilled and all the Gentiles might hear, and I was rescued out of the lion's mouth** (4:16–17). Paul describes his legal **defense**, the first stage in his trial, the *prima actio*, a preliminary hearing before the emperor or a magistrate that precedes the actual trial, *secunda actio*. The previous time he had had a two-year delay after the preliminary hearing (Acts 24:27;

---

107. Brownrigg 1971: 23.
108. Towner 2006: 631; Zahn 1953: 2:21–22; Kelly 1963: 216.
109. See also Hendricksen 1957: 324–25.
110. LSJ, 1973; BDAG, 1076; Thayer, 664. *Chalkeus* is a different term than silversmith (Acts 19:24) and contrasts with gold and silver in the NT (Matt 10:9; Rev 18:12).
111. *TLNT* 3:497.
112. Thayer, 26.
113. If Alexander was where Timothy was, why would Paul have to warn Timothy? If Alexander was in Rome, why would Paul warn Timothy now rather than wait until he arrived in Rome? (Zahn 1953: 2:16–17, 22). Also, an association of metalworkers existed at Troas (Towner 2006: 631).

28:30).[114] He notes **no one** had the courage to take a stand in court as his witness or advocate.[115]

The historian Tacitus mentions the conviction of "vast numbers" of Christians who were arrested and, "on their disclosures," convicted to squelch the rumor that Nero had ordered the fire in Rome (*Ann*. 15.44). In addition, Tacitus adds that their convictions were not so much because of the charge of "arson as for hatred of the human race." Suetonius mentions the punishment of Christians as a permanent practice. Ramsay explains that Suetonius "considered Nero to have maintained a steady prosecution of a mischievous class of persons, in virtue of his duty to maintain peace and order in the city, and to have intended that this persecution should be permanent."[116] The Romans felt that the Christians were turning them from their ancestral ways, Roman manners and laws, customs, and religious beliefs. Christians "were bent on relaxing the bonds that held society together; they introduced divisions into families, and set children against their parents."[117] Christianity greatly influenced its converts, resulting in marvelous reformations, enthusiastic devotion, and unbending resolutions. To be able to have such changes implied to some the practice of magic. The persecution of Nero began by diverting popular attention, but it "continued as a permanent police measure under the form of a general prosecution of Christians as a sect dangerous to the public safety."[118] Active persecution of Christians persisted between AD 64–66 but became sporadic between 66–68. Sulpicius Severus wrote that Nero's persecution in 64 was "the beginning of severe measures against the Christians. Afterwards the religion was forbidden by formal laws."[119] Even when Nero left Rome in AD 66, the prefect of the city would still be bound to follow the example set by the Emperor. Moreover, Nero's action served as a precedent to guide the actions of all Roman officials in every province toward the Christians. There would be no need for a general edict or a formal law. In contrast, in

---

114. Fee 1988: 296; Kelly 1963: 218; Sherwin-White 1963: 111–19. Eusebius thinks 2 Tim 4:16 refers to the first imprisonment (*Hist. eccl.* 2.22) but why would all desert him since the procurators had said his case was excellent?

115. Witherington III (2006: 380) suggests no *patronus* or legal defender came forward; Mounce 2000: 595.

116. Ramsay 1893: 230–31.

117. Ramsay 1893: 236; Acts 16:21; Luke 14:26.

118. Ramsay 1893: 241, 237; 242. See 2 Tim 2:9; 1 Pet 2:12.

119. Ramsay 1893: 243.

later persecutions, acknowledgment of the Name of Jesus alone sufficed for condemnation.[120]

Thus, it appears as if Alexander's accusation resulted in Paul's arrest. Despite the accusation and the lack of support, Paul was not convicted, but neither was he freed. As a Roman citizen, he continued to appeal to the Emperor's tribunal.

Paul had reminded Timothy that the Lord had rescued him from all the persecutions in Antioch, Iconium, and Lystra.[121] Even though Paul had at this first trial been left abandoned (4:16), the Lord **stood by**[122] Paul and **strengthened** him (4:17). Unlike humans, the Lord never **abandons** because God is a faithful, covenant-keeping God.[123] God not only was present with Paul but also strengthened or empowered him.[124]

God's presence and strengthening had a goal: **in order that through me the proclamation might be fulfilled and all the Gentiles might hear** (4:17b). This was Paul's ministry (cf. 4:5), to bring God's name before Gentiles and kings and the people of Israel.[125] As a result of the Lord's empowerment, Paul **was rescued out of the lion's mouth** (4:17c). The **lion** was a symbol of strength[126] and confidence,[127] but also death and destruction,[128] as in, "[T]he people rise up like a lioness and they rouse themselves like a lion that does not rest till it devours its prey and drinks the blood of its victims" (Num 23:24; TNIV). The **lion's mouth** would be the penultimate point of destruction. In the Messianic Psalm 22, David describes his enemies: "They open wide their mouths at me, like a ravening and roaring lion" and cries out, "Save me from the mouth of the lion" (vv. 13, 21)! Some rulers were compared to roaring lions: "tearing the prey, they have devoured human lives."[129] Daniel's account of being cast into a den of lions, but remaining

---

120. Ramsay 1893: 245, 251. Active persecution of Christians continued with Emperor Domitian (Eusebius, *Hist. eccl.* 3.17).

121. See 2 Tim 3:11.

122. *Paristēmi*, to stand beside or near (Thayer, 489) is used literally in Mark 14:47, 69–70; 15:35, 39). Cf. Exod 34:5.

123. Heb 13:5–6; Deut 4:31; 31:6–8.

124. See 1 Tim 1:12 (Spencer 2013).

125. Acts 9:15. See 1 Tim 2:7 (Spencer 2013).

126. 2 Sam 1:23; 17:10; Job 4:10; Arrian, *Epict. diss.* 4.5 (37).

127. Prov 28:1; 30:30.

128. 1 Kings 13:24; 21:36; 2 Kings 17:25–26; Job 10:16; Jer 4:7; Ezek 19:2–3, 6–7.

129. E.g., Ezek 22:25, NRSV; 32:2; Isa 5:29; Prov 19:12; 20:2. Paul may be alluding throughout to Ps 22 since his trial, death, and resurrection are patterned after Jesus'

unharmed because an angel stopped the lion's mouth, became proverbial in later Israelite and Christian accounts.[130] Peter aptly describes the Christian adversary, the devil, "as a roaring lion who prowls around, looking for someone to devour" (1 Pet 5:8).

Could Paul have been writing literally? Probably not, since during Nero's reign Christians were tortured, burned, and mauled by dogs (Tacitus, *Ann.* 15.44), but not so much eaten by lions. Later, the animal hunts would include lions.[131] Moreover, Paul as a Roman citizen would be executed, not sent to the coliseum. The **lion** could represent Nero, because of his "ferocity,"[132] or his representative, the *praefectus praetorii* as judge, or Satan working through Nero. For example, imprisoned Agrippa was told about Emperor Tiberius, "The lion is dead," giving Agrippa hope for his release (Josephus, *Ant.* 18.6.10 [228]). Tiberius, like a lion, was "quick to anger and relentless in action . . . It was his bent to turn savage in every case that he decided; and he inflicted the death penalty even for the slightest offences" (*Ant.* 18 [226–27]). To employ a lion to depict tyrannical rulers has been a long-standing practice that Paul used to describe how he was saved at the last moment from death. God, like a shepherd, rescued Paul from the lion's mouth (Amos 3:12).

Paul then summarizes: **The Lord will rescue me from evil work and will save me into his heavenly kingdom** (4:18a). Alexander did much evil (*kakos*) against Paul, but the Lord rescued him from his **evil** (*ponēros*) goals. **Evil works** are the works of the world against which Jesus testified (John 7:7). They are done by God's enemies (Col 1:21). God rescued Paul and will rescue him again (4:17–18), but now he emphasizes that God will save him for his kingdom, the **heavenly** one, not necessarily his earthly kingdom (4:18).[133] With this thought about his preservation for the heavenly kingdom, Paul, like many a rabbi, breaks out into a blessing: **to whom be the glory forever and ever, amen!** (4:18b). In the Pastorals, Paul has written about **glory** that is continuous and immeasurable (2:10) and now

---

passion (Towner 2006: 638–49; Laansma [Belleville 2009]; 214–17).

130. Dan 6:22; 1 Macc 2:60; 4 Macc 16:3; 18:13; Heb 11:33; 1 Clem 45:6.

131. E.g., *Mart. Pol.* 12.2; Eusebius, *Hist. eccl.* 5.1.

132. Eusebius, *Hist. eccl.* 2.22. Nero was preferred by the early Greek fathers (Zahn 1953: 2:23).

133. See 2 Tim 4:1; Rom 8:31, 35, 38–39.

he ascribes that same glory back to God (4:18). Jesus has such glory and his gospel has this glory.[134]

Greetings (4:19-22)

Paul concludes his letter by sending final greetings to coworkers who are with or near Timothy. He asks Timothy to **Greet Prisca and Aquila and the household of Onesiphorus** (4:19). These two households are dedicated to promoting God's reign. **Prisca** (her nickname in Roman style is lengthened to Priscilla) and Aquila are mentioned several times in the New Testament.[135] Aquila is a Jew from Pontus (near the Black Sea). Some have theorized that Aquila (and probably Prisca) had been in Jerusalem for Pentecost (Acts 2:9-10).[136] They had been living in Rome, Italy, and when Emperor Claudius in AD 49 had thrown the Jews out of Rome for their quarrels about the Christ,[137] they brought their tentmaking business to Corinth in Achaia, an important trade center. Paul stayed with them over a year and a half, becoming partners in tentmaking with them (Acts 18:5). Together in Corinth in AD 50-51, they joined Paul when he moved on, arriving in Ephesus in Asia around 51-52. Afterwards, Paul traveled back to his home church in Antioch (Acts 18:18-22). In Ephesus, about a year later, Prisca and Aquila more accurately expounded to Apollos Christian doctrine, in particular about baptism.[138] During their stay in Ephesus, Aquila

---

134. See Titus 1:2; 2:13; 1 Tim 1:11; 3:16. Forty-six percent of the references to *doxa* (**glory**) in the NT are used by Paul. A similar blessing for God also occurs in 1 Tim 1:17; Rom 11:36; 16:27; Gal 1:5; Phil 4:20.

135. Twice Aquila's name precedes Priscilla's and four times Priscilla's name precedes Aquila's. Luke presents Aquila's name first in a formal way (Acts 18:2). He always describes the wife as "Priscilla," her nickname, showing his affection for her, but afterwards mentions her name first as the predominant one in this teaching and pastoring couple (Acts 18:18-19, 24-28). Paul, like Luke, usually mentions her first, but calls her the more formal "Prisca" to give dignity to her as his teaching coworker (1 Cor 16:19; Rom 16:3; 2 Tim 4:19). Some later translations have reversed the order of their names in Acts 18:26 but the earliest best quality Greek manuscripts have "Priscilla and Aquila" (see the fourth-century codices Sinaiticus and Vaticanus).

136. Some scholars think Prisca was a Gentile. However, unlike Timothy's parents who are explicitly named as interreligious, Prisca is not said to be Gentile. Intermarriage between Jews and Gentiles was highly disproved since it was against Jewish laws and customs (Josephus, *Ant.* 18.9.5 [345]). Thus, if Prisca was a Gentile, I think, Luke would have mentioned it.

137. Acts 18:2; Suetonius, *Claudius* 25.4.

138. Acts 18:24-26; Spencer 1985: 107.

and Prisca greet the believers in Corinth. They are pastoring and teaching a church which met in their home (1 Cor 16:19). After Emperor Claudius dies in AD 54, they return to Rome. Paul describes them as coworkers, colleagues in ministry who prepare believers for ministry and to whom the churches were to be subject.[139] In Rome, by AD 57, again they have a church in their home (Rom 16:3–5). Paul reports they risked their own "neck" on behalf of his life (Rom 16:4), using the image of an execution where the prisoner "places" his/her neck "under" the sword.[140] Like Paul, they emphasized their ministry outreach to the Gentiles.[141] After Paul's release from imprisonment in Rome, they had returned to Ephesus (almost ten years after Romans was written), most likely, with Timothy, to continue their teaching ministry among the Gentiles.

Prisca and Aquila are remarkable for their ministering as a couple together and as equals. Even in a patriarchal culture, Priscilla was honored for her teaching abilities. They are always mentioned together and are always ministering together. Both were tentmakers by trade, both offered hospitality to Paul and to others, both were teachers, both traveled together, both were church overseers, and both risked their lives for Paul. They scheduled their business so that they could take church leadership positions wherever they went and offered their economic resources to other believers. Their time, money, and lives were given over to the promotion of God's reign. Possibly they informed Paul of the spiritual condition of the Roman churches before he wrote to the Romans. Paul had a special relationship with them. They are the first people whom he greets in his letter to Rome. They have the most extensive description in Romans 16:3–15. Prisca and Aquila ministered to many and were appreciated by many. They are a wonderful illustration of a couple who have taken seriously God's mandate for a married couple together to subdue the earth and have dominion over it.[142]

Remains of the homes of **Prisca and Aquila** are still recognized today in Rome. Near the Tiber River, the Church of Saint Prisca, in the area of Aventino, was built over the house of Prisca and Aquila. Archaeological excavations have unearthed an early Roman Christian place of worship

---

139. See 2 Tim 4:11.

140. *Hypotithēmi*; *Trachēlos* refers to "the whole neck and throat, the back part of the neck in human beings" (LSJ, 1811).

141. 2 Tim 4:17; Rom 16:4. Aquila and Prisca, as Jews, are partners with the Gentiles, symbolizing the ideal of a united, mutually loving Jewish and Gentile church which Paul extols to the Romans (Rom 1:16; 11:17–24; 15:7–16; Zahn 1953: 1:391).

142. Gen 1:28; Spencer 2009: 22–24.

and Mithras worship. Peter stayed with them for a while.[143] Further outside Rome, on the Via Salaria, an old Roman road used for commerce, near a main gate was a villa owned by Prisca and Aquila. The property was later donated by Prisca to the Christian community for burial (Catacombs of Saint Priscilla).[144] In one of the oldest areas of the catacombs under the original villa was found a burial inscription: "M(anio) Acilius c.v. ('most illustrious man') . . . and Priscilla C. (f.) ('most illustrious woman')." "C.V." indicates that both of them belonged to families of senatorial rank, the family of Acilius. Suetonius, in the *Life of Domitian* mentions that Emperor Domitian (AD 81-96) condemned to death "many senators, some of whom had been consuls, among them . . . Acilius Glabrione, the latter having been exiled. They were accused of wanting to introduce new things." This general charge, akin to that of atheism, would relate to the practice of calling Christianity an entirely "new concept," in contrast with that of idolatry, "where the brotherhood of all who had been baptized was recognized, with no discrimination for reasons of social condition or of national origin." Manius Acilii Glabriones is a relative of Pudens.[145] When Paul thanks Prisca and Aquila because "they placed their own neck" to help him and also the church of the Gentiles (Rom 16:3-4), possibly they used their senatorial rank to speak to proconsul Gallio in Corinth before Paul was brought to court, despite the danger of being themselves accused and executed (Acts 18:6-16).[146]

The household of Onesiphorus (4:19b), mentioned earlier, who had visited Paul in Rome, was now in Ephesus.[147] Paul mentions two coworkers about whom Timothy might have been concerned or whom he expected to be with Paul: **Erastus remained in Corinth, and I left Trophimus in**

---

143. The legend appears to confuse Prisca and Priscilla, describing Prisca, the daughter of Aquila and Priscilla, who accompanied Paul on missionary voyages, and was baptized by Peter. (Roman children were regularly called by the same name as their parents [Barnes 1933: 29-33; Morton 1937: 471].) In a similar manner, in some translations and by Latin church father Ambrosiaster (AD 384), "Priscilla" replaces "Prisca" in 1 Cor 16:19 and in Rom 16:3. But, the earliest Greek mss. support "Prisca" in those references. Peter later stayed on Via Nomentana near the Church of Saint Agnes (Barnes 1903: 34).

144. The pagans used to cremate the dead, but the Christians wanted to retain the bones of the dead so that they would be ready to be resurrected at the last judgment. Rich and poor were buried together in an egalitarian spirit.

145. Carletti 2007: 5, 9-11; Barnes 1903: 31-32.

146. Some traditions suggest that Aquila and Prisca went to Spain and were martyred there (Baring-Gould 1898: 7:183).

147. See 2 Tim 1:16-18.

Miletus, being sick (4:20). Possibly, they had begun to accompany Paul on his final journey to Rome. **Erastus** ("beloved")[148] probably is the same one mentioned in Acts 19, whom Paul sent ahead with Timothy from Ephesus to Macedonia. Described as "the ones ministering with" Paul (19:22), Erastus and Timothy are coworkers, Paul sending them ahead to Macedonia to prepare the churches for the collection for the Jerusalem Christians offering and to meet Titus there.[149]

Is this **Erastus** the same mentioned in Romans 16:23, a steward (*oikonomos*) of a city? A "steward" could be a manager of a household or here of a city-state, who would oversee the property, receive and pay bills, plan expenditures, apportion food, and oversee people.[150] A good manager would be trustworthy. If the Erastus of Acts had been in Ephesus with Paul and was traveling to Macedonia, how could he be functioning about the same time as manager of another city? Such an official would not be able to leave his city for a long period.[151] If Erastus is the same Erastus discovered in a first-century inscription on a marble in Corinth ("Erastus, commissioner for public works, laid this pavement at his own expense"),[152] then the Erastus mentioned in 2 Timothy 4:20 would have remained in his hometown, Corinth.

Trophimus and Tychicus were from Asia.[153] They, along with Timothy and others, had accompanied Paul from Achaia through Macedonia, Troas, and Miletus to Caesarea and Jerusalem to help guard the collection for the Jews in Jerusalem and, as well, to represent their churches and provinces (Rom 15:25–27). **Miletus**, where he was left sick, is a city right on the Aegean Sea, about thirty miles south from Ephesus (Acts 20:15, 17). Founded by Cretans, it was one of the oldest and most important cities in Ionia. With four harbors, it was an active and prominent harbor city. Jews lived there free to celebrate their festivals. The city had a synagogue.[154]

---

148. Thayer, 247.

149. Paul then writes 2 Cor together with Timothy from Macedonia (2 Cor 1:1; 9:2 [AD 56–57]; Spencer 1998b: 63).

150. See Titus 1:7.

151. Possibly Romans was written from Philippi in Macedonia during Acts 20:6 (Spencer 1998b: 63–65).

152. Cranfield 1983: 2:807.

153. Acts 20:4; see 2 Tim 4:12; Titus 3:12.

154. Trebilco 1994: 361–62; Yamauchi 1980: 115, 125; Strabo, *Geogr.* 14.1.4, 6 (Miletus and Ephesus are the "most famous" Ionian cities); Josephus, *Ant.* 14.10.21 (244–46).

Trophimus was a Gentile from Ephesus. Because he was present with Paul, some Jews from Asia falsely accused Paul of bringing this Gentile into the temple in Jerusalem (Acts 21:27–29). Thus, ultimately, Trophimus is responsible for Paul's arrest and first imprisonment in Jerusalem, Caesarea, and Rome (Eph 3:1). Paul never had the opportunity to explain in Jerusalem that Trophimus never entered the temple. In his defense speech, when Paul repeated the Lord's call to him: "Go, for, I myself, I will send you to Gentiles far away," the crowd became so wild, the tribune had to remove Paul (Acts 22:21–24). Apparently, Trophimus tried to accompany Paul on this journey almost ten years later, but, when Trophimus became **sick**, Paul left him behind at some household or inn to be healed.[155]

Paul now succinctly states his main reason for writing: **Make every effort, before winter, to come** (4:21a)! This is the third time Paul uses the imperative of *spoudazō* in this letter: **Make every effort** to present yourself to God (2:15) and make every effort to come to me quickly (4:9).[156] Because of dangerous **winter** weather, safe traveling was done between May through October (or, at the far limits, March 10 to Nov 10). The dangers of winter sailing were "scant daylight, long nights, dense cloud cover, poor visibility, and the violence of the winds doubled by the addition of rain or snow."[157] The trip from Ephesus to Rome might take anywhere from two weeks to two months.[158] Walkers averaged fifteen to twenty miles a day and coastal ships twenty-five to thirty-five miles a day. Timothy had a lot to do before he could arrive in Rome. Not only did he have to stop at Troas to pick up Paul's belongings (4:13) and follow all the directions Paul has given in 2 Timothy for the church in Ephesus, but he also had to do the many activities necessary before travel. Land or sea voyagers would have to bring their own clothing, supplies for cooking, eating, bathing, and sleeping (from pots and pans down to mattresses and bedding), and servants to pack, cook,

---

155. According to tradition, he became the first bishop of Arles in Gaul and, like Paul, he was martyred during Nero's persecution at Rome (Brownrigg 1971: 440; Baring-Gould 1897: 15:322–23).

156. I have chosen the rendering **make every effort** or "to be especially conscientious in discharging an obligation," rather than simply "to proceed quickly, hurry" (BDAG, 939), because in every NT reference to *spoudazō* and *spoudaios* outside of 2 Tim 4:9, 21 and Titus 3:12, "hurry" does not fit the context as well. For example, Paul exhorts Timothy to "make every effort to be approved" by God in 2 Tim 2:15. Also, even in 1 Thess where Paul does refer to a trip, as in 2 Tim 4:21, he made the effort but was not able to come (1 Thess 2:17–18).

157. Casson 1971: 272; Casson 1974: 150; Rapske 1994: 22.

158. Casson 1971: 297–98. See Titus 3:12; 2 Tim 4:9.

and prepare the beds. To travel by ship, Timothy would have to go to the waterfront and find a vessel scheduled to sail in the direction he wanted to go, then book a passage with the master of the ship, often applying for an exit pass and waiting for the herald's cry that the vessel was ready to leave.[159]

Paul now closes with greetings from Christians in Rome: **Eubulus greets you and Pudens and Linus and Claudia and all the brothers and sisters** (4:21b). Even though many have abandoned Paul, he was not abandoned by Eubulus, Pudens, Linus, and Claudia, and other believers. **Eubulus** literally signifies "prudent."[160] Rome has significant archaeological and traditional information on Pudens and Claudia. **Pudens** was probably a senator. A church was built over the home of Pudens and **Claudia** (now the Basilica of Santa Pudenziana). They had used their home for worship.[161] Pudens was a member of the Acilii Glabriones family (probably related to Aquila). His sons (Novatus and Timotheus) ran Roman thermal baths. Pudens married Claudia, who was British. After being captured by Emperor Claudius and sent to Rome, the family was set at liberty, eventually introducing Christianity into Britain.[162] According to a repeated tradition, Peter lived in their house in AD 64. Pudens and Claudia's daughters, Pudentiana and Prassede (Praxedes) are remembered today by churches in their names.[163] **Linus**, possibly an Italian from Tuscany, lived with Pudens. He became the second bishop in Rome, after Peter, and is buried near Peter in the Vatican under St. Peter's Basilica, where a coffin reads "Linus." The

---

159. Casson 1974: 153–55; 176–78; Ramsay 2001: 253–55.

160. LSJ, 707; Thayer, 257. These four people are mentioned only here in the New Testament. These five entities are presented in polysyndeton, treating each person or group of equal importance.

161. The first-century house and second-century baths remain under the current fourth-century church building.

162. Baring-Gould 1898: 9:82–86; 5:262. In contrast, other scholars conclude that the Claudia in 2 Tim 4:21 is not this Claudia (Zahn 1953: 2:21). Lightfoot (1890: 77–79) notes another tradition that considers Pudens's wife to be Sabinella and mentions a different married Pudens and Claudia in the imperial household.

163. After her father Pudens, brother Novatus, and sister Pudentiana died, Prassede used her wealth to build a church, where she concealed many Christians persecuted by Emperor Antonius Pius. Pudens, Pudentiana, and eventually Prassede died as Christian martyrs and were buried in the cemetery of St. Priscilla. However, later the remains of Prassede and Pudentiana were removed by Pope Paschal I (ninth century) to the Basilicas of Saint Prassede and Saint Praxedes in Rome. The Basilica of Saint Praxedes also honors the mother of Pope Paschal I, bishop ("Episcopa") Theodora.

bishops of Rome for two centuries all lived at Pudens's home at Via Urbana in Rome.[164]

Paul closes with a brief two-part benediction: **The Lord be with your spirit. Grace be with you** (4:22). The first sentence is addressed to Timothy since **your** is singular, while the second sentence is addressed to the church, since **you** is plural. The **Lord** had been present with Paul during his first defense and rescued him (4:17-18).[165] Paul would want the same benefits for Timothy as he joins him in suffering for Christ. Paul and Timothy could be assured the Lord was with them because Jesus promised it: "Behold I myself am with you all the days until the end of the age" (Matt 28:20).

Paul uses *pneuma* in the Pastorals to refer to the human **spirit** (2 Tim 1:7; 1 Tim 3:16) as well as to the Holy Spirit (2 Tim 1:14; 1 Tim 4:1; Titus 3:5). The human spirit is that inner aspect of a person that self-examines and reaches up to communicate to God's Spirit with the Holy Spirit's aid.[166] The human spirit, so necessary for life,[167] comprehends deep thoughts within oneself and within others.[168] Paul closes this letter with the same farewell as in 1 Timothy.[169] By using the plural **you**, he shows that, although he addresses Timothy, he writes to him in the context of the whole church. In 2 Timothy, **grace** was in Christ Jesus and revealed in the incarnation and is available to humans.[170] Thus, the Lord is present in a personal, compassionate, and merciful manner.

---

164. Barnes 1903: 42-43, 56-57, 72-74, 304, 310-12; Finegan 1981: 232, 234; Barnes 1933: 33-34; Morton 1937: 348-49, 470; Meisner 1988: 1-2; Gallio 2009: 1-2; McRay 1991: 348-49; Eusebius, *Hist. eccl.* 3.2, 4, 13, 21; 5.6; Irenaeus, *Haer.* 3.3.3.

165. In 2 Tim **the Lord** explicitly refers to Christ Jesus (1:2, 8) or is not specified (1:16, 18; 2:7, 19, 22, 24; 3:11; 4:8, 14, 17-18). The **Lord** in 2 Tim is also described as personal, merciful, giving understanding, a master who helps, and judges.

166. 1 Cor 2:10-13; Luke 1:47; Rom 1:9; 8:16; 1 Cor 14:14-15; 2 Cor 2:13. Towner defines the human spirit as "that dimension of human life which is characterized by the capacity for interrelating with God" (2006: 655).

167. Luke 8:55; 23:46; Jas 2:26.

168. Mark 2:8; John 11:33; 13:21; Acts 17:16.

169. See 1 Tim 6:21 (Spencer 2013).

170. 2 Tim 1:9-10; 2:1.

Fusing the Horizons: Coworkers

The Pastorals are letters that illustrate the work of team ministers and coworkers, including not only Paul, Timothy, and Titus, but also Onesiphorus' household, Demas, Crescens, Luke, Mark, Tychicus, Carpus, Prisca, Aquila, Erastus, Trophimus, Eubulus, Pudens, Linus, Claudia, Artemas, Zenas, and Apollos. Paul has worked with his coworkers in a variety of ways. Some serve as avant garde; others follow-up; some are replaced (Tychicus and Timothy). Some travel Paul commissions (sends or designates). Other travel is uncommissioned (Crescens, Titus) and some is desertion (Demas). Thus, some coworkers are faithful (Luke), others unfaithful.

Even as God is triune and a "team," so is ministry in God's name a team effort. Ministry teams have diverse people, in diverse stages of availability (e.g., illness limited Trophimus) and married and single people can take part and they should all have one purpose: to promote the good news. Team members can encourage each other in difficult as well as daily situations, since no one is too mature not to need a team.

Here are summarized some basic principles:

1. We need to *know* other Christians in order that their gifts can be discerned and then used in a cooperative ministry.
2. We need a *structure flexible* enough to allow different persons to come into a church periodically as they are needed.
3. *Team ministry* is biblical. The lone-ranger minister is not a biblical model. (Although even the Lone Ranger had Tonto.) Two is a minimum. However, not all Christians have to be under our own authority or in our program to be worth supporting or cooperating with.
4. Concern for a person and assistance in a ministry should be demonstrated in *material* as well as emotional terms. Presence is important.

Bibliography

Aune, David E. 1987. *The New Testament in Its Literary Environment*. LEC. Philadelphia: Westminster.
Barclay, William. 1966. *The First Three Gospels*. Philadelphia: Westminster.
Baring-Gould, S. 1897–1898. *The Lives of the Saints*. 16 vols. London: John C. Nimmo.
Barnes, Arthur Stapylton. 1903. *St. Peter in Rome: And His Tomb on the Vatican Hill*. London: Swan Sonnenschein.
———. 1933. *The Martyrdom of St. Peter and St. Paul*. London: Oxford University Press.
Bassler, Jouette M. 1996. *1 Timothy, 2 Timothy, Titus*. ANTC. Nashville: Abingdon.
Belleville, Linda L., Jon C. Laansma, J. Ramsey Michaels. 2009. *Cornerstone Biblical Commentary: 1 Timothy, 2 Timothy, Titus, Hebrews*. Carol Stream, IL: Tyndale House.
Bernard, J. H. 1922. *The Pastoral Epistles*. CGTSC. Cambridge: Cambridge University Press.
Branigan, Keith, and Michael Vickers. 1980. *Hellas: The Civilizations of Ancient Greece*. New York: McGraw-Hill.
Brooten, Bernadette J. 1982. *Women Leaders in the Ancient Synagogue: Inscriptional Evidence and Background Issues*. Brown Judaic Studies 36. Chico, CA: Scholars.
Brownrigg, Ronald. 1971. *Who's Who in the New Testament*. New York: Holt, Rinehart, and Winston.
Bruce, F. F. 1990. *The Acts of the Apostles: Greek Text with Introduction and Commentary*. 3rd ed. Grand Rapids: Eerdmans.
Calvin, John. N.d. *Calvin's Commentaries*. Vol. 10, *John-Acts*. Wilmington: Associated Publishers and Authors.
Campbell, Horace. 1987. *Rasta and Resistance: From Marcus Garvey to Walter Rodney*. Trenton: Africa World.
Carletti, Sandro. 2007. *Guide to the Catacombs of Priscilla*. Trans. Alice Mulhern. Vatican City: Pontifical Commission for Sacred Archaeology.
Casson, Lionel. 1971. *Ships and Seamanship in the Ancient World*. Princeton: Princeton University Press.
———. 1974. *Travel in the Ancient World*. Toronto: Hakkert.
Comfort, Philip. 1992. *The Quest for the Original Text of the New Testament*. Grand Rapids: Baker.
Cranfield, C. E. B. 1983. *A Critical and Exegetical Commentary on The Epistle to the Romans*. ICC. 2 vols. Edinburgh: T. & T. Clark.
Dibelius, Martin, and Hans Conzelmann. 1972. *The Pastoral Epistles*. Hermeneia. Trans. P. Buttolph and A. Yarbro. Ed. H. Koester. Philadelphia: Fortress.
Donaldson, T. L. 1985 "Thessalonica." In *Major Cities of the Biblical World*, edited by R. K. Harrison, 258–65. Nashville: Nelson.
Ellis, E. Earle. 1971. "Paul and His Co-Workers." *NTS* 17, no. 4, 437–52.
Fantham, Elaine, et al. 1994. *Women in the Classical World: Image and Text*. New York: Oxford University Press.

Farrar, F. W. 1883. *The Early Days of Christianity.* New York: Funk & Wagnalls.
Fee, Gordon D. 1988. *NIBC: 1 and 2 Timothy, Titus.* Peabody, MA: Hendrickson.
Finegan, Jack. 1981. *The Archeology of the New Testament: The Mediterranean World of the Early Christian Apostles.* Boulder, CO: Westview.
Gallio, Paola. 2009. *The Basilica of Saint Praxedes.* Rome: Monaci Benedettini Vallombrosani.
Gardiner, E. Norman. 1980. *Athletics of the Ancient World.* Chicago: Ares.
Gordon, Cyrus H. 1987. "Minoan Civilization." In *CE* 16:330–35.
Hansen, G. Walter. 1994. "Galatia." In *The Book of Acts in Its First Century Setting*, ed. David W. J. Gill and Conrad Gempf, 2:377–95. Grand Rapids: Eerdmans.
Hanson, A. T. 1982. *The Pastoral Epistles.* NCBC. Grand Rapids: Eerdmans.
Harris, Murray J. 1992. *Jesus as God: The New Testament Use of Theos in Reference to Jesus.* Grand Rapids: Baker.
Harris, R. Laird. 1969. *Inspiration and Canonicity of the Bible: An Historical and Exegetical Study.* 2nd ed. Grand Rapids: Zondervan.
Hawkes, Jacquetta. 1968. *Dawn of the Gods.* New York: Random.
Heine, Ronald E. 2002. *The Commentaries of Origen and Jerome on St. Paul's Epistle to the Ephesians.* Oxford Early Christian Studies. Oxford: Oxford University Press.
Hendricksen, William. 1957. *New Testament Commentary: Exposition of The Pastoral Epistles.* Grand Rapids: Baker.
Holmes, Michael W., trans. 2007. *The Apostolic Fathers.* 3rd ed. Grand Rapids: Baker.
Hood, Sinclair. 1971. *The Minoans: The Story of Bronze Age Crete.* New York: Praeger.
Horsley, G. H. R. 1987. "Early Evidence of Women Officers in the Church." *Priscilla Papers* 1, no. 4, 3–4.
Hunt, A. S., and C. C. Edgar, trans. 1932. *Select Papyri I.* LCL. Cambridge, MA: Harvard University Press.
Johnson, Luke Timothy. 1996. *Letters to Paul's Delegates: 1 Timothy, 2 Timothy, Titus.* New Testament in Context. Valley Forge, PA: Trinity.
Kearsley, R. A. 1994. "The Asiarchs." In *The Book of Acts in Its First Century Setting*, edited by David W. J. Gill and Conrad Gempf, 2:363–76. Grand Rapids: Eerdmans.
Kelly, J. N. D. 1963. *A Commentary on The Pastoral Epistles (1 Timothy, 2 Timothy, Titus).* HNTC. New York: Harper & Row.
Kohlenberger III, John R., Edward W. Goodrick, and James A. Swanson. 1995. *The Exhaustive Concordance to the Greek New Testament.* Grand Rapids: Zondervan.
Kroeger, Catherine Clark, and Mary J. Evans, eds. 2002. *The IVP Women's Bible Commentary.* Downers Grove, IL: InterVarsity.
Lampe, Peter. 1993. "The Family of New Testament Times." *Church and Society* 84, no. 2, 18–38.
Levine, Lee I. 2000. *The Ancient Synagogue: The First Thousand Years.* New Haven: Yale University Press.
Lightfoot, J. B. 1890. *The Apostolic Fathers. Part I. S. Clement of Rome 1.* New York: Macmillan.
———. 1913. *St. Paul's Epistle to the Philippians.* Grand Rapids: Zondervan.
Lock, Walter. 1924. *A Critical and Exegetical Commentary on The Pastoral Epistles.* ICC. Edinburgh: T. & T. Clark.
McRay, John. 1991. *Archaeology and the New Testament.* Grand Rapids: Baker.
Marshall, I. Howard. 1999. *A Critical and Exegetical Commentary on The Pastoral Epistles.* ICC. Edinburgh: T. & T. Clark.

Marshall, John W. 2008. "'I Left You in Crete': Narrative Deception and Social Hierarchy in the Letter to Titus." *JBL* 127:781–803.

Meisner, Joachin. 1988. *Saint Pudenziana's Basilica*. Rome: St. Pudentiana's Rectorate.

Metzger, Bruce M. 1953. "The Jehovah's Witnesses and Jesus Christ." *ThTo* 10, 65–85.

Metzger, Bruce M., and Bart D. Ehrman. 2005. *The Text of the New Testament: Its Transmission, Corruption, and Restoration*. 4th ed. New York: Oxford University Press.

Morton, H. V. 1937. *In the Steps of St. Paul*. New York: Dodd, Mead.

Mounce, William D. 2000. *WBC 46: Pastoral Epistles*. Nashville: Nelson,

Ngewa, Samuel. 2009. *1 and 2 Timothy and Titus*. African Bible Commentary Series. Grand Rapids: Zondervan.

Nilsson, Martin P. 1971. *The Minoan-Mycenaean Religion and Its Survival in Greek Religion*. 2nd ed. New York: Biblo and Tannen.

Poirier, John C. 2010. "Scripture and Canon." In *The Sacred Text: Excavating the Texts, Exploring the Interpretations, and Engaging the Theologies of the Christian Scriptures*, edited by Michael Bird and Michael Pahl, 83–98. Piscataway, NJ: Gorgias.

Ramsay, W. M. 1893. *The Church in the Roman Empire before A.D. 170*. London: Putnam's.

———. 2001. *St. Paul: The Traveler and Roman Citizen*. Edited by Mark Wilson. Grand Rapids: Kregel.

Rapske, Brian M. 1994. "Acts, Travel and Shipwreck." In *The Book of Acts in Its First Century Setting*, edited by David W. J. Gill and Conrad Gempf, 2:1–47. Grand Rapids: Eerdmans.

Richards, E. Randolph. 1998. "The Codex and the Early Collection of Paul's Letters." *BBR* 8:151–66.

Robertson, A. T. 1930–1931. *Word Pictures in the New Testament*. 6 vols. Nashville: Broadman.

———. 1934. *A Grammar of the Greek New Testament in the Light of Historical Research*. Nashville: Broadman.

Scheck, Thomas P., trans. 2010. *St. Jerome's Commentaries on Galatians, Titus, and Philemon*. Notre Dame: University of Notre Dame Press.

Schürer, Emil. 1979. *The History of the Jewish People in the Age of Jesus Christ (175 B.C.-A.D. 135)*. 4 vols. Edited by Geza Vermes, Fergus Millar, and Matthew Black. 2nd ed. Edinburgh: T. & T. Clark.

Sherwin-White, A. N. 1963. *Roman Society and Roman Law in the New Testament*. Oxford: Clarendon.

Sider, Ronald J. 2005. *The Scandal of the Evangelical Conscience: Why Are Christians Living Just Like the Rest of the World?* Grand Rapids: Baker.

Smith, James. 1880. *The Voyage and Shipwreck of St. Paul*. 4th ed. Grand Rapids: Baker.

Spencer, Aída Besançon. 1985. *Beyond the Curse: Women Called to Ministry*. Peabody, MA: Hendrickson.

———. 1990a. "God's Order Is Love." *Brethren in Christ History and Life* 13, 39–50.

———. 1994. *Joy Through the Night: Biblical Resources on Suffering*. Eugene, OR: Wipf & Stock.

———. 1998b. *Paul's Literary Style: A Stylistic and Historical Comparison of 2 Corinthians 11:16–12:13, Romans 8:9–39, and Philippians 3:2–4:13*. Lanham, MD: University Press of America.

———. 1998c. "Exclusive Language-Is It Accurate?" *RevExp* 95, no. 3, 383–95.

———. 2000. "Peter's Pedagogical Method in 1 Peter 3:6." *BBR* 10, no. 1, 107–19.

———. 2001. *2 Corinthians*. People's Bible Commentary. Oxford: BRF.

———. 2004. "Jesus' Treatment of Women in the Gospels." In *Discovering Biblical Equality: Complementarity without Hierarchy*, edited by R. W. Pierce and R. M. Groothuis, 126–41. Downers Grove, IL: InterVarsity.

———. 2005. "'El Hogar' as Ministry Team: Stephana(s)'s Household." In *Hispanic Christian Thought at the Dawn of the 21st Century: Apuntes in Honor of Justo L. González*, edited by Alvin Padilla, Roberto Goizueta, and Eldin Villafañe, 69–77. Nashville: Abingdon.

———. 2007. "The Denial of the Good News and the Ending of Mark." *BBR* 17, no. 2, 269–83.

———. 2013. *1 Timothy*, NCCS. Eugene, OR: Cascade.

Spencer, Aída Besançon, and William David Spencer, eds. 1998a. *The Global God: Multicultural Evangelical Views of God*. Grand Rapids: Baker.

Spencer, Aída Besançon, et al. 2009. *Marriage at the Crossroads: Couples in Conversation about Discipleship, Gender Roles, Decision Making and Intimacy*. Downers Grove, IL: InterVarsity.

Spencer, William David. 1989. "The Power in Paul's Teaching." *JETS* 32, no. 1, 51–61.

Stephens, William H. 1987. *The New Testament World in Pictures*. Nashville: Broadman.

Towner, Philip H. 2006. *The Letters to Timothy and Titus*. NICNT. Grand Rapids: Eerdmans.

Willetts, R. F. 1965. *Ancient Crete: A Social History, From Early Times until the Roman Occupation*. Studies in Social History. Toronto: University of Toronto Press.

Witherington, Ben, III. 2006. *Letters and Homilies for Hellenized Christians*. Vol. 1, *A Socio-Rhetorical Commentary on Titus, 1-2 Timothy and 1-3 John*. Downers Grove, IL: InterVarsity.

———. 2007. *The Letters to Philemon, the Colossians, and the Ephesians: A Socio-Rhetorical Commentary on the Captivity Epistles*. Grand Rapids: Eerdmans.

Yamauchi, Edwin M. 1973. *Pre-Christian Gnosticism: A Survey of the Proposed Evidences*. Grand Rapids: Eerdmans.

———.1980. *New Testament Cities in Western Asia Minor: Light from Archaeology on Cities of Paul and the Seven Churches of Revelation*. Grand Rapids: Baker.

Yarchin, William. 2012. "Scripture as a Spiritual Phenomenon: The Evidence of the 11Q Psalms Scroll Collophon." *BBR* 22, 363–81.

Zahn, Theodor. 1953. *Introduction to the New Testament*. 3 vols. Minneapolis: Klock & Klock.

Subject Index

Aaron, 111, 123, 133
Abraham, 23, 63–64
Adam, 21, 130
adultery, 14, 27
Agrippa, 66, 76, 93n, 144–45, 152
Alexander, v, 75, 109, 120, 127, 148–49, 151–52
Ananias, 79
Ananias, and Sapphira, 48
anger, 13, 17–19, 39, 42n, 115–16, 152
Antioch, 8, 36, 126, 151, 153
Apollos, 70–72, 153, 160
appearing (*epiphaneia*), 51, 86–87, 133–34, 142–43
Aquila. *See* Prisca, and Aquila.
Aretas, 60
argument(s). *See* heterodoxy.
Aristotle, 16, 42, 46, 62
Artemas, 68–70, 72, 160
Artemis, 3–4
Asia, 70, 75–76, 80, 90–92, 145, 147, 153, 156–57
athlete (athletics), 19, 31, 98–99, 139–41
attack, not open (*anenklētos*), 14–15, 17, 41, 45
beast(s) (*thērion*), 25–26
beloved, 47, 70, 79–80, 145, 156
belly (*gastēr*), 26
Bible. *See* Scriptures.
blaspheme. *See* slander.
Brooten, Bernadette, 34–35
Callimachus, 24
calling, 86–88, 113–14
Calvin, John, 12n
Carpus, 147, 160
Cerinthus, 29–30

charge(s) (*katēgoria/diamartyromai*), 14–15, 17, 52, 105, 133–35, 138, 150, 155.
See also attack, not open.
child(ren), 13–16, 20, 36, 40–43, 55, 68, 79, 83, 91, 94, 110, 119, 128, 135n, 150, 155n
Cicero, 24
circumcision (*peritomē*), 12, 14, 18, 20–23, 26–27, 29–31, 48, 54n, 59, 67, 107, 119
Claudia, v, 158, 160
Claudius, 153–54, 158, 160
clean. *See* pure.
Clement, 54, 57n
Clement, of Alexandria, 24
cloak, 147
conscience, 20, 22, 30, 67, 81, 88, 95, 97, 107, 109, 114, 148
Cornelia, 83
coworker(s), v, 1, 8, 10, 15, 68–70, 91, 106, 142–47, 153–54, 156, 160
Crescens, v, 75, 144, 160
Crete, 3–4, 8–10, 12, 14–16, 18–19, 21, 24–26, 28, 34, 36, 40–41, 44–45, 54, 58–60, 64, 75, 156
crown, 8n, 98, 140–42
Daniel, 151–52
David, 9, 93n, 100, 104, 151
days, last, 117–21
death, 42, 75, 79, 86–88, 100, 102–3, 109, 139, 151
Demas, v, 75, 91n, 110, 142–44, 149, 160
demeanor (*katastēma*), 33, 35, 38
deny, 49–50, 59, 85, 104, 120
devil, 38–39, 116–18, 121, 152. *See also* slander.

165

drinking. *See* wine.
education, 31–32, 58, 83, 94–95, 108, 123, 128–29. *See also* teaching.
elder(s), 10–14, 18–20, 24, 27, 33–41, 44, 47–49, 95, 119. *See also* overseer.
elect, 101–2
Elizabeth. *See* Zechariah.
empty talk (*mataiologia*), 10, 20–22, 52, 105, 107–9, 112, 114
encourage (*parakaleō*), 20, 27, 52–54, 70, 136
Epaphroditus, 51
Epictetus, 122, 131
Epimenides, 24
Erastus, v, 17, 155–56, 160
Essene(s), 28–29
Eunice, 83, 128
Eubulus, v, 158, 160
Eupolus, 98
Eusebius, 68, 115
evangelism (evangelist), 41–42, 56–57, 84, 134–35, 137–38
Eve, 21
faith (faithful), 82–84, 89, 96, 113, 124–25
farmer, 98–99
gangrene, 109
Genymede, 26
genealogy. *See* myth(s); heterodoxy.
Gentile(s), 8, 15, 21, 23, 27, 29, 36, 51, 54, 71, 83, 143–44, 151, 154–55, 157
gentle(ness), 13, 28, 47, 56–58, 60–61, 113–16, 119, 129, 131, 136
genuine, 6, 8, 72, 79–80, 82–84, 88, 95, 106, 114, 117, 120
gift, spiritual, 8, 37, 69–71, 83–84, 95–96, 137–39, 144, 160
glory, 8, 49, 99, 101–2, 106, 120, 141, 152–53
Gnosticism, 29–30, 110
God, 19, 49, 53, 60–63, 92, 104, 125, 151. *See also* grace.
godliness (*eusebeia*) (ungodliness), 6–7, 10, 22, 36, 39, 49–50, 77, 87, 105, 107, 109, 114, 118, 120, 126, 131
good news/gospel, 60–65, 86–88, 101
Gortyn, 9, 12, 14, 34, 45
grace, 6, 8, 49, 51, 59–60, 63, 66, 72–74, 86–87, 94, 100, 106, 114, 119–20, 140, 159. *See also* mercy.
haughty, 117–18
health: 6, 73; character traits, 37, 40, 44–45, 61; teaching, 20–21, 26–28, 31–33, 35–37, 40, 43–45, 48–49, 53, 65, 89, 108–9, 117, 131, 136–37. *See also* teaching.
heir(s). *See* inheritance.
Hermogenes, 75, 90–91, 94, 110, 143n
heterodoxy, 20–23, 28, 45, 66–68, 73, 75, 105–6, 108, 114–15, 136–37. *See also* myth(s).
holiness. *See* righteous(ness); honor(able).
honor(able) (*semnos/kosmeō*), 36, 44, 48–49, 112, 119
household, 3, 10–11, 14–18, 20, 25, 36, 40, 42–48, 64, 75–76, 91–93, 111–12, 114, 121, 153, 156
human(s) (*anthrōpos*), 96
Hymenaeus, 107, 109–11
Iconium, 126, 151
imprisonment. *See* prison.
inheritance, 62–66, 103
Irenaeus, 30
Isaiah, 49, 55, 57
Jannes, and Jambres, 123–24, 127
Jesus, 6, 19, 31, 48, 51–52, 85–88, 93, 100–101, 120, 134. *See also* God; ransom; Savior.
John the Baptist, 20, 49, 57, 66
Joseph, 11, 48, 59
Josephus, 9n, 18, 65, 129
Jubilees, 29
Judas Iscariot, 120

judgment (s), 25, 34, 52, 67, 87, 98, 106, 108, 110–11, 117, 122, 126–27, 132–34, 141–42
Knossos, 12, 24
Korah, 111
law (lawless), 10, 15, 19, 21–23, 25, 27, 29–32, 39, 47, 49, 52, 60, 66–67, 71, 83, 95, 99, 107–9, 115, 129
Lazarus, 82
life, eternal (*aiōn*), 6–7, 9, 28, 39, 59–60, 64, 78, 95, 103, 133–34
Linus, v, 158, 160
lion, 25, 75, 151–52
Lock, Walter, 124
Lois, 80, 83, 128
love, 85, 88–89, 113, 118, 120, 122. See also marriage.
Lucian, 24–25
Luke, v, 1–2, 9–10, 61, 71, 129, 142–45, 160
Lydia, 36, 92
Lystra, 10, 83, 98–99, 124, 126, 151
magic(ian), 30, 123–24, 127, 150
maiestas minuta law, 14
Mamertine Prison, 76
Mannine, 34
Marcion, 68
Marianne, 38
Mark, John, 146–47
marriage, 40–42, 45, 66, 112, 154. See also one-woman man.
mercy, 60–62, 73, 80n, 89, 91–93, 104, 136. See also grace.
Miletus, 156
minister(s)/deacon(s), 35–36, 38, 160
Minos (Minoan), 3–4, 12, 16, 18–19, 25
money/wealth, 18, 23, 30, 48, 98, 118, 131
Moses, 11–12, 19, 23, 58, 61, 68, 74, 83, 111, 123
myth(s) (*mythos*), 20, 22 – 29, 55, 66, 75, 78, 107–8, 114–17, 124, 133, 136–37.
    See also heterodoxy.
Nero, 8, 14, 56, 101n, 115, 150, 152

Nicodemus, 62
Nicopolis, 68–69, 144
Noah, 19
one-woman man, 14, 40. See also marriage.
offering, drink, 139
Onesimus, 70, 146
Onesiphorus' household, v, 75–76, 80, 85, 90–94, 106, 114, 153, 155, 160
overseer (*episkopos*), 11–13, 17–20, 35, 38, 62, 115–16, 154. See also elders(s).
parent(s), 14–16, 28, 42, 54, 79, 80–83, 94, 117–18, 132, 150
passion(s) (*epithymia*), 10, 19, 22, 37n, 47, 49–50, 58–60, 85, 87, 112–14, 121–23, 136–37
Pastoral Epistles, defined, 1
paterfamilias, 15, 42
Paul, 6, 59, 75–76, 79, 81–84, 88, 102, 124–27, 139–42. See also prison.
Pergamum, 148
Philetus, 107, 109–11
Philo, 19, 51
Phoebe, 51
Phygelus, 75, 90–91, 94
Plato, 25 – 26
Polybius, 18, 26, 58
Polycarp, 68
polysyndeton, 52, 67n, 85n, 158n
prayer(s), 13, 37–38, 59, 80–83, 112, 114, 119n
priest, 38, 41–42, 61–63, 66, 103, 111–12
Prisca, and Aquila, v, 43, 76, 90, 115, 153–55, 158, 160
prison (imprisonment), 56, 61, 70, 75–76, 81, 84–86, 88, 92–95, 101, 106, 115, 117, 121–22, 138, 142–50, 152, 154, 157
prophet(s), 24, 27, 42, 47, 120, 130, 144
Ptolemy, 9, 24
Pudens, v, 155, 158–60

Subject Index

pure (clean) (*katharos/hosios*), 22, 30–31, 33, 40–41, 43–44, 54n, 66–67, 95, 106, 112, 140
Quashie, 48
ransom, 49, 52, 63, 87, 103. See also Jesus.
rebuke (*elenchō/epitomaō*), 27–28, 53, 66, 130–31, 133–35
reprove. See rebuke.
resurrection (*anastasis*), 21, 51, 64, 87, 91n, 107–10, 143
righteous(ness) (*dikaios*), 13, 17–19, 23, 50, 54–55, 60–63, 87, 106, 109, 111–13, 120, 130–31, 134, 140–42
Savior (salvation) (*sōtēr*), 6, 8, 45, 48–49, 51, 60–63, 86–88, 94, 96, 100, 102, 129–30. See also Jesus; God.
saying (*logos*), 65, 72, 75, 102–3
Scriptures, 83, 113, 117, 127–32, 134–35, 136, 148
self-control, 13, 17–19, 36–37, 39–40, 84–85, 117, 119, 138
Sharp, Granville, 51n
silence (*epistomizō*), 20, 23–24, 28, 45
Simon Magus, 29–30
slander (blaspheme) (*diabolos*), 10, 22, 33, 35–36, 38–39, 43, 49, 56–57, 108, 117–19, 126
slave(s) (slavery), 6, 10, 14, 16, 33, 35–36, 42, 45–52, 58, 64–65, 91, 97, 114, 145
sober. See wine.
soldier, v, 3, 57, 76, 84–85, 92n, 96–99, 115, 139
Sophia, 34
Sparta, 3, 34, 40n
Spicq, Ceslas, 84
Spirit, Holy, 27, 47, 60, 62–63, 82, 89–90, 94, 116, 130, 134, 159
steward (*oikonomos*), 10–11, 13, 17–18, 28, 48–49, 156. See also overseer.
straight (*orthos*), 4, 10, 20, 49, 57, 106–8, 131
Stygian, 60

stylistics, 1
submit (*hypotassō*), 42, 46, 56
suffering, 75, 80, 85–88, 90, 96–97, 99n, 100–103, 118, 125–27, 138, 143–44
Sulpicius Severus, 50
synecdoche, 23, 102
Synod, of Laodicea, 35n
Tacitus, 150
teaching, 20–21, 33, 38–40, 44, 49, 65, 89, 95–96, 115–16, 125, 128–31, 136; false, 28–31, 99. See also education; health.
tears, 82, 84
Thessalonica, 81, 142–43
Tiberius, 83, 144, 152
time (*chronos, kairos*), 7, 87
Timothy, 8, 44, 53, 79–82, 84–85, 90, 94–95, 121, 127, 159
Titius Justus, 36
Titus, 6, 8, 10, 44–45, 52–54, 69, 71–72, 75, 144
Towner, Philip, 98, 100n, 147n, 159n
travel, 1, 9, 69, 72, 145n, 156–58, 160
trial, 53, 62, 76, 97n, 133, 149–51
Troas, 10n, 145–47, 149, 156–57
Trophimus, v, 90, 155–57, 160
truth, 7, 27–28, 116, 135
Tychicus, n, 68–70, 72, 76, 90–91, 147, 156, 160
understand, 99–100
ungodliness. See godliness.
Varus, 24
vessel(s) (*skeuos*), 57, 105, 111–13, 131, 146
washing/cleansing, 62–63. See also pure.
wealth. See money.
widow (s), 13–14, 22–23, 26, 92n, 122
Willetts, R. F. , 12
wine, 18, 33, 35–39, 47, 59, 116, 137–39
wisdom (wise), 36–37, 39–40, 42–43, 50, 99n, 106, 119, 129–30, 132

witness, 13, 17, 28, 39, 53, 55, 85,
    94–95, 133, 150. *See also*
    attack, not open.
women: elder(s), 33–39, 42–43, 47,
    75, 95 – 96; in Crete, 4, 64;
    in Ephesus, 85, 107–8, 114,
    121–23; learners, 128, 145.
work, good, 57, 61–62, 72–73, 86–87,
    112, 131
Xenophon, 40, 42–43
youth, 12n, 26, 33, 35, 41, 43–44, 49,
    54, 65, 85, 87, 112–13, 123,
    146
Zechariah, and Elizabeth, 19
Zenas, 68, 70–72, 160
Zeus, 4, 21, 24–26, 28, 31, 71n, 141

www.ingramcontent.com/pod-product-compliance
Lightning Source LLC
Chambersburg PA
CBHW030112170426
43198CB00009B/594